TO THE ORDINARY CITIZEN, even one who has given the map of Canada no more than a casual glance, the province of Ontario is an immense territory. From east to west it borders the entire chain of the Great Lakes and a considerable reach of the St. Lawrence River. From its southernmost tip in Lake Erie, which touches the parallel of latitude joining Boston and northern California, it extends northward to the boreal waters of a great arm of Hudson Bay.

This summary description, though true and impressive, is but a simple thumbnail sketch compared with the detailed picture seen by the naturalist. He sees the province as an irregular tract divided by nature into diverse zones and regions, each with its special types of flora and fauna or with special geological and topographical phenomena, the zones themselves in many cases subdivided into lesser zones and regions, each with its special natural traits.

As through the years settlement has advanced and population has spread, knowledge of the diverse phenomena of this wide-flung network of tracts has increased and names of places associated with them have become widely known. Unfortunately these places are so far apart that the naturalist from one region finds it hard to plan in advance well-arranged field trips in a distant region. What handbook has he at his easy disposal to acquaint him with routes and timetables and with the many other sundry bits of information the careful traveller seeks to know? Frankly, he has at his command no chart, no system of signposts to show the way! Surely it is plain that Ontario needs a Baedeker, or someone of his kind, very soon.

In an earnest attempt to meet the need, A *Naturalists' Guide to Ontario* has been prepared and published by the Federation of Ontario Naturalists and other allied agencies. Although its authors are well aware of its shortcomings they hope their manual will prove to be at least a very successful first step in widening appreciably the field of natural history study in Ontario.

W. SHERWOOD FOX
*Hon. President, F.O.N. (1959–1964)*
*London, Ontario*

THIS GUIDE to the natural history of Ontario will be of great interest and assistance to the naturalist planning a trip in the province. Whether he wants information that will aid him in mapping out an interesting route or whether he has already decided on where he is going but wants more information on the natural history of the regions through which he will pass; whether he wants a long trip or a day's excursion; whether his interests are general or specific, he will discover that this book serves several useful purposes.

In the first two sections, he will find that the general descriptions of Ontario's geology and flora and fauna provide a helpful introduction to the province's natural history as well as an indication of what he might expect to encounter in various regions of Ontario.

This information will lead him to the next and largest section of the book, the regional guides. Here, the province has been divided up into regions, each of which has been named according to the city, town, county, or other geographical designation that best identifies the area. To determine the location of these various regions or to select those on or near his route of travel, the naturalist can look at Figure 1. If he wishes to visit a specific point of interest but does not know in which region it is located, he can turn to the back of the book where there is an index of all geographical names that appear in the text. Similarly, if he is interested in a particular species of plant, tree, bird, or mammal, the index of species will refer him to the regions in which the species is mentioned.

When he has decided upon the areas he wishes to visit, the naturalist can then consult the appropriate regional guides. These are arranged alphabetically in the text. Under each heading, he will find directions on how to reach the region itself as well as the localities within each region that are of interest to the naturalist. Because of the unpredictability of most living things, it is not

FIGURE 1. MAP OF ONTARIO SHOWING LOCATION OF REGIONS DESCRIBED IN THIS BOOK
(h = highway)

1. Algonquin Provincial
   Park
2. Bancroft
3. Barrie
4. Belleville
5. Brantford
6. Brockville
7. Bruce County
8. Bruce Trail
9. Cape Henrietta Maria
10. Chatham
11. Collingwood
12. Fort William and Port
    Arthur
13. Georgian Bay Islands
    National Park

14. Hamilton
15. Hudson Bay Lowlands
16. Kingston and Gananoque
17. Kirkland Lake
18. Kitchener and Waterloo
19. London
20. Long Point
21. Manitoulin Island
22. Muskoka
23. Niagara Falls
24. Niagara Peninsula
25. Ottawa
26. Owen Sound
27. Perth
28. Peterborough
29. Point Pelee National Park

30. Port Hope and Cobourg
31. Porcupine District
32. Presqu'ile Provincial Park
33. Quetico Provincial Park
34. Rondeau Provincial Park
35. St. Lawrence Islands
    National Park
36. St. Thomas
37. Sarnia
38. Sault Ste. Marie
39. Sibley Provincial Park
40. Toronto
41. West Lorne

possible to give infallible directions to the precise spot where an interesting plant or bird can be found, but in this book there are more than three hundred directions to general locations which the naturalist will find easy to follow and which will greatly simplify and reduce the searching that in an unfamiliar area he would otherwise be forced to do.

Also under each regional heading, the naturalist will find descriptions of the geology, plants, trees, birds, and mammals that are typical of the locale. Rare and unique species that he might discover in the area are often listed. If he wishes to learn more about the region, each guide provides him with information on how to contact the local naturalist or the nearest nature club, and gives the titles of regional natural history publications.

In the final section of the book, the naturalist will find the two indexes referred to above and a list of various manuals that will aid him in the identification of plants and animals found in the province of Ontario.

This book has been prepared with the co-operation of the various naturalists and nature clubs, and it is to be hoped that all persons who benefit from their information herein or call upon them for additional assistance will heed their advice both to ask permission for access to various areas and to preserve existing vegetation and wildlife. Only thus will these regions be of continuing interest to nature lovers.

## ❀ CONTENTS

FOREWORD, by W. Sherwood Fox                                    v

HOW TO USE THIS BOOK                                           vii

NOTES ON THE GEOLOGY OF ONTARIO, by Walter M. Tovell            1

AN OUTLINE OF THE VEGETATION AND FAUNA OF ONTARIO,
by J. B. Falls, and J. H. Soper                               19

REGIONAL GUIDES                                               37

| | | | |
|---|---|---|---|
| Algonquin Provincial Park | 39 | Manitoulin Island | 117 |
| Bancroft Area: Haliburton and | | Muskoka | 120 |
| Hastings Counties | 45 | Niagara Falls (Geology) | 123 |
| Barrie | 49 | Niagara Peninsula | 131 |
| Belleville | 52 | Ottawa | 135 |
| Brantford | 53 | Owen Sound | 142 |
| Brockville | 55 | Perth | 149 |
| Bruce County and the Bruce | | Peterborough | 150 |
| Peninsula | 60 | Point Pelee National Park | 155 |
| The Bruce Trail | 63 | Port Hope and Cobourg | 159 |
| Cape Henrietta Maria | 67 | Porcupine District | 160 |
| Chatham | 70 | Presqu'ile Provincial Park | 162 |
| Collingwood | 73 | Quetico Provincial Park | 163 |
| Fort William and Port Arthur | 76 | Rondeau Provincial Park | 165 |
| Georgian Bay Islands National | | St. Lawrence Islands National | |
| Park | 81 | Park | 170 |
| Hamilton | 84 | St. Thomas | 172 |
| Hudson Bay Lowlands | 87 | Sarnia | 173 |
| Kingston and Gananoque | 93 | Sault Ste. Marie | 175 |
| Kirkland Lake | 103 | Sibley Provincial Park | 178 |
| Kitchener and Waterloo | 108 | Toronto | 180 |
| London | 111 | West Lorne | 185 |
| Long Point | 115 | | |

SOURCES OF IDENTIFICATION OF PLANTS AND ANIMALS              189

INDEX TO SPECIES OF INTEREST                                 193

INDEX TO POINTS OF INTEREST                                  201

## ❀ ILLUSTRATIONS

TEXTUAL FIGURES

Figure 1. Map of Ontario Showing Locations of Regions
    Described in This Book                                     viii

Figure 2. Geological Map of Ontario                      4

Figure 3. Generalized Topography of Southern Ontario    7

Figure 4. Generalized Structure Map of Southern Ontario    10

Figure 5. Vegetation Regions of Ontario                  22

Figure 6. The Stratigraphic Section at Niagara Falls     125

Figure 7. The Subdivisions of the Niagara Gorge      127


DRAWINGS BY SYLVIA HAHN

Pigeon Hawk                                         30

Wolf                                              44

Walking Fern                                      65

White-winged Crossbill                         79

Wild Turkey and Pitch-Pine                  102

Whistling Swan                                  116

Parula Warbler                                  122

Showy Orchis                                  144

Prickly Pear                                  157

Cerulean Warbler                           168

# Notes on the Geology of Ontario

By WALTER M. TOVELL

*Curator of Geology, Royal Ontario Museum/University of Toronto*

✸ THE GEOLOGIST interprets the distant past from the rocks of the earth's crust. To most people a rock is hard, but to a geologist soft materials are also rocks. To differentiate between the two, he calls the hard materials bedrock and the soft material overburden. Where bedrock is visible, it is called an outcrop. In Ontario, most of the overburden is of glacial origin, and in many areas it completely masks the bedrock so that outcrops are very scarce.

Rocks are made of minerals. In fact about 10 minerals out of a total of approximately 2,000 known mineral species make up most of the rocks. The classification of rocks is based on their mineral content and their textures, or on the pattern and size of the constituent minerals. As an example, the rock "granite" may be composed of the minerals quartz, feldspar, and black mica. These minerals can be recognized with the naked eye or a hand lens, so granite is said to be "coarse-grained." However, the rock "rhyolite," which may be composed of the same minerals as granite, is "fine-grained" because the minerals can only be recognized under a microscope.

The rocks of the earth's crust were formed in three different ways: on the basis of their origin, they are called *igneous, sedimentary,* or *metamorphic.* Igneous rocks are those that are "born of fire" referring to the fact that they were once molten. They may form from lavas at the earth's surface, or cool (crystallize) slowly from a magma deep within the earth, as in the case of granite. Rocks formed at depth in this manner become exposed to view by crustal movements and the removal of overlying material through erosion.

Sedimentary rocks owe their origin to the deposition and accumulation of fragments of rocks and minerals: for example, mud accumulating on the bottom of a lake, pond, or ocean, and sand accumulating on a beach or desert. With time, these loose particles become cemented to form shale and sandstone, respectively. Such deposits are usually bedded or "stratified." Another type of sedimentary rock is "till" which is composed of clay, sand, pebbles, and boulders. This material is the result of deposition from a

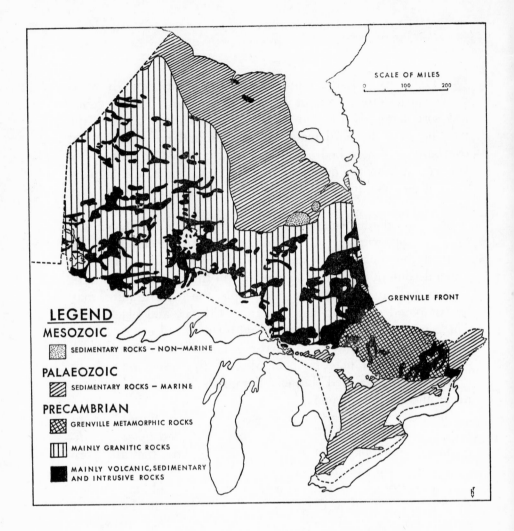

SCALE OF MILES
0      100      200

GRENVILLE FRONT

LEGEND

MESOZOIC
SEDIMENTARY ROCKS — NON—MARINE

PALAEOZOIC
SEDIMENTARY ROCKS — MARINE

PRECAMBRIAN
GRENVILLE METAMORPHIC ROCKS

MAINLY GRANITIC ROCKS

MAINLY VOLCANIC, SEDIMENTARY
AND INTRUSIVE ROCKS

FIGURE 2. GEOLOGICAL MAP OF ONTARIO

The map shows the distribution in a general way of the major rock types
and their ages, with the surficial deposits of glacial debris and soils removed.
Detailed maps should be consulted for local areas.

glacier and is unconsolidated. However, consolidated tills—called tillites—occur in the Precambrian sequence of Ontario.

Igneous and sedimentary rocks, with time and changing physical environments, become metamorphosed—that is, altered to form metamorphic rocks. With metamorphism, a shale may be transformed into a slate or a schist, and sometimes into a rock that looks something like a granite but is called gneiss. Gneisses and schists are foliated rocks, and the former are often banded. Foliation and banding may be mistaken for bedding, but in reality they result from the pressures that assist in the metamorphism, and hence may bear no relationship to bedding.

Once a rock has been identified as to its type and origin, the next task is to "date" it so that correlations can be made between various bodies of rock found in different areas, and the historical sequence of geological events established. Modern methods, based on isotope studies, permit the dating of rocks in "years." Geologists also use the Standard Geological Time Scale, which is a relative time scale based on the distribution of fossils within sedimentary rocks. It contains a series of time periods, which might be likened to chapters in a book and to which rocks and events may be correlated.

The Standard Geological Time Scale is given in Table I. It goes back only 600 million years, but the age of the oldest rocks of the earth's crust are known to be of the order of 3,000 million years. The age of the earth itself is about 4,500 million years. No physical record exists of what happened between the time of the origin of the earth and the oldest rocks; it can only be concluded that during this time the earth evolved, and a crust developed. The time from the age of the oldest rocks (3,000 million years) to 600 million years ago, is called Precambrian time, so Precambrian time represents nearly 80 per cent of all geological time recorded in the rocks.

THE TOPOGRAPHY OF SOUTHERN ONTARIO

Southern Ontario, though apparently quite flat, may be divided into a series of highlands which, in turn, are separated by lowlands. The subdivision between these features, for illustrative purposes, is made using the 1,000-foot contour as shown in Figure 3. The area occupied by the Grey County Highlands is bounded

## TABLE I
### The Standard Geological Time Scale and the Ontario Record in Outcrop

| Era | Period | The Ontario Record | Million years |
|---|---|---|---|
| CENOZOIC | | The glaciation of the Pleistocene Epoch is thought to have begun one million years ago or less. The ice retreated from southern Ontario 10,000–12,000 years ago. This is the age of Niagara Falls. | |
| | | | 63 |
| MESOZOIC | CRETACEOUS | Shales and lignites of the Hudson Bay Lowlands. | |
| | | | 135 |
| | JURASSIC | No record. | |
| | | | 180 |
| | TRIASSIC | No record. | 230 |
| PALAEOZOIC | PERMIAN | No record. | |
| | | | 280 |
| | PENNSYLVANIAN | No record. | ? |
| | MISSISSIPPIAN | Youngest Palaeozoic rocks in southern Ontario. Exposed in Port Lambton area. | |
| | | | 345 |
| | DEVONIAN | Southwestern Ontario and the Hudson Bay Lowlands. | |
| | | | 405 |
| | SILURIAN | Niagara Escarpment; Lake Timiskaming; Hudson Bay Lowlands. | |
| | | | 425 |
| | ORDOVICIAN | Below Niagara Escarpment, east and northeast to Precambrian Shield; in fault blocks of the Ottawa-Bonnechère Graben including Lake Timiskaming; Hudson Bay Lowlands. | |
| | | | 500 |
| | CAMBRIAN | Eastern Ontario; scattered outcrops. | |
| | ? ? ? ? ? ? ? ? ? | | 600 |
| PRECAMBRIAN | | Extends back to the age of the oldest rocks of the earth's crust—i.e., about 3,000 million years. The Ontario record is fragmentary. The oldest rocks have been dated at about 2,500 million years. | |

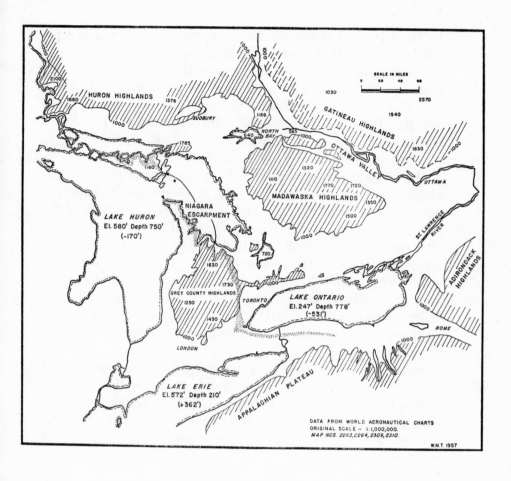

FIGURE 3. GENERALIZED TOPOGRAPHY OF SOUTHERN ONTARIO

Highlands and lowlands may be separated by the 1,000 foot contour. Notice the straight contour lines that parallel the Ottawa River. These indicate the topographic effect of faults that form the Ottawa-Bonnechère Graben. The major topographic trend that includes the Grey County Highlands, the Madawaska Highlands, and the Gatineau Hills is a reflection of the Algonquin Arch (see Figure 4).

by the Niagara Escarpment on the north and east, and is separated from the Madawaska Highlands by the Lake Simcoe and Trent River lowlands. The Madawaska Highlands are separated from the Gatineau Hills in Quebec by the Ottawa Valley, a branch of which runs westward through Lake Nipissing, separating the Huron Highlands from the Madawaska Highlands. Another branch runs northward through Lake Timiskaming to separate the Gatineau Hills from the Huron Highlands.

The Niagara Escarpment is perhaps the most important topographic feature of southern Ontario. It divides southwestern, or peninsular Ontario, from the central and eastern portions of the province. It forms part of the shoreline of Georgian Bay, and in the vicinity of Osler Bluff and the Blue Mountains the elevations are over 1,700 feet. The escarpment is responsible for numerous waterfalls of which Niagara Falls is the most important. It contains indentations along its face, such as the Dundas and Beaver valleys, which reflect periods of pre-glacial erosion. The escarpment exists because of the hard bedrock (dolomite) that forms its crest.

Superimposed on the major topographic features are minor features too numerous to detail. Suffice it to say that they are formed in some areas by bedrock control, or by glacial action which includes both erosional and depositional features. In addition, of course, streams in some areas have cut deep valleys of recent origin.

THE REGIONAL STRUCTURE OF SOUTHERN ONTARIO

The fundamental structural or architectural feature of Ontario is the Precambrian (or Canadian) Shield. The portion of the shield that lies in Ontario is but a part of the total area of the shield as it is known throughout Canada. The term is essentially geographic in that it refers to the large area of outcropping Precambrian rocks, but the shield is actually more widespread than the term would suggest; bore holes drilled through sedimentary strata encounter Precambrian rocks beneath the prairies of western Canada, the peninsula of southern Ontario, and the Hudson Bay Lowlands. The shield, therefore, is also a basement or platform upon which younger sedimentary rocks have been deposited.

In southern Ontario, the buried Precambrian surface occurs in the form of a broad arch that plunges to the southwest, called the Algonquin Arch (see Figure 4). This structural feature underlies the Grey County Highlands and the Madawaska Highlands; the Gatineau Hills of Quebec appear to be a continuation of this structural trend.

The Ottawa Valley and the Nipissing Lowlands owe their origin to a large structural feature called the Ottawa-Bonnechère Graben. The term *graben* means that large blocks of rock were down-faulted; geologists, therefore, refer to these lowlands as being "structurally controlled."

Small patches (outliers) of Palaeozoic rocks are found in the Ottawa Valley. These are remnants of a once continuous blanket of sedimentary rocks that covered most of southern Ontario. They have been preserved in the graben because they were down-faulted and hence protected from erosion. The fact that these rocks are present indicates that the faulting occurred after the deposition of the early Palaeozoic sediments. The exact age of the structure, however, remains unknown.

THE PRECAMBRIAN RECORD

The Precambrian rocks of Ontario are between 2,500 million and 800 million years old. The use of isotopes to determine the ages of rocks has confirmed other data, and together they suggest that the shield is made up of distinct geological provinces, each with its own geological history. In Ontario, portions of two of these provinces, Grenville and Superior, are recognized. The Superior province contains the oldest rocks of the Precambrian Shield. Called Keewatin, they are about 2,500 million years old, and consist of thick deposits of volcanic and sedimentary materials, the former predominating. Keewatin rocks are followed in the succession mainly by sedimentary rocks which are called Timiskaming. The Keewatin-Timiskaming rocks occur in patches throughout the Superior province of the shield in Ontario, and important mineral deposits, such as the gold in the Porcupine and Kirkland Lake areas, are associated with these rocks. An interesting feature about the Keewatin-Timiskaming rocks is that the volcanic rocks have been metamorphosed to form what is commonly called "greenstone." These greenstones have characteristic structures in them which are called "pillow lavas," discrete masses

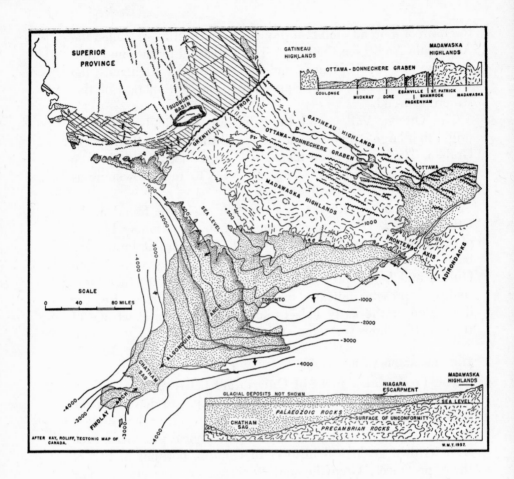

FIGURE 4. GENERALIZED STRUCTURE MAP OF SOUTHERN ONTARIO

The map shows the major subdivisions of the Precambrian Shield in southern Ontario, and the major structures therein. The contour lines show the elevations of the Precambrian rocks with respect to sea level. The contours beneath the Palaeozoic cover rocks define the Algonquin Arch. This structure controls the shape of southwestern Ontario.

formed in succession upwards from the bottom of the lava-flow, each succeeding pillow having adjusted its form to those directly below it. A good locality to see pillow lavas is at the divide between the Hudson Bay drainage and the Atlantic drainage, on Highway 11 north of Kirkland Lake.[1]

Keewatin-Timiskaming rocks have been intruded by igneous rocks of many types, which, for convenience, can all be lumped together as "Early Precambrian Intrusives." The intrusions are in the form of dikes, stocks, and batholiths, granite being a common constituent of the latter. The Keewatin-Timiskaming rocks and the Early Precambrian Intrusives form what is generally considered to be a basement complex.

Overlying this basement complex is a succession of sedimentary rocks, broken by a maze of faults, and in some places flexed and warped into folds. These rocks, referred to as Huronian, are characteristic of the areas along the north shore of Lake Huron, and extend from that region up to the Cobalt area. In the Blind River district, some of these sedimentary rocks are the host rocks for the uranium-bearing minerals. The Huronian succession of sedimentary rocks also contains evidence of Precambrian glaciation. The evidence lies in the tillites—consolidated till—which are well-known from the areas mentioned and which form characteristic outcrops along the highways. They can be recognized because tillites are conglomerates, but the pebbles vary in size from a fraction of an inch up to two or three feet in diameter in certain places. Excellent outcrops occur north of Elliot Lake on Highway 108 and at the intersection of Highway 11 and 66 west of Kirkland Lake. Outcrops of the tillite are also common in the Cobalt area.

The youngest rocks in the Superior province are called Keweenawan, and are of igneous and sedimentary origin. In the Nipigon area, the sedimentary rocks are in part bright red shales, which stand out quite prominently in outcrops. In the same area, the igneous intrusions are in the form of sills of diabase, named the Logan[2] Sills, which cap the mesas that are such a prominent

[1]The divide is very clearly marked on Highway 11 just eight miles north of the junction with Highway 66.

[2]After Sir William Logan, the first Director of the Geological Survey of Canada.

feature of the landscape around Thunder Bay. A diabase sill is also responsible for the famous "Sleeping Giant" at the foot of the Sibley Peninsula, and for Mount McKay at the Lakehead. Along the north shore of Lake Huron, Keweenawan rocks occur as intrusions, in the form of dikes and irregular masses. The rocks that form the Sudbury Basin are considered to be Keweenawan in age.

The rocks of the Grenville province are of metamorphic origin; they are well exposed, and familiar to many in the Georgian Bay, Muskoka, and Haliburton districts of southern Ontario. The rocks are mainly gneisses and schists, but marbles and rocks of volcanic origin occur as well. It is thought that originally these rocks were shales, limestones, and lavas, and that with crustal movements they became deeply buried and recrystallized (metamorphosed). This process probably took place at depths of between five and ten miles within the earth's crust some billion years ago. The Grenville rocks are cut intricately by pegmatite dikes which are masses of coarsely crystalline, igneous rocks composed primarily of quartz and feldspar. The formation of these dikes is considered to be part of the metamorphic process.

The formation of the Grenville rocks probably took place in the roots of an old mountain system. The Grenville complex, therefore, is considered by some geologists to be the evidence for a lofty mountain range—the Muskoka Mountains—which existed one billion years ago, but were reduced to a nearly flat plain before the Palaeozoic seas spread over the area.

The boundary between the Grenville and Superior provinces in Ontario appears to be very sharp, and is called the Grenville Front. It is marked by a zone of intense metamorphism, and in some places has been considered a fault of large magnitude. There are not as yet enough good exposures to permit a complete description of this intriguing structure.

The Precambrian rocks have both economic and scientific importance. The shield contains the bulk of Ontario's (and Canada's) mineral wealth in rich, large ore deposits of many different types. The gold camps of Timmins and Kirkland Lake, the nickel-copper ores of the Sudbury Basin, and the uranium of Blind River offer examples of the contrasting ways in which mineral wealth may be located. The scientific importance of the shield lies in the fact that Precambrian rocks contain the evidence for the early history of the earth's crust. From present information it would seem that we shall not be able to get direct evidence of the nature of the earth from the time of its formation (4,500 million years ago) to about 3,000 million years ago, the date of the oldest rocks of the shield. However, with patience, time, and ingenuity, geologists should be able to reconstruct Precambrian history from about 3,000 million years ago to the beginning of the Palaeozoic era. Since many of the rocks exposed within the shield area were formed deep within the earth's crust, detailed studies of these rocks make it possible to interpret some of the physical and chemical processes that operate at depth within the earth.

### THE PALAEOZOIC RECORD

In the area lying to the south of the Precambrian Shield, and mainly covered by the Pleistocene (Glacial) deposits, are strata of sandstone, shale, and carbonate rocks (limestones and dolomites). These rocks contain abundant fossils—the petrified remains of the marine life that thrived in Palaeozoic ancient seas. The sedimentary rocks, therefore, originated as sand and mud on these sea floors; the age of the rocks is between 530 and 310 million years.

These bedded or stratified rocks appear to be flat when viewed in the outcrop. Detailed surveys and drilling indicate, however, that they slope gently to the southwest. Younger and younger strata, therefore, appear in the outcrops towards the southwest corner of the province. Below the Niagara Escarpment the marine sedimentary rocks belong principally to the Ordovician period, though in eastern Ontario there are a few outcrops of Cambrian sandstone.

Small patches of Palaeozoic rocks occur along the Ottawa Valley and on islands in Lake Nipissing. These outliers are associated with the Ottawa-Bonnechère Graben and indicate that the Palaeozoic seas in which these sediments were deposited were much more widespread than first would appear. Probably all of southern Ontario and a good deal of northern Ontario was covered at one time with Palaeozoic sedimentary rocks. These deposits were removed by erosion, exposing the rocks of the Precambrian Shield.

The Palaeozoic sedimentary rocks have been studied in great detail from the point of view of their lithology and fossil content. Such studies lead to a subdivision of the strata into formations, and permit a detailed reconstruction of the environment of deposition of the original sediments. The data indicate, for example, that at one time coral reefs flourished in southern Ontario, while at another time "Dead Sea" conditions persisted in southwestern Ontario, at which time much salt was deposited. Certain rocks of the Niagara Escarpment may be recognized as part of a delta built out from rising mountains that were located in what is now the eastern United States. The deposits of these Palaeozoic seas, therefore, reflect to the trained observer the record of an ever changing environment.

Palaeozoic rocks also form a significant portion of the lowlands surrounding James and Hudson bays (see Figure 2). The rocks are comparable in age and type to those of the peninsula of southwestern Ontario.

### THE MESOZOIC RECORD

A small area of non-marine shales, with beds of lignite and fireclay, occur in the Moose River Basin of the James Bay Lowlands. Fossil plants indicate an early Cretaceous age for the strata.

### THE CENOZOIC RECORD

Within Ontario, the Cenozoic rocks are the glacial deposits of the Pleistocene Epoch. The Pleistocene began about one million years ago, when the whole of the northern part of North America was covered with glacial ice. The glaciers crept very slowly across the area from northern Canada, modifying the pre-existing rock surface and removing all weathered debris; and the moving ice produced the round, smooth bedrock surfaces that are so characteristic of the Precambrian rock surfaces. In addition, the moving ice, with the incorporated rock fragments, scratched and grooved the bedrock surfaces locally.

Detailed studies of the glacial or Pleistocene history of southern Ontario have established that the glacial advance took place primarily in the form of lobes which spread over the area from three different directions. One lobe emerged from the Georgian Bay and Lake Huron basins, another from the Lake Ontario Basin, and a third from the northeast advancing towards the southwest over the Peterborough district. Studies also reveal that the glaciers did not advance just once, but several times. This information has been derived from a study of the Pleistocene deposits of the Don Valley Brick Yard and Scarborough Bluffs in Metropolitan Toronto, and elsewhere.

A final effect of the Ice Age was the development of the Great Lakes. Prior to glaciation, the basins now occupied by the Great Lakes were large valleys with rivers flowing within them. The advancing glaciers followed these valleys in part and deepened them. As the ice withdrew, the melt waters became impounded in the valleys. In the initial stages, the lakes stood at higher levels; the shorelines can be recognized in many places around the borders of the present lakes. In Toronto, for instance, the bluff that forms the "Avenue Road Hill" may be followed almost continuously across the city and marks the shoreline of Lake Iroquois, the forerunner of Lake Ontario. At Waubaushene, three distinct levels of old water-planes of Lake Algonquin may be observed.

Immediately following the withdrawal of the ice, the salt waters of the St. Lawrence River entered the Ottawa Valley and Lake Ontario so that marine flooding of the eastern part of the province took place. This "sea" is referred to as the Champlain Sea. This small marine invasion was made possible because the weight of the glaciers was sufficient to depress the earth's crust below its present level. This may sound surprising, but it should be borne in mind that the glacial ice may have been a mile or more in thickness over Ontario. This figure is admittedly a guess, but it is not out of order, because measurements taken during the International Geophysical Year have indicated that the glacial ice at the South Pole is over a mile and a half thick. Gradually, as the ice melted, the crust slowly rose, causing a withdrawal of the marine waters. This crustal rise also modified the drainage pattern of the Great Lakes, diverting the outlet from the Ottawa Valley to the Niagara River and through Lake Ontario. The small earthquakes that occur in the Ottawa and St. Lawrence valleys today are evidence that the earth's crust in this area still is undergoing minor adjustments that are thought to be associated with the withdrawal of the glaciers.

These few remarks are but a capsule comment on the well-documented glacial history of southern Ontario. Because the glacial deposits form such a prominent part of the landscape, they have received considerable attention from many geologists. For fuller details, therefore, it is suggested that the reader consult the references below.

Although present-day southern Ontario lacks the spectacular scenery of mountains, the fireworks exhibited by present-day volcanoes, and the quiet beauty of coral reefs, the rocks tell us that such phenomena did exist in this area at one time or another. It is easy, therefore, to visualize the tremendous changes that take place even locally within the vast span of geological time. "Here today and gone tomorrow" is the geologist's creed, with the "todays" and "tomorrows" measured in millions of years.

REFERENCES

CHAPMAN, L. G., and D. F. PUTNAM, The Physiography of Southern Ontario (University of Toronto Press, 1951), pp. i–xxi, 1–284.

CLARK, THOMAS H., and STEARN, COLIN W., The Geological Evolution of North America (Ronald Press Co., 1960), pp. i–vi, 1–434.

DEANE, R. E., Pleistocene Geology of the Lake Simcoe District, Ontario, Geological Survey of Canada, Dept. of Mines and Technical Surveys, memoir 256 (1950), pp. i–vii, 1–108.

GEOLOGICAL SURVEY OF CANADA, Geology and Economic Minerals of Canada, Geological Survey of Canada, Economic Series no. 1, 4th ed. (1957), pp. i–xiii, 1–517.

GRAVENOR, C. P., Surficial Geology of the Lindsay-Peterborough Area, Ontario: Victoria, Peterborough, Durham and Northumberland Counties, Ontario, Geological Survey of Canada, memoir 288 (1957), pp. 1–60.

HOUGH, JACK L., Geology of the Great Lakes (University of Illinois Press, 1958), pp. i–xviii, 1–313.

KARROW, P. F., Pleistocene Geology of the Hamilton-Galt Area, Ontario, Department of Mines, Geological Report no. 16 (1963), pp. i–vi, 1–68.

WILSON, ALICE E., A Guide to the Geology of the Ottawa District, Canadian Field-Naturalist, LXX, 1 (1956), pp. 1–68.

*Topographic Maps.* Obtain from:
> Map Distribution Office,
> Map Compilation and Reproduction Division,
> Department of Mines and Technical Surveys,
> Ottawa, Ontario

or

> Ontario Department of Lands and Forests,
> Maps Division, Room 2431,
> East Block, Parliament Buildings,
> Queen's Park,
> Toronto 5, Ontario.

*Geological Maps and Reports*
Federal Publications. Obtain from:
> Geological Survey of Canada,
> 601 Booth Street,
> Ottawa, Ontario.

Provincial Publications. Obtain from:
> Ontario Department of Mines,
> Publications Office, Room 1532,
> East Block, Parliament Buildings,
> Queen's Park,
> Toronto 5, Ontario.

# An Outline of the Vegetation and Fauna of Ontario

By J. B. FALLS

*Department of Zoology, University of Toronto*

and J. H. SOPER

*Department of Botany, University of Toronto*

❀ ONTARIO SPANS over 1,000 miles from south to north and almost as much from east to west. In the frozen north a narrow strip of Arctic tundra borders the coast of Hudson Bay. At the other extreme, in what is the most southerly part of Canada, is a sample of the deciduous forest that covers much of southeastern North America. Between these extremes, on a surface here of scarred rocks and there covered by deep glacial drift—both evidences of the ice age—we find a varied pattern of plant and animal communities.

However, it is not a static pattern, for changes are taking place in the environment. The climate has fluctuated many times since the ice retreated, and a warming trend is currently bringing a new wave of invaders from the south. Some animals have extended their ranges beyond the plant communities with which they were formerly associated. Man has drastically changed the natural patterns of the landscape and continues to do so, replacing forest habitats with fields and settlements and replacing the plants and animals of the forest chiefly with those of open country, some from other parts of North America or from the Old World.

On this varied landscape naturalists look for patterns of distribution of natural communities, and this section of the guide points the way to interesting samples of these communities— some, remnants of conditions encountered by the pioneers; others, much modified by human activities.

In Ontario, the main pattern of natural vegetation consists of broad belts of forest running in an east-west direction. Although they have been given various names there is general agreement about their number and description. These regions are shown on the accompanying map (Figure 5). The boundaries are taken from J. S. Rowe's *Forest Regions of Canada* with the exception of the southernmost boundary which is based on Fox and Soper's study of the distribution of Carolinian trees and shrubs. From this map it should be possible to determine into which of these natural regions the various geographical areas (discussed below under "Regional Guides") fall. Table II indicates the names used

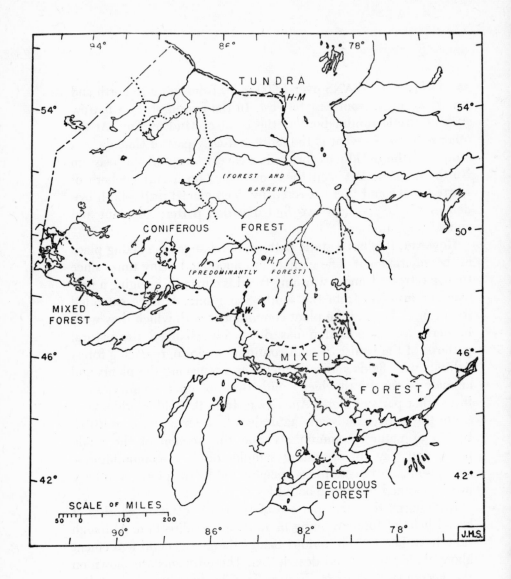

FIGURE 5. VEGETATION REGIONS OF ONTARIO

H-M = Cape Henrietta Maria; K = Kenora; P = Port Arthur; F = Fort William; H = Hearst; W = Wawa; N = New Liskeard; G = Grand Bend; L = London; T = Toronto.

here for these regions as well as other names commonly used for approximately the same areas.

### TABLE II
#### NATURAL REGIONS IN ONTARIO

| Terms used here | Terms used by | |
| --- | --- | --- |
| | Rowe | Merriam |
| Deciduous Forest Region | Deciduous Forest Region | Upper Austral (Carolinian) Life Zone |
| Mixed Forest Region | Great Lakes–St. Lawrence Forest Region | Transition (Alleghenian) Life Zone |
| Coniferous Forest Region (a) Predominantly Forest (b) Forest and Barren | Boreal Forest Region (a) Predominantly Forest (b) Forest and Barren | Canadian Life Zone Hudsonian Life Zone |
| Tundra Region | Tundra Region | Arctic Life Zone |

Although these natural regions can be characterized by their dominant trees and other common or unique plants and animals, they are not sharply delimited. There are few plants and even fewer animals whose distributional limits coincide with the boundaries of any of these regions, but this situation is to be expected from the dynamic nature of distribution already referred to above. It does not invalidate the use of the regions themselves, because the latter indicate the broad outlines of major biotic communities which have developed in response to climatic and topographic variations in the environment. Most of the boundaries in Ontario seem to be related to temperature as expressed in the length of the growing season, although the northern section of the Coniferous Forest differs mainly in topography from the rest of that region (see *Atlas of Canada*, 1957).

The following descriptions of the flora and fauna of the different regions are based chiefly on the occurrence of trees, breeding birds, and mammals, because these are the most conspicuous and best known forms. Some reference is made to other vascular plants and vertebrate animals. It should be realized that the species listed here are only a small fraction of those that occur in the communities they represent. A more complete listing is beyond the scope of this guide. Animals are referred to only by common names in general use. Names of birds are taken from the 1957 *A.O.U. Check-List.*

DECIDUOUS FOREST

This is a unique forest region containing a number of species of deciduous trees which are found nowhere else in Canada. It occupies a comparatively small area north of Lake Erie between the southern end of Lake Huron and the western end of Lake Ontario.

Although often referred to as a beech-maple forest, this area contains several other species which seem to be equally important. The dominant trees are Sugar-Maple (*Acer saccharum*), Basswood (*Tilia americana*), Red Oak (*Quercus rubra*), White Oak (*Q. alba*), Beech (*Fagus grandifolia*), White Ash (*Fraxinus americana*), Black Cherry (*Prunus serotina*), Ironwood (*Ostrya virginiana*), Red Maple (*Acer rubrum*), and Blue Beech (*Carpinus caroliniana*). Also common in this region are White Elm (*Ulmus americana*), Shagbark-Hickory (*Carya ovata*), and Butternut (*Juglans cinerea*).

The typical southern species which reach their northern limit in this forest association and thereby distinguish it from other deciduous or mixed forest in Ontario are Sassafras (*Sassafras albidum*), Black Walnut (*Juglans nigra*), Wild Crab (*Pyrus coronaria*), Swamp-White Oak (*Quercus bicolor*), and Flowering Dogwood (*Cornus florida*). Formerly the Chestnut (*Castanea dentata*) was an important member of this group but it has practically been exterminated by a parasitic fungus. Other southern species with more restricted ranges within this forest region are Tulip-tree (*Liriodendron tulipifera*), Pawpaw (*Asimina triloba*), Red Mulberry (*Morus rubra*), Sour Gum (*Nyssa sylvatica*), and Chestnut-Oak (*Quercus prinus*).

Although the broad-leaved deciduous trees give this forest its characteristic appearance, some conifers are also present, notably White Pine (*Pinus strobus*), Hemlock (*Tsuga canadensis*), White Cedar (*Thuja occidentalis*), and Red Cedar (*Juniperus virginiana*). These are found either scattered among the deciduous trees or locally abundant in clumps or groves. The Deciduous Forest is also characterized by the absence of certain typically northern species such as Balsam-Fir (*Abies balsamea*) and White Spruce (*Picea glauca*) and by the restriction of certain others such as Black Spruce (*P. mariana*) and Tamarack (*Larix laricina*) to isolated bogs or cool wet woods.

In addition to trees, the forest contains many southern species of shrubs and herbs. Some of these are confined to the region and are therefore excellent indicators, for example, Running Strawberry-bush (*Euonymus obovatus*), Wild Yam Vine (*Dioscorea villosa*), and Stoneroot (*Collinsonia canadensis*). Other species are characteristic but extend beyond the region, for example, shrubs such as Witch-Hazel (*Hamamelis virginiana*), Spicebush (*Lindera benzoin*), Bladdernut (*Staphylea trifolia*), American Hazel (*Corylus americana*), Leatherwood (*Dirca palustris*), Burning-bush (*Euonymus atropurpureus*), Wild Black Currant (*Ribes americanum*), Prickly Gooseberry (*R. cynosbati*), Snowberry (*Symphoricarpos albus*), Maple-leaved Viburnum (*Viburnum acerifolium*), Choke-Cherry (*Prunus virginiana*), Poison Ivy (*Rhus radicans* var. *rydbergii*), and several species of shadbush (*Amelanchier* spp.). There are a few climbing vines such as Bittersweet (*Celastrus scandens*), Virgin's-bower (*Clematis virginiana*), Bristly Catbrier (*Smilax hispida*), and the climbing variety of Poison Ivy (*Rhus radicans* var. *radicans*).

As a result of extensive cultivation, settlement, and industrialization, this region has lost most of its original vegetation. Only a few areas remain where remnants of this characteristic forest can be observed. Some of these are in the Niagara Peninsula, the vicinity of Turkey Point and Long Point, and in Rondeau Provincial Park, Backus Woods and White's Bush.

The Deciduous Forest probably has the richest fauna of any part of Ontario. Cold-blooded vertebrates are particularly well represented here as compared with other areas. Although not part of the forest, the lakes and streams contain more kinds of fish than more northerly waters. Many species, for example, several minnows and darters, the Lake Chubsucker, and the Green Sunfish, reach their northern limits in Ontario here. Approximately twenty species of amphibians and twenty-seven species of reptiles have been found in the region, but only a few rare ones, like the Cricket Frog and the Blue Racer, are confined to this part of the province.

Common birds of the forest include the Great Crested Fly-catcher, Orchard Oriole, Eastern Wood Pewee, Wood Thrush, Red-eyed Vireo, Ovenbird, American Redstart, and Scarlet Tanager. Although these species are also found in the mixed forest, several less common birds reach their northern limits in Ontario here. Some, for example, the Acadian Flycatcher, Carolina Wren, Blue-gray Gnatcatcher, Prothonotary and Cerulean Warblers, Louisiana Waterthrush, and Yellow-breasted Chat, occur regularly in certain localities; others, such as the Red-bellied Woodpecker, Tufted Titmouse, Mockingbird, Blue-winged and Hooded Warblers, are found occasionally. Although it once occurred farther north, the Bobwhite is now confined to this region; the Turkey was formerly a bird of the Deciduous Forest.

Common mammals of the forest are the Eastern Gray Squirrel, Eastern Chipmunk, White-footed Mouse, and Raccoon. Although there are no mammals whose ranges exactly coincide with the boundaries of this region, the Little Short-tailed Shrew, Eastern Mole, and Pine Vole reach their northern limits in Ontario in this region. The Deciduous Forest has a rich invertebrate fauna including many southern insects and a variety of molluscs.

Because of the elimination of the major portion of the original vegetation in this region, many animals of open country, forest edge, and second growth forest (to be mentioned under the Mixed Forest) are common here.

MIXED FOREST

The Mixed Forest is essentially a transitional type between the southern Deciduous Forest and the northern Coniferous Forest, containing hardwoods and conifers in various combinations. It is divided into two parts as shown on the map: a large eastern section and a smaller western section, separated by Lake Superior.

The common deciduous species of this forest include such northern hardwoods as White Birch (*Betula papyrifera*), Yellow Birch (*B. lutea*), Trembling Aspen (*Populus tremuloides*), and Balsam-Poplar (*P. balsamifera*), as well as other species common to the Deciduous Forest Region, namely, Sugar-Maple, Red Maple, Red Oak, Ironwood, White Elm, Beech, and Basswood. Some of the latter are rare in the northern parts of this region and others are entirely restricted to the southernmost areas. Black Ash

(*Fraxinus nigra*) is a common tree of low swampy woods; Bur Oak (*Quercus macrocarpa*), Large-toothed Aspen (*Populus grandidentata*), and Showy Mountain-Ash (*Sorbus decora*) may be locally abundant; Butternut is restricted to limestone and other basic soils south of the Canadian Shield.

The common conifers are White Pine, White Spruce, Balsam-Fir, and White Cedar. Hemlock is important in the southern parts of the region; Red Pine (*Pinus resinosa*) and Jack-Pine (*P. banksiana*) may be locally abundant along lake shores and on sand plains; Black Spruce and Tamarack are common in poorly drained situations, often forming dense stands.

Many shrubs and herbs are conspicuous in the understory and on the forest floor. Some of the common shrubs of the Mixed Forest are Beaked Hazel (*Corylus cornuta*), Fly-Honeysuckle (*Lonicera canadensis*), Bush-Honeysuckle (*Diervilla lonicera*), Choke-Cherry, Red-berried Elder (*Sambucus pubens*), Mountain-Maple (*Acer spicatum*), Speckled Alder (*Alnus rugosa*), Round-leaved Dogwood (*Cornus rugosa*) and Skunk-Currant (*Ribes glandulosum*). Other shrubs may be locally abundant or more restricted in their distribution, for example, Prickly Gooseberry, Pin-Cherry (*Prunus pensylvanica*), American Yew (*Taxus canadensis*), Snowberry, Green Alder (*Alnus crispa*), and Striped Maple (*Acer pensylvanicum*). Among the characteristic herbs of the forest floor are various club-mosses (*Lycopodium* spp.), Rattlesnake-Fern (*Botrychium virginianum*), Wild Lily-of-the-valley (*Maianthemum canadense*), Twisted-stalk (*Streptopus roseus*), Goldthread (*Coptis groenlandica*), Wood-Sorrel (*Oxalis montana*), Sarsaparilla (*Aralia nudicaulis*), Bunchberry (*Cornus canadensis*), Star-flower (*Trientalis borealis*), Bedstraw (*Galium triflorum*), Partridge-berry (*Mitchella repens*), Twin-flower (*Linnaea borealis*), and Large-leaved Aster (*Aster macrophyllus*).

The fauna of this region is also a mixture of southern and northern elements found in the corresponding plant associations with many species reaching their northern or southern limits. Most of the nineteen amphibians and twenty-three reptiles which occur here do not extend to the northern boundary of this area. In general, fewer animals are active in winter and more birds migrate than in the Deciduous Forest Region.

Today, many of the commonest animals which live in this region and other parts of southern Ontario are not those of the mature forest, but species of open country, forest edge, or second growth woods. Examples are the American Toad, Leopard Frog, Brown Snake, Garter Snake, several hawks, Killdeer, Mourning Dove, Yellow-shafted Flicker, Eastern Kingbird, Barn Swallow, Blue Jay, Common Crow, House Wren, Catbird, Brown Thrasher, Robin, Yellow Warbler, Bobolink, Eastern Meadowlark, Red-winged Blackbird, Brown-headed Cowbird, Indigo Bunting, American Goldfinch, Rufous-sided Towhee, Savannah, Chipping, and Song Sparrows, Red Fox, White-tailed Deer, Woodchuck, Meadow Vole, Eastern Cottontail, and Striped Skunk.

Common birds and mammals of the deciduous woods in this region are similar to those listed for the Deciduous Forest, although the Deer Mouse replaces the White-footed Mouse in the north. Among the birds and mammals which reach their northern limit in this area are the Wood Duck, Screech Owl, Great Crested Flycatcher, Rough-winged Swallow, Catbird, Brown Thrasher, Wood Thrush, Veery, Loggerhead Shrike, Yellow-throated and Warbling Vireos, Pine Warbler, Scarlet Tanager, Rose-breasted Grosbeak, Rufous-sided Towhee, Field Sparrow, Hairy-tailed Mole, Eastern Gray Squirrel, Eastern Cottontail, and Long-tailed Weasel.

A similar list of species whose southern limits fall within the region would include the Snowshoe Hare, Northern Flying Squirrel, Woodland Jumping Mouse, and Porcupine, and the breeding range of the Myrtle Warbler and White-throated Sparrow. With the exception of the Jumping Mouse these species are common in coniferous woods along with the Red Squirrel, although the latter extends further south.

One species whose breeding range fits the region fairly well is the Black-throated Blue Warbler, a bird of deciduous woods. In the northern part of the region a number of animals listed as typical of the Coniferous Forest occur in predominantly coniferous woods and reach their southern limits. These are mentioned in the Algonquin Park guide. This fact, together with the different elements mentioned in the present account, indicates the aptness of the term Transition Zone for this area.

In his report on the fauna of the western Rainy River District, L. L. Snyder draws attention to the rich and varied fauna of the section of the Mixed Forest west of Lake Superior. Birds and mammals of this area include northern species such as three-toed woodpeckers, Marten, and Fisher; southern species such as the Red-headed Woodpecker, Scarlet Tanager, and Eastern Gray Squirrel; and prairie species such as Sharp-tailed Grouse and Franklin's Ground Squirrel. Snyder attributes this variety to warm summer temperatures, the proximity of prairie, mixed forest, and boreal islands, and the effects of clearing, forestry, and forest fires.

CONIFEROUS FOREST

The Coniferous Forest is the most extensive formation in Canada, reaching from Newfoundland westward across northern Quebec and Ontario, thence northwestward to the Yukon. In Ontario this region may be divided into two sections (as shown by the dotted line on the map): a southern one, which is predominantly forest, and a northern one which is a mixture of forest and barren and is essentially a transition zone.

The Coniferous Forest is predominantly evergreen and contains five species of conifers, White Spruce, Black Spruce, Balsam-Fir, Tamarack, and Jack-Pine, but the two spruces are the dominant species throughout most of the region. The hardwoods are limited to three main species, White Birch, Trembling Aspen, and Balsam-Poplar.

The southern section may have different associations of trees, for example, Spruce-Fir-Birch or Spruce-Fir, or in the case of large poorly drained areas such as the Clay Belt it may have a pure stand of Black Spruce. Shrubs of the Coniferous Forest include Showy Mountain-Ash, Prickly Rose (*Rosa acicularis*), Bracted Honeysuckle (*Lonicera involucrata*), Squashberry (*Viburnum edule*), Blueberry (*Vaccinium myrtilloides*), Green Alder, and Laborador-tea (*Ledum groenlandicum*). The ground is carpeted with mosses, and the herbaceous and low woody species of the forest floor are rather few in number, presenting a uniform type of ground cover. The latter species include Bristly Club-moss (*Lycopodium annotinum*), Bunchberry, Twinflower, Sarsaparilla, Star-flower, and Miterwort (*Mitella nuda*), At the southern boundary of this region there are other trees and shrubs characteristic of the Mixed Forest.

PIGEON HAWK

In the northern section there are extensive areas covered by Black Spruce muskeg and Tamarack bogs. The ground in these low wet forests is covered with mosses, especially species of *Sphagnum*. The shrubs and herbs include Labrador-tea, Leather-leaf (*Chamaedaphne calyculata*), Bog-Laurel (*Kalmia polifolia*), Bilberry (*Vaccinium uliginosum*), Dwarf Birch (*Betula pumila* var. *glandulifera*), Skunk-Currant, sedges (*Carex* spp.), cotton-grasses (*Eriophorum* spp.), and Three-leaved False Solomon's-seal (*Smilacina trifolia*). A common type of vegetation in the Hudson Bay Lowlands is the Lichen–Black Spruce woodland, which is very open and park-like with scattered trees on a uniform dense carpet of lichens with very few herbs or shrubs. In this area also are many open bogs and fens, with occasional low stands of Tamarack and Dwarf Birch. White Spruce is confined to river banks and other well-drained sites; aspen and poplar become less common; and Black Spruce is dominant throughout, both on wet and dry soils.

The Coniferous Forest has a fairly distinct fauna although many of the typical species are also found in the northern part of the Mixed Forest Region, and some occurred still further south in former times. Only seven amphibians, mostly frogs, and one reptile, the Garter Snake, are widely found in the region.

Typical birds and mammals that are confined to the region or do not extend much further south include the Spruce Grouse, Black-backed and Northern Three-toed Woodpeckers, Yellow-bellied Flycatcher, Gray Jay, Common Raven, Boreal Chickadee, Tennessee Warbler, Cape May Warbler, Bay-breasted Warbler, Pine Grosbeak, Eastern Phenacomys, Marten, Fisher, and Caribou. Other species which are common in the Coniferous Forest but also occur considerably further south include Swainson's and Hermit Thrushes, White-throated Sparrow, Snowshoe Hare, Red Squirrel, Eastern and Least Chipmunks, Beaver, Deer Mouse, Red-backed Vole, Porcupine, Black Bear, Timber Wolf, Lynx, and Moose.

The northern section of this region contains the breeding ranges of the following birds: Canada Goose, Great Gray and Boreal Owls, Gray-cheeked Thrush, Blackpoll Warbler, Common Redpoll, Tree, White-crowned, and Fox Sparrows. Apparently, no mammals are confined to this section. Because the Coniferous

Forest Region has a very severe winter, the fauna changes markedly with the seasons and about 80 per cent of the breeding birds are migratory leaving behind mainly seed-eaters and predators. Many of the mammals hibernate or remain inactive and a few turn white in winter.

Among the invertebrates, biting insects and those that attack the foliage and bark of trees are abundant.

### TUNDRA

There is a narrow strip along the Hudson Bay shore in Ontario where trees do not occur. In the vicinity of Cape Henrietta Maria this strip becomes a belt ten miles or more in width and is the only extensive area of tundra in the province. The limits of this area are marked by the appearance of scattered individuals of spruce and Tamarack as one goes inland.

The vegetation of the coastal tundra is not truly Arctic but does include a number of species of "low-Arctic" affinity. There are beach ridges and sandy or gravelly shorelines with such species as Lyme-Grass (*Elymus arenarius*), Sandwort (*Arenaria peploides*), Lungwort (*Mertensia maritima*), and Thrift (*Armeria maritima*). There is also a heath-like cover, varying from an open to a dense mat of mosses and lichens with a low stratum of woody plants and scattered individuals or clumps of herbaceous perennials in a wide variety. Some of the woody plants include Labrador-tea (*Ledum groenlandicum, L. decumbens*), Rosebay (*Rhododendron lapponicum*), Avens (*Dryas integrifolia*), Bilberry, Mountain-Cranberry (*V. vitis-idaea* var. *minus*), Ground Birch (*Betula glandulosa*), Bearberry (*Arctostaphylos rubra*), Crowberry (*Empetrum nigrum*), Soapberry (*Shepherdia canadensis*), Juniper (*Juniperus communis* var. *depressa*), and various willows (*Salix arctica, S. reticulata,* et al.). In addition to grasses and sedges, a list of herbs would include the following: Moonwort (*Botrychium lunaria*), Bistort (*Polygonum viviparum*), Chickweed (*Cerastium alpinum*), Bladder-Campion (*Melandrium apetalum*), Anemone (*Anemone parviflora*), Buttercup (*Ranunculus pedatifidus* var. *leiocarpus*), Baked-apple (*Rubus chamaemorus*), Milk-Vetch (*Astragalus alpinus*), Large-flowered Wintergreen (*Pyrola grandiflora*), louseworts (*Pedicularis* spp.),

Groundsel (*Senecio congestus*), and Goldenrod (*Solidago multiradiata*).

No reptiles occur in this region but there is a record for one amphibian, the Wood Frog, at Cape Henrietta Maria.

The distinctive fauna of the northern coast of Ontario is made up partly of marine mammals such as the White Whale, Polar Bear, and seals and partly of birds and mammals of the tundra. These include the following: Arctic and Red-throated Loons, Snow Goose, Oldsquaw, eiders, Willow Ptarmigan, about eight sandpipers and plovers, Parasitic Jaeger, Arctic Tern, Water Pipit, longspurs, and Arctic Fox. The Snowy Owl and Snow Bunting occur regularly in the summer but there are no records of these birds nesting in Ontario.

Other features of this region are discussed in the guide for Cape Henrietta Maria.

### CHANGES IN THE FAUNA AND FLORA

Glacial retreat from different parts of Ontario probably occurred between five and twelve thousand years ago. It must have taken some time for plant communities to become established on the barren landscape which was uncovered. Plants and animals that had survived the glacial period in different areas came to Ontario from different directions. Much of northern Ontario was populated from the west, while southern Ontario was invaded from the west, south, and east. This can still be detected in the present fauna, particularly if subspecies are considered.

For aquatic animals the barriers to dispersal are particularly rigid and the distribution of many Ontario fishes gives evidence of the routes by which they entered the province following glacial retreat. For example, many fishes of the Great Lakes, and especially of Lake Erie, also occur in the Mississippi watershed which at one time served as an outlet for the Great Lakes. On the other hand, the presence of such marine species as the Three-spined Stickleback, Alewife, and Sea Lamprey in Lake Ontario can be explained by the marine invasion of this region following the disappearance of ice from the St. Lawrence Valley.

Judging from fossil evidence, a warm period followed the

retreat of ice and some plants and animals occurred considerably further north than similar forms do today. After about 1,000 B.C., the climate became cooler and life zones gradually retreated southward again. Changes in moisture accompanied some of these temperature changes and at one time prairie is believed to have extended into southern Ontario. Within historic times minor fluctuations in climate have continued to occur and during the last hundred years mean annual temperatures in southern Ontario have increased by four to five degrees Fahrenheit. All these events have left their mark on the present fauna and flora of Ontario.

Coinciding with the most recent climatic change, many animals —especially insects, birds, and mammals—are changing their distributions as pointed out by Urquhart *et al.* (1957). Most of the recorded movement has been of southern animals moving northward and northern species withdrawing. The most spectacular cases are those of birds such as the Cardinal and Turkey Vulture, which have moved 200 miles or more in the last half century. Mammals that have moved north include the Moose and White-tailed Deer. Some southern species such as the Gray Fox and Opossum seem to be more numerous in recent years than formerly. The Spruce Grouse and Caribou are examples of species that have withdrawn northward.

Although the main directions of movement are those to be expected in view of the climatic trend, it is not possible to prove that they are caused by climate. Indeed, many changes in distribution can undoubtedly be attributed to habitat alterations brought about by lumbering, clearing for agriculture, and the subsequent abandonment of farms to second growth. It has already been remarked that many common animals of southern Ontario are those of fields and forest edge. Some present-day movements are invasions of species such as the Western Meadowlark, Brewer's Blackbird, Clay-colored Sparrow, and Brush Wolf from the prairies into Ontario; and some of the species extending northward such as the Mourning Dove, Bobolink, and Eastern Meadowlark are moving into the more recently cleared land of northern Ontario.

Man has also altered the fauna of Ontario by bringing in animals from abroad. Some of the introductions have been accidental as a by-product of commerce, for example, the Norway Rat and the House Mouse as well as scores of insect pests that inhabit buildings or infest agricultural crops or gardens. A few are forest pests. Many natural enemies of insect pests have been intentionally introduced. Among these are a number of small predacious insects and the Starling and House Sparrow. A few species have been introduced as game or food sources, such as Carp, Gray Partridge, Ring-necked Pheasant, and European Hare. Most of the accidental and intentional introductions are found in the man-made habitats provided by agriculture and settlement.

We have only a hazy and conjectural picture of how the vegetation moved back into Ontario after the last retreat of the glaciers. Very little is known about the rate of migration of our native plants either as individual species or as associations such as occur in the forests. Normally the rate may be so slow that it is difficult to measure accurately except over long periods of time. Some data are available, however, for the rate of spread of certain introduced plants, chiefly our important weeds and conspicuous exotics.

Man has introduced hundreds of species of plants into Ontario since settlement first began. Many cultivated species have not strayed far from their planted sites, but some have escaped to fields, roadsides, or waste places. Other species, either intentional or accidental introductions, have spread and established themselves rapidly, becoming so thoroughly naturalized that they now appear as part of the wild flora. Only by knowing their history can we say whether they actually were part of the original flora. In this category belong such plants as the Common Field Buttercup (*Ranunculus acris*), Bladder-Campion (*Silene cucubalus*), Cinquefoil (*Potentilla recta*), St. John's-wort (*Hypericum perforatum*), Wild Carrot (*Daucus carota*), Blueweed (*Echium vulgare*), Ox-eye-Daisy (*Chrysanthemum leucanthemum*), Milfoil (*Achillea millefolium*), Chicory (*Cichorium intybus*), and Orange Hawkweed (*Hieracium aurantiacum*). Introduced species may be considered as troublesome weeds when they appear in fields of agricultural crops or as wildflowers when found in disused pastures or along roadsides.

Although many trees and shrubs have been introduced into Ontario very few have escaped from cultivation and become weedy. The main proportion of weeds are herbaceous annuals, biennials, or perennials. In some areas as much as 25–30 per cent of the flowering plants may be introductions from other countries. The percentage drops off as one goes north or away from centres of settlement and agriculture and is relatively small in the forested regions. The number of weeds inside a forest association is usually very small, the introduced species being conspicuous only in clearings, along trails, and at the edges of the woods. This is because most exotic species are unable to compete with the native species in the closed community.

A notable example of an introduced species occurring both in open areas and in more or less undisturbed forest habitats in southern Ontario is the Helleborine (*Epipactis helleborine*), which, however, appears to be restricted to calcareous soils. Some species, for example, the Selfheal or Heal-all (*Prunella vulgaris*), are thought to have both a native variety and an introduced variety within our province.

REFERENCES

AMERICAN ORNITHOLOGISTS' UNION (A.O.U.), Check-List of North American Birds, 5th ed. (1957), pp. i–viii, 1–691.

CANADA, DEPT. OF MINES AND TECHNICAL SURVEYS, GEOGRAPHICAL BRANCH, Atlas of Canada (1957), 110 plates.

FOX, W. S., and SOPER, J. H., The Distribution of Some Trees and Shrubs of the Carolinian Zone of Southern Ontario, part III, Transactions of Royal Canadian Institute, 30 (1955), pp. 99–130.

MERRIAM, C. H., Life Zones and Crop Zones of the United States, U.S. Dept. of Agriculture, Biological Survey, bull. 10 (1898).

ROWE, J. S., Forest Regions of Canada, Canada, Dept. of Northern Affairs and National Resources, Forestry Branch, bull. 123 (1959), pp. 1–71.

SNYDER, L. L., A Faunal Investigation of Western Rainy River District, Ontario, Transactions of Royal Canadian Institute, 22 (1938), pp. 157–213.

URQUHART, F. A. *et al.*, Changes in the Fauna of Ontario (University of Toronto Press, 1957), pp. i–iv, 2–75.

# Regional Guides

APPROXIMATELY 2,900 square miles in area, Algonquin Park lies on a southern extension of the Precambrian Shield between Georgian Bay and the Ottawa River. Once mountainous country, this land has been eroded and glaciated to form a rolling, hilly upland, which is higher than the surrounding country. Streams and rivers flow through it and down almost 1,000 feet to the Mattawa and Ottawa rivers on the north and east, and the Muskoka and South rivers on the south and west.

Farming was tried in a few places in the park for a short period during the 1800's, but could not be established on a permanent basis because of the characteristically thin soil of this area. For the main part it is forest, in which four general forest types are to be seen. The western two-thirds, on the hills, are composed of Sugar-Maple–Yellow Birch–Hemlock forest, while in the low-lying areas spruce forests predominate. The remaining one-third, on the east side, is made up of large sand plains and long, rocky ridges. The forest here is White, Red, and Jack-Pine, with maple in higher or more silty locations. Much of the park has been burned over by forest fires within the past eighty years, and heavily and repeatedly burned areas are now overgrown with aspen, White Birch, spruce, and Balsam-Fir.

Essentially a wilderness, the park contains birds and mammals not normally seen close to civilization. The more persistent observer may encounter the Black Bear, Timber Wolf, Moose, Otter, Mink, Marten, Fisher, Goshawk, Osprey, Bald Eagle, Barred Owl, Pileated and both Three-toed Woodpeckers. The casual observer will see the White-tailed Deer, Beaver, Red Fox, Blue and Gray Jays, Black-capped and Boreal Chickadees, White-throated Sparrow, many species of warblers, Spruce and Ruffed Grouse, and the ever present Common Raven. Field species are comparatively rare because of the scarcity of suitable habitat.

The best way to see Algonquin Park is to travel by canoe or on foot. One may spend weeks in the interior on water routes seemingly made for the canoeist, and in the southern part of the park there are a number of good hiking trails.

Access to the park is limited. By rail one can enter the north side on the main line of the C.N.R., operating between North Bay and Ottawa. The landing of aircraft within the park is restricted to certain lakes. Access by road is largely limited to Highway 60, which runs through only the southern portion. A bus service operates between Huntsville and Renfrew. Some park perimeter points may also be reached on a few gravel roads open in summer only. For up-to-date information on the points of access contact the District Forester at Pembroke.

The Ontario Department of Lands and Forests employs a permanent park naturalist in Algonquin Park, who, with a summer staff, conducts a programme of evening talks, guided hikes, and special features for park visitors. In addition, as part of the programme, labelled nature trails, a nature museum, and a pioneer logging exhibit are in operation during the spring, summer, and fall months. These naturalists are also available to help visitors in any way they can, and will assist organized groups if arrangements are made in advance.

The Department of Lands and Forests issues the following useful publications which may be obtained free of charge at the Nature Museum in the park, or by writing to the District Forester, Department of Lands and Forests, 162 Agnes Street, Pembroke, Ontario: *Algonquin Provincial Park (General Information)*; *Canoe Routes, Algonquin Provincial Park*; *A Guide to Angling in Algonquin Provincial Park*; *Reptiles of Algonquin Park*; *Check-Lists of Birds, Plants, Reptiles and Amphibians*. Maps are also available from the District Forester. *Lands and Forests Map 47A* (2 miles to 1 inch), costing 75 cents, covers the whole park, and the *National Topographic Series* (1 mile to 1¼ inches), at 55 cents each, covers the areas of Algonquin, Whitney, Opeongo, Lake Lavieille, Burnt Root, Achray, Kawagama.

Because of the large size and extensive wilderness of Algonquin Park, a thorough guide would be a book in itself. As most visitors enter the park on Highway 60 and remain close to the highway, the following guide refers only to this area. One should keep in mind that this region is heavily used during July and

August, and that trips to the interior may prove more fruitful for nature study.

The possibilities of winter travel in the park should not be forgotten. The main highway and a few roads used for logging are open year round. Thirty to forty inches of snow may accumulate on the ground by February, and from then until spring it is usually ideal for snowshoeing, with warm, sunny days and cool nights. This is the time of year to see winter birds and evidence of non-hibernating mammals.

Along Highway 60 from the West Gate (Mile 0.0) to the East Gate (Mile 36.5) there are mileage markers to assist in locating the various points of special interest and facilities. The following list contains only a few of the places with particular attractions for the naturalist. It should be emphasized that many in-between points may be well worth investigating.

PARK BOUNDARY. This is 3 miles west of the West Gate at Park or Long Lake. In spring and fall the marshy shoreline is much used by migrating birds, and some are always present in summer.

MILE 0.0, WEST GATE. A checkpoint for vehicle entry permits and guns, this gate is set in the midst of an advanced maple forest. Jays, warblers, and woodpeckers may be seen from the parking area.

MILE 1.0, HERON CREEK. Lined on both sides by thick spruce forest, the area abounds in northern shrub species, such as Leather-leaf, Sweet Gale, and Labrador-tea. Spruce Grouse and Boreal Chickadees are the exceptional birds to look for.

MILE 1.0, OXTONGUE RIVER PICNIC AREA. The picnic ground is surrounded by a mixture of different types of forest, and one may expect a great variety of wildlife. Two paths follow the river for some distance.

MILE 3.2, DEPARTMENT OF HIGHWAYS GRAVEL YARD. Still in a mixed forest, one may find jays, warblers, crossbills, and Pine Siskins around this small cleared area, which extends from the highway to the river.

MILE 4.3. The highway still parallels the Oxtongue River at this point. There are many footpaths to the river which should prove fruitful for the birdwatcher and botanist.

MILE 6.3, COOT LAKE. This lake is on the south side of the highway. In July and August there are usually Black Ducks and Common Mergansers, and in spring and fall migrant ducks are always present.

MILE 8.9, HAINS MEMORIAL LOOKOUT. On a hill overlooking Smoke Lake, this area combines a short nature trail, picnic ground, and lookout into a worthwhile stop. This is one of the few places in the park where one may see Red Oak, and there is a rich variety of ground cover plants. Red-eyed Vireo, Rose-breasted Grosbeak, Black-and-white Warbler, Black-throated Green Warbler, and Winter Wren are among the birds to be expected.

MILE 11.2, DEER LAKE TRAIL. Sometimes used as a nature trail, a good path travels for one mile through mature hardwood forest to marshy Deer Lake.

MILE 13.0, ALGONQUIN PARK NATURE MUSEUM. Open May 15 to Thanksgiving (Canadian), the museum portrays some of Algonquin's natural and human history. A park naturalist is on duty to answer inquiries.

MILE 13.8, LITTLE MADAWASKA RIVER. There are interesting marshy areas on both sides of the highway. The first park specimen of Blanding's Turtle was killed by a car at this point.

MILE 14.4, ABANDONED RAILWAY ROADBED. The old railway may be followed for some distance in either direction and runs through much promising territory. A short distance to the southeast, towards Cache Lake, a typical spruce-Tamarack swamp is frequented by Olive-sided Flycatchers and other birds characteristic of that habitat.

MILE 15.5, CACHE LAKE. Turn south on either of two roads leaving the highway. Common Loons and Common Mergansers breed on the lake, and there are extensive marshes nearby.

MILE 17.5, JACK LAKE TRAIL. A marked trail leads to the lake, about one mile from the highway. The trail runs through mixed forest as well as mature stands of hardwood and Hemlock. A good place for such birds as Three-toed Woodpeckers and Solitary Vireos.

MILE 18.3. A little-used gravel road on the south side leads to a small lake quite close to the highway. There is usually an active Beaver colony here and a possibility of seeing Black Ducks and Hooded Mergansers.

MILE 19.0, ENTERING THE TWO RIVERS BASIN. From this point eastward the predominant forest type along the highway is Spruce–Balsam-Fir–Aspen–White Birch. This area has been recently and extensively burned.

MILE 19.5, MEW LAKE. The extensive mud-flat shoreline is a botanist's delight, and the surrounding spruce-grown plain, both north and south of the highway, shelters Spruce Grouse and Boreal Chickadees.

MILE 20.0, AIRFIELD. A road to the south, just east of a small bridge on the highway, leads to an emergency landing field maintained by the federal Department of Transport. Although no exceptional species may be encountered, it is of interest to find Bobolinks, Eastern Meadowlarks, Vesper and Savannah Sparrows, and an occasional Grasshopper Sparrow well established in a small opening surrounded by many miles of unbroken forest. The north and west branches of the Madawaska River enter Lake of Two Rivers here, and marshes and alder swamps contain a great deal of material awaiting the exploration of a naturalist.

MILE 23.5, BLACK FOX LAKE ROAD. The old lumber road north from the highway may be followed 3 miles to Black Fox Lake. This area has been both lumbered and burned in comparatively recent times, but the resulting forest of Aspen–Spruce–Balsam-Fir is ideal cover for birds and mammals. There is a possibility of meeting with almost any kind of wildlife found in the park, from a Winter Wren to a Moose.

MILE 26.0, LOOKOUT TRAIL. This trail offers a variety of habitat and at its end an exceptional view over a vast area of Algonquin Park. This is good thrush country, and the Wood, Hermit, and Swainson's Thrush and Veery have all been found here.

MILE 26.5, ROCK LAKE ROAD. The well-travelled road south from the highway follows the course of a marshy stream on which there are a number of Beaver dams and ponds and a rich variety of other wildlife and plants associated with this type of habitat.

MILE 31.0, OPEONGO ROAD. From the highway to Lake Opeongo,

WOLF

approximately 3 miles, this road roughly parallels the winding course of Costello Creek, which is bordered throughout most of its length by marshes and bogs containing great numbers of birds, mammals, plants, and insects.

MILE 34.5, SMITH LAKE ROAD. This partly overgrown road, which must be travelled on foot, was once a railway between Whitney and Lake Opeongo. Like the Black Fox Lake Road area, it has been heavily lumbered and burned, but the resulting "scrubby" forest cover provides excellent habitat for a variety of living things. The road passes through boggy areas where Pitcher-plant, sundew, Pogonia, and many other aquatic and shoreline plants abound, and it is one of the few areas in this part of the park where the little rock fern, Rusty Woodsia, may be located.

MILE 36.5, PIONEER LOGGING MUSEUM. A display here tells about the early days when the great pine forest was being removed by lumbering. The present semi-open surroundings make it a very good area, particularly for such birds as the Hermit Thrush and White-throated Sparrow.

A. F. HELMSLEY

## ❀ BANCROFT AREA: HALIBURTON AND HASTINGS COUNTIES

THIS GUIDE COVERS Haliburton County and the northern half of Hastings County. The focal point is Bancroft. It is a perfect area for the naturalist who likes to explore on reasonably good back roads and wishes to walk for miles on old logging trails. This area abounds in lakes and rivers, large and small, named and unnamed. The terrain is ever changing with long stretches of dense woods, immense spruce-Tamarack bogs and swamps, steep hills and rock cuts, dotted with rolling farm lands. It is an area of special appeal to the naturalist interested in rocks and semi-precious stones. It has an Algonquin-type terrain and flora and fauna as far as the lower boundary of Haliburton which crosses

Highway 28 just north of Apsley. There, at the Haliburton sign post, you can hear all of the common Ontario thrushes singing in summer, except, of course, the Gray-cheeked Thrush.

As the crow flies (or the raven) Bancroft is about 25 miles from Algonquin Park. It is a wonderful area for birds, particularly because there is an overlapping of northern and southern species. Such northern species as the Red and White-winged Crossbills, Evening Grosbeak, and Black-backed Three-toed Woodpecker can be seen there in summer, along with such southern species as Indigo Bunting, Mourning Dove, and Brown Thrasher. Some of the common summer birds are Wood Duck, Broad-winged Hawk, Osprey, Ruffed Grouse, Whip-poor-will, Belted Kingfisher, Pileated Woodpecker, Eastern Wood Pewee, Cedar Waxwing, Black-throated Blue Warbler, Rose-breasted Grosbeak, Purple Finch, and White-throated Sparrow. In the winter, possibly one of the finest stretches of good road in all of southern Ontario on which to see northern birds extends from Burleigh Falls to Bancroft along Highway 28.

The highway into and through the Haliburton-Hastings area on the west is Highway 35 from Lindsay, entering Haliburton just past Norland and passing through Minden and Dorset and connecting with Highway 60 at Dwight. On the north, Highway 60 from Huntsville enters Haliburton near Dwight and goes through Algonquin Park to Whitney, Madawaska, and Barry's Bay to Ottawa. Some of the highest points of altitude in the province are on Highway 60 near Barry's Bay and Killaloe. On the east, Highway 62 runs up from Madoc through Bancroft to Barry's Bay on Highway 60. Centrally, Highway 28 goes from Peterborough, through Burleigh Falls, to Bancroft. Bancroft is the hub of a number of lesser roads, all of great interest to the explorer. Highway 127 is the route from Maynooth to Whitney and Algonquin Park, and Highway 500 runs through Bancroft, east to McArthurs Mills and west to Wilberforce and Gooderham. An interesting gravel road, Highway 507, runs south from Gooderham to Highway 36 and passes Catchacoma and the Mississauga Lakes.

There are no natural history clubs in the area closer than Peterborough but a new mineral club has been organized at Bancroft. It is called the Bancroft Mineral Society and hopes to make Bancroft the "Mecca" of "rock hounds" and other mineralogists for the American continent. Conducted tours are planned to noted mineral sites of the district and regular field trips are taken every Thursday evening. There has been very little published on the flora and fauna of the area. Margaret K. H. Mitchell published in the *Canadian Field-Naturalist* of October 1929 a list of the summer birds of Miners Bay and vicinity in Haliburton County and a revised list in the same journal in November 1937. George Toner has published articles on the flora and fauna of the Bancroft area periodically in the *Bancroft Times,* and E. V. Stark has published the Audubon Christmas Census for the past ten years.

Two uranium mines still active in 1960 were Bicroft on Paudash Lake (turn left off Highway 28 on to Highway 109 just past the head of the lake) and Faraday on Highway 28, 3 miles east of Highway 109 on the left side. An inactive mine, Dyno is located on Dyno or Cheddar Road running west off Highway 28, 2 miles south of Paudash Lake. The Bancroft area is liberally dotted with abandoned mine properties that may prove interesting to the rock and mineral collector. These mines and other rock outcroppings can be located by using the following provincial and federal mine surveys: *Ontario Dept. of Mines Annual Report,* no. 52, "Mineral Occurrences in the Haliburton Area," see map no. 52A; *Annual Report,* no. 62, "Geology of Brudenell-Raglan Area," Nat. Geological maps nos. 31F4 and 31F5; *Annual Report,* no. 64, "Dungannon and Mayo," maps 31F4 and 31C13; *Annual Report,* no. 66, "Geology of Cardiff and Faraday Townships," maps 31F4, 31C13, and 31SW.

The Department of Lands and Forests has established several small parks and roadside camps in the area and is reserving Crown lands, especially the sand beaches, for the public on all newly developed lakes. A fine picnic site is situated at Eel's Creek (9.1 miles north of Burleigh Falls) on Highway 28. Department of Lands and Forests District Headquarters is located at Lindsay where the Chief Ranger and the Biologist are stationed. There are two Chief Ranger Headquarters, at Minden and Gooderham, and two Deputy Chief Ranger Headquarters, at Apsley and Haliburton. There are ten conservation officers in the Lindsay district. Tourist accommodation is good at the resort lakes. The main highways are excellent and secondary roads are good. But for real adventure, explore the back roads and hike up the old logging trails.

The Haliburton area is noted for the beauty of its autumn colouring. One can take an exceptionally beautiful colour tour by driving north from Burleigh Falls, where the vivid colour begins, to Bancroft via Highway 28 and "Old Monck Road." If the Burleigh Falls bridge is taken as the starting point for this tour, the following mileages and directions would apply.

7.4, Peterborough Game Preserve.

9.1, Department of Highways roadside camp at Eel's Creek with tables, fireplaces, and rest rooms.

17.4, town of Apsley; take either road through town, or bypass.

24.8, Eel's Lake, road to left but do not turn.

25.9, Eel's Creek.

27.9, Haliburton County line.

28.6, Lands and Forests camping site on Eel's Lake (poor road in and incomplete camp).

29.9, turn left from Highway 28 on Dyno Mine or Cheddar Road (Highway 648, paved).

30.2, pass the Dyno townsite on left.

32.7, Dyno Mine on right side (now closed down).

37.5, junction with Highway 121; turn right and follow Highway 121.

42.2, Cardiff townsite. Turn left to townsite then right along edge of townsite, with townsite on left side. You are now on the Old Monck Road which is a very winding and narrow road, but in good condition.

43.0, steep winding hill (low gear); on top stop for a panoramic view of the surrounding countryside.

45.2, crossroad, but continue straight ahead.

51.2, Highway 28 just south of Bancroft; turn right for return to Burleigh Falls.

54.3, Faraday Mine on right.

57.6, Highway 109 (paved) to Bicroft Mine.

57.8, Paudash Lake. You are now on route back to Burleigh Falls by Highway 28.

For another enjoyable trip go north from Bancroft on Highway 62 to Maynooth, north on Highway 127 to Highway 60, east on Highway 60 to Barry's Bay, south on Highway 62 through

Combermere, Maynooth, and back to Bancroft, a tour of about 115 miles. This area is the Madawaska Valley.

An equally interesting and enjoyable trip is the Scenic Drive from Dorset to Minden on Highway 35 (see guide for Muskoka).

EARL STARK

## ✤ BARRIE

BARRIE IS SITUATED at the western extremity of Lake Simcoe at the end of Kempenfelt Bay. This long bay stretches eastward from Barrie for 9 miles, with a width of approximately 1½ miles, widening into the main lake at the eastern boundary of Simcoe County. The city is approached from the north and south by Highways 11, 400, and 27, and from the west by Highways 90 and 26.

The local natural history club is the Brereton Field Naturalists' Club which meets about six times a year and holds Saturday morning hikes in spring and fall. A list of the executive is on file at the Public Library for the convenience of anyone wishing to get in touch with the officials of the club.

The club's area of interest is, in the main, Simcoe County. This provides much scope, Simcoe being the fourth largest county in Ontario, with considerable variety in types of habitat. In the following accounts of points of interest to naturalists, the routes start from Memorial Square on Dunlop Street in the city of Barrie directly north of the C.N.R. station on the waterfront, which is approximately the centre of the county.

THE WATERFRONT. Migrating waterfowl in spring and fall may be seen along the shore of Kempenfeldt Bay. The mud flats southeast of Allandale Station sometimes harbour wading birds. From Memorial Square follow Dunlop Street west 5 blocks. Bear left at stop light to Bradford Street. Go south on Bradford Street 5 blocks. Turn left into C.N.R. station. Walk southeast along shore to boat houses.

SEED PLANT AT ANGUS. A wooded and landscaped area surrounds the buildings of the Department of Lands and Forests seed extracting plant. Migrants and nesting birds may be seen in season. Grounds are open 8.00 A.M. to 5.00 P.M. Monday to Friday. From Memorial Square on Dunlop Street go west to signs for Highway 90. Follow highway to Angus, about 11 miles, and inquire for seed plant.

MINESING SWAMP. This is an extensive swamp in the valley of the Nottawasaga River. It lies north of Highway 90 and south of Highway 26, and between Concession XI of Vespra Township on the east and the town line of Vespra and Sunnidale on the west. Going in from the west side one can reach a very large Great Blue heronry. Anyone wishing to visit the heronry should arrange to be guided by a member of the Brereton Club, or by one who is familiar with the area. Rubber boots are a necessity. The roads around the swamp area are of much interest to naturalists, especially in April, May, and June.

HENDRIE FOREST. From Memorial Square on Dunlop Street drive west one block, turn north and follow the signs for Highways 27 and 26 until Highway 26 turns off to the left. Follow Highway 26, and after crossing a railway track turn right at the third road running north. Follow this to the first crossroad. On the northeast corner is a wooded area which is part of the Hendrie Forest. Some three or four acres here contain a boggy area in which will be found flora and fauna similar to that of a northern bog.

LITTLE LAKE AND WILLOW CREEK (adjacent to Little Lake). Little Lake is a small, shallow lake about 2 miles north of Barrie. Its marshy shores provide nesting cover for wrens, terns, shorebirds, and waterfowl. Migrating birds, from warblers to geese, use it. The hills on the north and south side of the lake support upland birds and assorted other species. It is easily accessible and usually worth looking at. Three approaches to the lake and creek are possible. (1) Start from Memorial Square and proceed east on Dunlop Street until Dunlop runs into Blake Street. Follow Blake one block and turn north on St. Vincent Street. Continue on St. Vincent, crossing Highway 400. Two and one-half miles north of Highway 400 is a bridge crossing Willow Creek. (2) From Memorial Square go north on Owen Street one block, east on Collier Street one block, north on Mulcaster Street 4 blocks and east on Penetang Street to Duckworth Street which runs to Little Lake. Boats may be rented here. (3) Proceed west from Memorial Square on Dunlop Street one block, turn right, following the signs for Highway 27 to Highway 400. Follow Highway 400 east 3.2 miles to the bridge over Willow Creek. Cross the highway to the parking lot northwest of the bridge. Walk ½ mile along the shore of the creek to Little Lake.

HOLLAND MARSH. This large marsh, partly in Simcoe and partly in York counties, is now almost totally reclaimed for vegetable gardens. However, the few acres which are left in their natural state still provide nesting grounds for many interesting species including such rarities as Yellow Rails and LeConte's Sparrows, and one or two other species which do not nest elsewhere in southern Ontario. It is worth a visit at any time of the year. Go south from Barrie on Highway 11, through Bradford and across the bridge over the Schomberg River (still on Highway 11). Take the first road to the left, that is, north, and continue as far as possible.

ORR LAKE. Here, waterfowl may be seen in migration. Follow Highway 11 from Memorial Square on Dunlop Street to junction of Highway 93. Follow Highway 93 north for about 15 miles to Orr Lake.

BEAVER POND ON HIGHWAY 90. From Memorial Square on Dunlop Street proceed west, following the signs for Highway 90 for approximately ¾ of a mile to a White Rose service station on the left. Climb the fence on the left and go 200 yards to the pond. Ducks and shorebirds occur in season, also nesting Common Snipe.

CONCESSION X OF VESPRA. From Memorial Square on Dunlop Street go west 6 blocks to Parkside Drive. Turn north on Parkside Drive 3 blocks to Sunnidale Road. Drive west on Sunnidale Road about 3 miles to Concession VIII. Just past the house at the corner on the right is a field where Grasshopper Sparrows nest. Continue about 2 miles to Concession X. Turn north on X and proceed about 3½ miles to a small bridge crossing Willow Creek. There are nesting marsh birds and ducks in season in the marsh area on the left. Continue north about 2 miles to crossroads of Minesing village, and west for 2 concessions. The fields here are flooded in spring and provide stopping places for migrating water birds.

STAYNER SPEEDWAY. Follow directions for Hendrie Forest above to Highway 26. Follow Highway 26 for about 12 miles to sign for Stayner Speedway. Upland Plovers nest in these fields.

MARL LAKE. Marsh birds and migrants occur here in season. Follow Highway 26 (see Hendrie Forest above) to second concession road past bridge over Nottawasaga River (about 9 miles). Go north about 6 miles to Wasaga Beach Country Club. Take next road to right down to the lake.

*Brereton Field Naturalists' Club*

 **BELLEVILLE**

ROUTES TO POINTS of interest start from the intersection of Highways 2 and 14 in Belleville.

HUFF'S ISLAND. Go 6 miles south on Highway 14 in Prince Edward County. The island is east of the highway and is surrounded by extensive marshes which support a population of marsh birds.

LAKE ON THE MOUNTAIN. Go 20 miles south on Highway 14 to Highway 33, then 10 miles east on Highway 33 through Picton to Glenora and Lake on the Mountain. Now a provincial park, this area affords a view of fine scenery and interesting geological formations.

SANDBANKS AREA. Go 20 miles south on Highway 14 to Highway 33. The sandbanks extend westward between the highway and Lake Ontario as far as Wellington which is on Highway 33, 8 miles west of the intersection of Highways 14 and 33. This is the finest example of active sand dune formation in southern Ontario. It is an excellent habitat for shorebirds and has a very interesting dune-succession flora.

AMELIASBURG INLIER. Go 5 miles south on Highway 14. The inlier is ½ mile east of the highway and is an interesting geological formation with a filled-in cave.

SHANNONVILLE INLIER. Go 10 miles east on Highway 2 to Shannonville, then one mile north from the main intersection. This inlier is another odd and interesting geological formation.

SCUTTLE HOLE. Go north on Highway 37 to village of Latta, turn right at the main intersection and go 2 miles to the bridge on the Moira River. On the east bank of the river is the Scuttle Hole which shows caves and unusual rock formations and is an excellent habitat for wildlife. Visiting children should be attended by adults.

*Quinte Field Naturalists' Club*

## ✻ BRANTFORD

BRANTFORD IS SITUATED in Brant County approximately 24 miles north of Lake Erie, in the valley of the Grand River. The banks, flats, and marshes of the valley provide habitats suitable for many species of plant and animal life. The surrounding area is typical southern Ontario farmland, with open fields and wooded areas. To the south lies Norfolk County which contains some of the finest areas in Ontario for the naturalist. Points of interest for Simcoe and Long Point mainland are included in this section.

Brantford is approached from the east and west by Highways 2 and 53 and from the north and south by Highway 24. Routes to points of interest start at the grounds of the Canadian National Institute for the Blind, at the southwest corner of Brant and St. Paul avenues at the junction of Highways 2 and 24.

This city is represented in the Federation of Ontario Naturalists by the Brantford Nature Club. Meetings are held at Glenhurst Gardens at 8.00 P.M. on the first Tuesday of each month, January to March, September to November. Visitors may contact members of the club by phoning the Brantford Public Library.

GLENHURST GARDENS. From starting point go west on Brant Avenue one block to bridge approach and Ava Road. Continue west on Ava Road ¼ mile to gates of Glenhurst, a public park and art centre of the city of Brantford. It contains formal gardens and a nature trail through a wildflower garden with many native flowers and trees.

MOHAWK PARK. From starting point follow Highway 2 east through city approximately 2 miles—Brant Avenue to Colborne to Linwood Drive and entrance to Mohawk Park, a public park of the city of Brantford. It has camping facilities and a playground, and wooded areas and a lake provide good birding in spring and fall.

PINEHURST PARK. From starting point follow Highway 2 west to Highway 24A in the town of Paris. Pinehurst is between Paris and Galt on Highway 24A, 6 miles north of Paris, 7 miles south of Galt. This park of more than 100 acres is operated by the Grand Valley Conservation Authority, and access is by toll during summer months. There are camping, picnic, fishing, and swimming facilities, and a nature trail with over 100 varieties of native trees, including Sassafras, and plants labelled. Cerulean Warbler and Blue-gray Gnatcatcher are summer residents.

MAPLE GROVE SWAMP. From starting point go south 6½ miles on Highway 24 to the village of Mount Pleasant. Continue approximately one mile to first concession road west, then west one concession 1¼ miles, south one concession ½ mile and west about 350 yards. Continue west from this point on narrow unpaved lane to Maple Grove Swamp. Access is by permission of local owners. There are several miles of cedar swamp and hardwood forest, many varieties of native plants, including some orchids. Birding is fair to excellent with the season.

COPETOWN BOG. From starting point go north 5 miles on Highway 24 to Osborne Corners, the junction of Highways 5, 24, and 99. Go east on Highway 99 approximately 12 miles to Copetown, then south at main corner in village ¾ mile to the bog. It is a well-known nesting place for wild ducks. A project of the Hamilton Naturalists' Club, the area is under option to that club and is open to naturalists.

TURKEY POINT. This area is on Lake Erie 12 miles south and west of the town of Simcoe. From junction of Highways 3 and 24 in Simcoe proceed south on Highway 24 to the point where it turns east. Continue south on paved county road, following road signs and map to Turkey Point. The road to Turkey Point Gun Club provides access to excellent birding and botany. Access to posted areas is by permission of local owners. The cliff is steep and the heavily wooded area above the cliff consists mainly of reforested Crown lands. The Turkey Point area contains several species of wildflowers, trees, and birds not normally found in other parts of Ontario.

ST. WILLIAMS FORESTRY STATION. Three concessions (about 3 miles) north of village of St. Williams, there is a provincial forestry station with public park and picnic grounds. Feeding stations are maintained by resident employees during winter. This is a fine area for warblers in spring. One concession west of this point is a nesting area of Prairie Warblers.

BACKUS WOODS. From village of St. Williams go west 3 miles to intersection marked with historical site sign for Backhouse Mill. Proceed north past the mill to the next concession road. From this intersection continue north into woods on unimproved road. Backus Woods consists of over 600 acres of virgin forest and offers a variety of plant and animal life. Flowering Dogwood is abundant, and there are several Tuliptrees. It is also the nesting site for such species as the Northern Waterthrush, and Pileated Woodpecker.

LONG POINT. See guide for Long Point.

K. BEEMER
*Brantford Nature Club*

 **BROCKVILLE**

THE TOWN OF Brockville is located on the westerly edge of the Ottawa Valley, where the Frontenac Axis borders the valley lowlands. Thus, on its east is located a fairly prosperous farming area while on the west is the rougher country given over to dairy farming. Because it is situated on the St. Lawrence River at a spot which seldom freezes over completely in the winter it is a wintering spot for many species of waterfowl. The rough area to the west and north provides many lakes, ponds, marshes, woods, swamps, and bogs, all of which supply habitat for many species of birds, mammals, and flowers in a wide range of soil and moisture conditions. Brockville is reached by Highways 2 and 401 from the east and west, and by Highways 16, 29, and 42 from the north.

The local natural history club is the Brockville Nature Club which holds its meetings at 8.00 p.m. in the basement room of the Public Library located on Buell Street one block north from King Street, on the second Friday of each month from September to May inclusive. Visitors to the area can get in touch with officials of the club by phoning the Brockville Public Library (DIamond 2-3936).

Routes to points of interest to naturalists, in the following account, start at the war memorial (cenotaph) located in the Court House Square at the junction of King Street and Broad Street, in the heart of the town.

SHERWOOD FOREST (local name only). Leaving the cenotaph go east along King Street about 1½ miles and take the first lane going north from Highway 2 east of the Ontario Hospital property. Proceed north about ½ mile to the railroad, park car, and walk, crossing the railroad to the woods beyond. This area is about one mile square and is made up of a mixed wood-lot, partly second growth. There is considerable Buckthorn in shallow topsoil on limestone, and there is an old quarry and pasture. This area is little used and provides excellent cover for mammals and birds. There are many birds which nest in this spot. It also has much good winter cover and feed.

JOHNSTON PROPERTY. From the cenotaph go east along King Street and Highway 2 about 2½ miles to the Ralph Dairy. Directly across from it is a lane running down to the river. Permission to enter should be obtained from the owners, the Johnstons, who live at the foot of the lane. This property consists of about ten acres sloping gradually from the roadway to the river. There are two benches in this slope, formed by the old river-bed cutting at the soft limestone of the shore. The property is partly cleared and partly covered in a fairly dense mixture of Hawthorn, grape vines, Red and Sugar Maple, White Cedar, Choke-Cherry, White Birch, willow, locust, sumac, Apple, and Virginia Creeper. Thus it provides excellent cover for summering, nesting, and wintering species of birds. There are few people in the immediate neighbourhood, so many species of smaller mammals live here undisturbed.

ST. LAWRENCE RIVER. Going east from the cenotaph along Highway 2 the visitor will find that the road runs very close to the river for many miles and that much of this area is excellent for observing waterfowl and aquatic mammals during both summer and winter. From the Iroquois area eastward the observer will find that the new lake formed by the dam at Cornwall has provided wonderful nesting cover for ducks and geese. There are many nesting Blue-winged Teal, Mallards, Pintails, Black Ducks, and even Shovelers in these shallow marsh areas. There is also a Great Blue heronry in the woods lying between Highways 2 and 401 about 5 miles east of Iroquois.

LONG SWAMP. From the cenotaph go east along King Street about ½ mile, 11 blocks (counting on the north side of the street) to North Augusta Road. Turn north and proceed about 2½ miles up this street, crossing Highway 401, and proceed past the Drive-in Theatre to the woods which are about ½ mile beyond the theatre. This is a large wood extending many miles in both directions. In spring particularly, the roadway running across the swamp here provides an excellent spot for observing the migration of small birds. The edges of the swamp provide excellent cover for many nesting species.

LONG SWAMP POND. Follow the same directions above to the Drive-in Theatre. At this point turn west and go about one mile to just over the first railway crossing. This spot is for those with canoes and for those who wish to observe waterfowl and aquatic plant life. Proceed up the small stream that will be found here to the large pond which is about ½ mile up. This pond is about one mile square. At present it is surrounded by farms which are given over largely to grazing, as the soil is insufficiently productive for crops. The pond therefore is not generally frequented and so provides an excellent breeding ground for most marsh birds and for Black Terns, as well as for aquatic and other mammals. Marsh and swamp plants and insects are found here in great profusion.

LONG SWAMP BOG. Follow the same directions outlined above to the Drive-in Theatre. At the theatre continue north another 2½ miles. Shortly after passing a church on the right side of the road one will come to a bog area which extends along both sides of the highway. It is the most southerly bog in this area, and has characteristic plants of the northern bogs, such as Black Spruce and Sphagnum Moss as well as some wild orchids.

LEE'S POND. This area is frequently used by the public but permission to enter it should be obtained from the owner, Mr. Fred Grant, R.R. 3, Brockville, whose telephone number may be found in the Brockville section of the telephone book. From the cenotaph proceed west about 1½ miles on Highway 2 to a road going north to Lyn village. Follow this road to the village. On entering this village one finds a Y-intersection. Take the right-hand road leading north for about 2½ miles to the "North Star Farm"; turn right once more at this point and follow the road for about one mile to the first laneway leading right. Park the car and walk along the road allowance going *left* down to the lake. The lake provides a mixed habitat of marsh and swamp with many Mallards, Black Ducks, Blue-winged Teal, Wood Ducks, Green Herons, Great Blue Herons, and Osprey nesting around its shores.

ST. PETER'S CEMETERY. Leave the cenotaph and go west along King Street about 1¾ miles to the first cemetery which will be found on both sides of the road. The area next to the river is most profitable for observing birds and consists of about twenty acres bounded on the south by the St. Lawrence River. The shore here is screened with a narrow band of willow shrubs. The west boundary is the creek, which contains a large area of marsh that harbours many marsh-breeding birds. The creek usually provides some mud flats on which shorebirds may be found in spring and fall. Across the creek is a large number of tall White Pine in which owls and Bald Eagles frequently roost in winter.

LILY BAY. Proceeding west from the cemetery another mile one will come to a place where the river makes a bay coming in towards the roadway. There is a little lane leading down to the property surrounding this bay. The area immediately east of this lane and extending about ½ mile along the shore of the river consists of a mixed woodlot, river front, and a marsh of about 200 acres. There are a large number of nesting species here as well as quite a few varieties of flowers.

LYN ROAD AND HIGHWAY 401. Follow the same directions as to Lee's Pond. When proceeding north on the road from Highway 2 to Lyn, stop at the area where Highway 401 crosses. The fresh rock cut here east of the road and along Highway 401 shows good fresh exposures of Precambrian gneiss. An abandoned iron mine is located nearby to the north.

JONES CREEK. Go west from the cenotaph along either Highway 2 or 401 approximately 7 miles, being sure to take Highway 401 from the point where they join at Long Beach. About 7 miles from Brockville the highway crosses a river. This is Jones Creek. Access to the area is best made by boat but one may also walk. The area may be approached from the north as well as from the south but is most accessible from the south. The river here, at its mouth, has cut through the limestone to leave a cliff about 100 feet high with flat land on the top, and a sloping bottom land going down to the creek itself. Much of the area is covered with sparse woodlot which has been heavily grazed. The junction of limestone and gneiss is apparent along this creek. An extensive marsh all along the shore of the creek and its various branches (which extend for many miles) provides wonderful nesting areas for marsh birds as well as good cover and food for mammals, reptiles, and fish.

NARROWS LANE. This is on Highway 401 about 14 miles west of Brockville and about one mile west of Mallorytown Landing. It is the first lane west of the landing and leads south. Permission to enter the observation area should be obtained from Mrs. David May. The property consists of sixteen acres of dense woodland, hills, and a valley, with a little marsh at the front near the highway. Many species of birds, mammals, trees, flowers, reptiles, and fish may be observed in this vicinity in both winter and summer.

MALLORYTOWN LANDING. See guide for St. Lawrence Islands National Park.

*Brockville Nature Club*

❀    BRUCE COUNTY AND THE BRUCE PENINSULA

KINCARDINE HARBOUR. Turn off the main street in Kincardine and go west to the railroad station which is right at the harbour. The Penetangore River empties into the harbour, and as long as there is open water in the winter it is a favoured place for gulls and winter ducks.

BAIE DU DOREE (pronounced locally "Betty Door"). From Underwood on Highway 21, go west 4 miles to Lake Huron. The bay extends into a marshy area frequented by ducks and other marsh birds.

GREENOCK SWAMP. From Walkerton follow Highway 4 west for 5½ miles to Greenock corner; turn north and go 3¾ miles to Chepstowe; turn left and after travelling 3¾ miles, you enter an extensive wooded swamp area of about 7,000 acres. The road goes through the centre of the tract and makes easy access both north and south.

ELDERSLIE ISLAND. From Paisley go 3 miles north on the Elora Road to Concession 10 of Elderslie, then east on this concession road for 2 miles. Shorelines and other features of this former island of a few hundred acres in glacial Lake Warren are quite evident.

ARRAN LAKE. From Burgoyne corner, on the Elora Road between Paisley and Southampton, go east 3¾ miles and then north 3 miles. Here, access to this lake is made at the township park. This is a shallow lake with marshy areas attractive to ducks and other water birds. It is drained by a branch of the Sauble River which passes through a flat and in places through flooded Red Maple–Elm swamp which attracts many resident nesting birds as well as migrants in spring and fall.

GRIMSTON FLATS. Go north from Chesley for 6 miles to Dobbinton corner, then east 1¼ miles and turn north on the county line between Bruce and Grey counties. The next 4 miles is a low and flat area along the Sauble River. Often flooded in the spring, it is an attractive place for geese, ducks, and waders.

PORT ELGIN SEWER OUTLET. This is in Port Elgin, just north of the breakwater at the harbour. Shorebirds and ducks congregate here in spring, and it is a favoured stopping place for shorebirds during the latter part of August.

CHANTRY ISLAND. This is a federal wildlife sanctuary in Lake Huron about one mile from Southampton. It has one of the larger nesting colonies of Herring and Ring-billed Gulls in Lake Huron and is also a stopping place for shorebirds and other migrants in the migration seasons.

SAUBLE BEACH. From Hepworth on Highway 6, go west for 7 miles. Turn north along the Beach Road. About ½ mile north there is a section behind the cottages of the subdivided area which contains some of the old windblown White Pines, White Cedars, and Hemlocks. It is a favoured place for orchids and heath plants, and for nesting and migrating birds. By following the road 2 miles further north, the mouth of the Sauble River is reached. When not disturbed by tourists, it is an attractive stopping place for water birds.

WIARTON HARBOUR. Going north on Main Street at Wiarton, follow the road to the right instead of going up the hill. The bay here usually remains free of ice longer than the water on the lake Huron side of the Bruce Peninsula and shelters winter ducks, gulls, and Common Loons. During migration seasons it is a good place to observe a variety of water birds. A little further south, around the bay at the park, shorebirds are often found during the August migration.

WIARTON QUARRIES. About 3 miles west of Wiarton on the Oliphant Road, a series of limestone quarries provide an interesting place for finding fossils of the Ordovician Period.

OLIPHANT. Follow the county highway west from Wiarton for 7 miles and you come to a flat shoreline, in some places sandy and in other places covered with vegetation. The extensive flats make this one of the best places for shorebirds along Lake Huron. The adjoining wooded area has many interesting varieties of plant and bird life. (See also guide for Owen Sound.)

FISHING ISLANDS. Along the west side of the lower part of the Bruce Peninsula there is a group of islands varying in size from small shoals to islands of about 100 acres. These islands extend from Oliphant in the south to Pike Bay in the north.

Some of the less common orchids are found here, and there are several nesting colonies of Herring Gulls, Ring-billed Gulls, Common Terns, and Great Blue Herons. The islands can be reached by boat from Oliphant, Howdenvale, or Pike Bay.

SKYE, ISAAC, AND BOAT LAKES. From Mar corner on Highway 6, turn west and follow the road for 2 miles to Skye Lake. Access to the other lakes can be made by boat through the river channel at the southwest corner of this lake. Isaac Lake can also be reached by car by turning off Highway 6, 1¼ miles south of Mar, and following the road 2 miles to the lake. Permission to enter can be received from the property owner who lives at the farm near the lake. Boat Lake can be reached by car by turning west off Highway 6, one mile south of Wiarton, and following the road for 4½ miles. These three lakes are all shallow with plenty of growing vegetation. Black Terns, Pied-billed Grebes, Common Gallinules, and Common Loons nest through the area, and migrating ducks are particularly evident in spring. The road to Isaac Lake passes through a flat area which is flooded in spring and which is favoured by ducks and geese as a stopping place during migration.

HOPE BAY AND BARROW BAY CAVES. For those interested in caves, there are several interesting ones in the cliff along the north side of Hope Bay and the south side of Barrow Bay on the Georgian Bay side of the Bruce Peninsula. One of these has been described as the most beautiful cavern in southern Ontario and is situated midway between Hope Bay village and Shoal Cove in the cliff on the north side of Hope Bay.

PIKE BAY. Turn west off Highway 6 at the corner 6¼ miles north of Mar corner. Go 2½ miles west, then south one mile, and west another mile to this inlet of Lake Huron. The east end of the bay is shallow with a flat shoreline and is usually a stopping place for a few Whistling Swans in the spring. The road running on the north side of the bay to Lake Huron and the road running around the south side and continuing along the lake to Howdenvale are both excellent places to see warblers in the May migration.

LAKE IRA. Five miles north of Stokes Bay, the "old highway" curves around the west side of this lake. It is a good example of a lake that has been filled in naturally with marshy areas and floating vegetation. Grebes, ducks, rails, and Black Terns nest on and around the lake.

DORCAS BAY. About 6 miles south of Tobermory on Highway 6, a sign indicates the road leading west to Dorcas Bay on Lake Huron. This is a shallow, sandy bay often used by shorebirds and other northern nesting birds as a resting place. Inland from the bay are marshy and wooded areas with many interesting plants, including some of the less common orchids. Some birds which typically nest farther north and which have been found here in the nesting season include Magnolia, Myrtle, Cape May, and Parula Warblers, Red-breasted Nuthatches, Ruby-crowned Kinglets, and Olive-sided Flycatchers.

ST. EDMUNDS MARSH. Two miles south of Tobermory on Highway 6, stop at Hatt's Dairy. A ½ mile walk west leads to a bog area containing Sheep-Laurel and other heath plants, various mosses and other bog plants. Ask permission to enter at the dairy.

FLOWERPOT ISLAND. See guide for Georgian Bay Islands National Park.

OTHER PARTS OF THE BRUCE PENINSULA. Besides the various places listed, there are many others of interest through the Bruce Peninsula. Some of these are easily accessible from the roads running off Highway 6 and some can be reached only on foot. The Lake Huron side is the best for birds and the more rugged areas and rocky cliffs of the Georgian Bay side are noted for the prevalence of various ferns. One of Ontario's native rattlesnakes, the Massasauga, inhabits the Bruce Peninsula. Each of the numerous inland lakes has its own interesting plant and animal species. Directions for getting to these other places can be obtained from local residents or, in some cases, by simply following the road signs.

*Grey-Bruce Nature Club*

 **THE BRUCE TRAIL**

THE BRUCE TRAIL originated as a result of the foresight of a Hamilton metallurgist and naturalist, Raymond Lowes. His concept was to establish a walking trail along the total length of the Niagara Escarpment from Queenston to Tobermory, in the belief that this unique natural feature was insufficiently appreciated as a recreational and wildlife area. An unbroken footpath, created by volunteers, and depending on the permission of landowners and a high standard of public respect for the environment, could create havens of peace for those seeking fine landscapes and native flora and fauna; it could link together the many activities associated with the escarpment—hiking, camping, birdwatching, skiing, snowshoeing, sketching and photography—and thus be a signal contribution to the outdoor recreation of Ontario.

The general plan for such a trail was suggested to the Federation of Ontario Naturalists by letter on March 11, 1960. The F.O.N. executive immediately appreciated the merit of the proposal and suggested that a committee be formed to investigate the feasibility of the idea. Accordingly, the Bruce Trail Committee was formed at Hamilton on September 23, 1960. It quickly became apparent to this committee that the trail should and could be built, and they resolved to proceed with it. The cooperation and understanding of the Canadian Youth Hostels Association, the Conservation Council of Ontario, numerous planning bodies, naturalist groups, and private citizens, and enthusiastic and generous press, radio, and television support resulted in such a favourable climate of opinion that a brief submitted to the Atkinson Foundation resulted in a grant to the F.O.N. for their Bruce Trail project. The grant was received on April 6, 1962, and it enabled the project to be greatly accelerated by the appointment, for a one-year term, of a full-time trail director. In his year of office the general route was established, local interested groups were brought together in "Bruce Trail Clubs," and large parts of the trail were actually completed. In order to maintain progress and establish a firm foundation for the future of the whole concept a provincial charter was obtained for the Bruce Trail Association. This was granted on March 13, 1963, and it established a federation of the various clubs and enabled local groups to relate their efforts to the general framework. In addition, liaison was established with parallel groups in the United States in the hope that there might ultimately be a continuous route from Ontario to the Appalachian Trail.

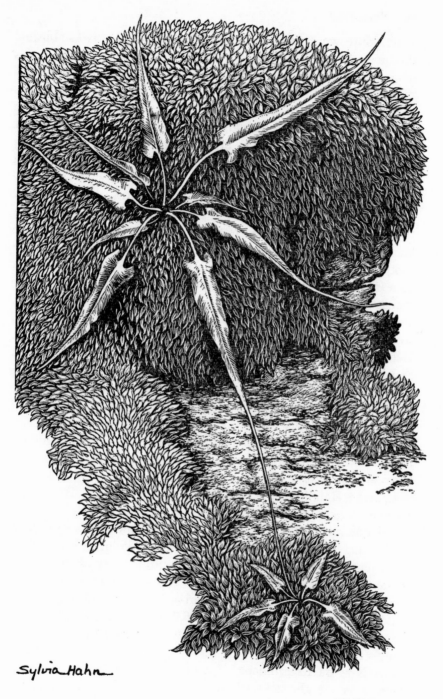

Sylvia Hahn

**WALKING FERN**

Response was rapid, and almost half the trail was established in the first year of operation; the response of landowners was generous, and with standard manuals and markers the accomplishments are already indicative of the great need for facilities of this kind in an area which has urbanized rapidly and all too often had little respect for natural habitat. It is to be hoped that the regeneration of interest in the escarpment will result in a fuller understanding of the meaning of all the natural phenomena associated with it.

In the Niagara Peninsula, the trail originates near the Brock Monument and traverses lands of the Niagara Parks Commission; thence it follows fairly closely the crest of the escarpment to the Hamilton vicinity, where it crosses Red Hill Creek, enters the footpath system of the City Parks Board, and crosses an urban area in surroundings of sylvan splendour. In the peninsula, many plants (not seen further north) are found not far from the trail, and there are numerous natural and historic features of interest, such as the Twin Locks on the Welland Canal at Thorold, the Decew Falls area, Beaver Dams reminiscent of Laura Secord, and the Stoney Creek Battlefield with its legends of Billy Greene; dramatic features such as the Devils Punchbowl at Stoney Creek, the ravine of the Fifteen Mile Creek at Rockway, the Balls Falls ravine at the Twenty Mile Creek; the magnificent vistas from the Forty Mile Creek at Grimsby, and within the city of Hamilton from Felkers Falls ravine, and expansive scenes across the harbour and the bay.

Leaving Hamilton, the trail crosses the Dundas Valley, enters Spencer Creek gorge to Websters Falls, Tews Falls, and the Royal Botanical Gardens Rock Chapel area, and winds its way to the heights of Mount Nemo and Rattlesnake Point in Burlington, and thence across the outskirts of Toronto by way of the Forks-of-the-Credit. Seldom out of sight in this section are numbers of Turkey Vultures wheeling overhead—and even a Golden Eagle nested at Rattlesnake Point in 1963! In the deep valleys the cheerful burble of the Winter Wren can be heard coming from many a ferny dell.

The Niagara Escarpment, of course, does not meander across Ontario as an abrupt wall (capped by dolomitic limestone); rather in many places it is obscured by great deposits of glacial debris. Thus from the Caledon Hills north (to the Hockley Valley, Mono Mills, Horning Mills, Lavender, the Pretty Valley, the Devils Glen) to Craigleith, the observant naturalist will discover varied landscapes. The appreciation of this area—and, indeed, of the entire trail—is much improved if some of its geological history is read first. The Beaver Valley cuts a wide notch in the escarpment and the trail takes a curve in appreciation of this fact. Reluctantly it again sweeps west to Walters Falls, skirts the urban area of Owen Sound, and finally turns north to Wiarton and all the magic of *The Bruce Beckons* (now available in paperback, by Dr. W. Sherwood Fox). In this countryside there is a succession of scenic gorges and ravines, magnificent secret waterfalls, clear trout streams, and unequalled vistas across cliff and water. Rare plants such as the Hart's-tongue Fern, Dwarf Iris, and Bird's-eye Primrose await the curious and careful.

The Bruce Trail Association intends to complete the trail by the anniversary of Confederation, and it is intended to establish at regular and convenient intervals along its length the necessary youth hostels and camping sites that fuller use will necessitate. Obviously, it is impossible to give a complete account of the great variety of natural history interests along the trail. Further details regarding access points, organized hiking trips, and membership in the Bruce Trail Association or any of its federated clubs should be obtained by writing directly to the secretary of the association, Mr. R. N. Lowes, 33 Hardale Crescent, Hamilton, Ont.

NORMAN PEARSON
*Bruce Trail Association*

## ❁ CAPE HENRIETTA MARIA

ONE OF THE largest truly flat and continuously swampy areas in the world has its northeastern extremity at 55° 09′ N, 82° 20′ W at Cape Henrietta Maria. Untilted strata of Ordovician and Devonian limestones form the bedrock which, until only a few thousand years ago, lay beneath the sea. Old beach-lines near Willowbark Lake, 216 miles southwest of the cape, mark the limit of marine submergence. An absence of old beaches between this area and the area 30 to 40 miles from the present coast suggests that emergence from the sea was rapid. The land is still rising slowly and as many as seventy-five beaches can be counted in some places within 20 miles of Hudson Bay. In the inland areas the marine clay between the beaches now carries a thick layer of peat. However, insufficient time has elapsed to permit much of an accumulation of plant debris close to the present coast.

The old beach-lines and better drained sites support a stunted forest of Black Spruce and Tamarack with some White Spruce and Balsam-Poplar. The intervening poorly drained sites support a sedge marsh community with a heath-lichen complex on the hummocks.

The whole area experiences long cold winters and short summers with some hot days. Within a few miles of the Hudson Bay coast sea fogs are frequent in summer. These effectively lower mean temperatures so that the plant and animal communities are those found in a sub-Arctic climate. Cape Henrietta Maria itself probably has an Arctic climate.

It is possible to fly to the cape area and land on wheels on the airstrip at site 415 at 54° 48′ N, 82° 21′ W. Float landings can be made by small aircraft at site 415 on a small lake and on parts of the James Bay coast from Duck Creek north to the tip of the cape. At high tide fairly deep water can be found adjacent to a well developed beach. It is possible that additional float landing places can be found on some of the inland lakes and on the sea at high tide on the east shore of Walrus Island and in the mouth of the Sutton River near Little Cape, but these sites must be explored by boat before they can be declared safe for use by aircraft. The shallow nature of the sea and numerous boulders constitute a constant hazard for the unwary.

Cape Henrietta Maria can be reached by boat from Winisk, a journey of 116 miles, and from Attawapiskat, a journey of 160 miles. The coast is a dangerous one and inexperienced travellers should always hire a competent Indian guide. At low tide the boulder-strewn mud flats extend sometimes for miles from the shore, and at all times it is necessary to travel by outboard well out to sea to avoid hitting rocks.

Break-up of the sea ice on Hudson Bay comes late, and pack ice may drift about off shore as late as August. Wind and tide may drive it close to some of the points of land, for example, Ekwan Point and the coast just south of the cape on James Bay. These hazardous ice conditions can prevent travel for extended periods; indeed, during some summers a visitor should consider himself lucky if he gets one day per week really suitable for travel.

Good camping places which can be approached closely by boat at high tide and with a supply of palatable fresh water are scarce. One day's journey, 60 miles approximately, east of Winisk there is an excellent camping site on Little Cape at the mouth of the Sutton River. Care must be exercised in entering the river because of reefs, and except at high tide boats should stay in the river-bed. There is an elevated beach which serves as an excellent landmark on the east bank of the river. At the northern end of this beach the mud flats are not as extensive as elsewhere, and it is possible at half tide to beach a boat without having to carry gear too far. Tents can be set up above the high-tide mark close to the northern end of the elevated beach or a hundred yards inland, and sometimes further to the northeast close to some fresh water ponds. At this latter place a dip in the ground provides the only truly sheltered campsite on the whole coast.

Another day's journey to the east, about 48 miles, there is another campsite ½ mile west of the mouth of the Mukataship River. A low gravel ridge can be seen from the sea. This must be approached at right angles to the coast because of the shallow nature of the bay. It is necessary to walk over ½ mile from this campsite for fresh water.

It is possible to land at other places along this coast if the traveller is forced ashore by bad weather. The Indians know how to find these places. Their judgment should always be accepted on matters of when and where to head for shore and on the suitability of the weather for travel.

The Cape Henrietta Maria area is of interest to naturalists because of the Arctic element in its fauna and flora. Polar Bears, Arctic Foxes, and Bearded Seals can be seen at certain seasons.

King Eiders, Dunlins, Pectoral, Stilt, and Semipalmated Sandpipers, Northern Phalaropes, Parasitic Jaegers, and Lapland Longspurs have all been recorded breeding there. One of the finest
sights in Ontario is the breeding colony of Snow Geese which
nest between Kwinabiskak Lake and a nameless river which flows
into the sea east of Cape Nemaskamagow. Characteristic plants
of this region include several species in the genera *Salix, Betula,
Cerastium, Arenaria, Anemone, Ranunculus, Draba, Saxifraga,
Astragalus, Oxytropis,* and *Hedysarum.*

Those considering a visit to the cape following the James Bay
coast should bear in mind that the trading outpost at Lake River
is usually not occupied during the summer and supplies may not
be available there.

H. G. LUMSDEN
*Ontario Department of Lands and Forests*

## 🏵  CHATHAM

CHATHAM IS ON the lower Thames River well inside the Carolinian Zone (Deciduous Forest Region). Highway 2 leads into
Chatham from both London and Windsor, and Highway 40 from
the north also leads into Chatham. The surrounding farmland is
flat, with small hardwood woodlots.

The Kent Nature Club meets indoors on the third Friday of the
month from October to April. Outdoor meetings take place in
May, June, September, and October. Information may be obtained from the Chatham-Kent Museum, 59 William Street North.

Routes to the following areas start at the Federal Building
(Post Office) in the centre of the city.

BOWDEN'S WOODS (Dogwood Bush). Follow Highway 2 east 10
miles to Kent Bridge, turn right across Thames River and go
south ¾ mile, turn left on first road and go east 2¾ miles. Turn
right and go ¾ mile south across railway, then turn left on
first road, and go one mile east to Bowden's Woods. It is a dry,

sandy area, part hardwoods, part pasture, with a notable stand of Flowering Dogwood and scattering of Black Gum, Hackberry, Chestnut (sprouts), and Pawpaw. It is a good area for small land birds. Access is by permission of local farmers.

SINCLAIR'S WOODS. From Federal Building follow Queen Street south 7 miles to Charing Cross, then take Highway 98 southeast 5 miles to Blenheim. Follow Highway 3 almost 3 miles and turn right at first road past big bend to the east, going south one mile to turn of road in woods. Of interest here are hardwood woodlots, sugar-making in spring, a patch of Pawpaw just east of turn in road, and many local species of trees and plants. It is a good birding area for small woodland species. Access is by permission of local landowners.

THAMES RIVER OXBOW. From the Federal Building follow Highway 2 down Queen Street to Park Avenue East, turn left and follow Park Avenue across the C. and O. Railroad track; turn left at the first sideroad, cross the C.N.R. track, and turn right on the river road. Follow the river road to the Maple City Golf and Country Club. Many interesting flowering plants may be found along the river that abuts the golf course. These include Bladdernut, White Dog's-tooth-Violet, Virginia Bluebell, Hop-tree, Moosewood (*Dirca palustris*), and Hackberry. Bobwhite and Eastern Bluebirds are frequently seen here.

WALPOLE ISLAND. From Federal Building follow Highway 2 down Queen Street to Richmond Street, turn right and go 2 blocks to Raleigh Street, turn right and follow Highway 40 to Wallaceburg. Continue on Highway 40 west to Baldoon Monument (about 4 miles) and the ferry which takes you to the north end of Walpole Island. The island is an Indian Reserve, and large parties of visitors or those wishing to explore remote portions should obtain permission of the Indian Agent to do so. Many Carolinian trees and smaller plants are found, such as Tulip-tree, Black Gum, Blue Ash, Yellow Iris, Golden-seal, Blazing-star, and gentians. Redhead, Ruddy Duck, and Canvasback nest in the vicinity and many other marsh birds and small land birds may be found.

MINER'S SANCTUARY. From Federal Building follow Highway 2 down Queen Street to Richmond Street, turn right and continue on Highway 2 to Tilbury. Take Highway 401 to the Belle River cloverleaf and turn left. Cross Highway 98 and follow the paved road through Woodslee to Cottam. Go left on Highway 3 for ½ mile, then turn south on paved road. Watch for the Jack Miner sign on the side of a garage. Turn right and follow road for ½ mile to the sanctuary. In open fields along the road, large numbers of Canada Geese may be seen from mid-November to the end of December, and between mid-March and mid-April. Birds are fed at 4.00 P.M. when a good flight may be seen. A few Snow Geese and Blue Geese are usually present in the fall. The public is admitted to the sanctuary daily except Sunday, when birds may be seen from the public road. A good collection of penned waterfowl is visible from the road.

BRADLEY'S MARSH. From Federal Building follow Highway 2 down Queen Street to Richmond Street, turn right and go 2 blocks, turn right on Highway 40 across the Thames River, and turn left on Grand Avenue. This becomes the North River Road in Dover. Follow it all the way to the Bradley farmstead (14–15 miles). Inform Mr. Bruce Bradley or family that you are a naturalist, and you will be free to explore the area. The marsh includes 1,500 acres, and a road runs all around the property. It is an excellent location for waterfowl, shorebirds, and warblers in season. Hundreds of Whistling Swans rest here each spring, along the lakeshore. Golden Plover are seen almost every spring, north of Bradley's in Dover Township; take Highway 40 north of Chatham, turn left at Concession 8 and follow it towards the lake. Carefully examine unploughed corn lands and newly ploughed fields. Later in May Black-bellied Plover may be seen. A striking plant in the marsh is the American Lotus. In summer, Egrets are often seen in marshy areas from the Thames River north to Walpole Island.

DETROIT RIVER. From Federal Building go south on Queen Street to Richmond Street, turn right and follow Highway 2 to Tilbury and Highway 401 to Windsor. The area along Highway 18 from Windsor through Amherstburg, east to Big Creek, is inhabited by many birds at all seasons. The slips for industrial purposes and the many marshes provide havens for migrants such as Whistling Swans and also for other waterfowl which nest or winter here. Two large heronries, both with Great Blue Herons, Black-crowned Night Herons, and Common Egrets nesting, always provide an opportunity to observe these birds. One heronry is on an island in the Detroit River near Grosse Ile in the United States and the other, at Big Creek, is on the mainland in Ontario. Big Creek has other species nesting there such as ducks, American Coots, terns, rails, Bald Eagles, and owls. The farmers' fields and very small patches of deciduous woods provide habitat for other types of birds. During the past four or five years the Eastern Massasauga has been increasing, particularly around La Salle.

*Kent Nature Club*

### ❀ COLLINGWOOD

THE TOPOGRAPHICAL ASPECTS of this area are such that it offers a wide and interesting flora and fauna for the student of natural history. Within the confines of this area are extensive swamps, heavily wooded areas, ranges of high hills, and wide and lengthy stretches of lakeshore.

SUNSET POINT PARK. This is a public park within the town proper. Here the visitor will find several species of native trees, cedar, spruce, elm, Red Ash, birch, and Manitoba Maple, with thickets of willow and alder. This cover attracts some fifteen species of warblers during the spring migration, May 1–20. It also harbours several winter bird residents. Some 100 species of birds have been recorded in this general area over the years. Proceed north on Main Street to the third stop light, then turn right and drive ¼ mile east to the lake. Any citizen can direct the visitor.

COLLINGWOOD HARBOUR. During early spring and fall until freeze-up this area offers to the visiting naturalist a view of many waterfowl and shorebirds. Some sixteen species of ducks are commonly observed during the spring migration, as are

Whistling Swans. Fifteen species of shorebirds are generally observed during the spring and fall in this area. A colony of Cliff Swallows breeds each summer at the Collingwood Terminal elevator. Proceed north on Main Street to the third stop light, turn right to first left turn at shipyard office. To observe shorebirds, retrace route from harbour to north end of Main Street, proceed west to Birch Street, and turn right to lake.

OSLER BLUFFS ON THE BLUE MOUNTAINS. From the junction of Highway 24 and Sixth Street in Collingwood go west 5 miles, then south 5 miles to the bluffs. Here the visitor will find many interesting forms of plant life growing on the shales and limestones of which this area is chiefly composed. The Hart's-tongue and Walking Ferns, the Common Polypody, Maidenhair-Fern and Maidenhair Spleenwort, and several of the wood ferns grow here. It is suggested that the visitor camp here for the weekend, as a convenient area is cleared for a campsite. During the early morning hours in the early summer, the camper will hear the songs of Wood Thrush, Scarlet Tanager, Rose-breasted Grosbeak, Winter Wren, and several other birds. Also, Turkey Vultures, Red-tailed and Red-shouldered Hawks can be seen. Although the elevation on the crest of the bluffs is some 1,400 feet, it can easily be reached by car. The visitor is afforded from this elevation a splendid view of the surrounding countryside, and particularly a large area of the ancient Algonquin Lake plain, now the Nottawasaga watershed and drainage system. As the visitor walks along the edge of the cliffs he will observe, in the limestone rock, large crevasses that have developed over the centuries, forming caves.

BYRNES AVENUE WOODS. This wood is located 6 miles south and east of Collingwood between Highway 26 and the shore of Nottawasaga Bay. It is in the midst of a heavily populated area, and its continued existence cannot be guaranteed as it is expected that it will eventually be included in the adjoining development area. The cover of this fifteen-acre wood is composed of mature pines, cedar, Hemlock, Red Oak, birch, and Red Maple. It is a very old wood and consequently a heavy cover of duff exists on the forest floor, thus encouraging an interesting and varied flora. Here grow many orchids, including the Calypso, Ram's-head Lady's-slipper, Early and Spotted Coral-roots, Rattlesnake-plaintain, Round-leaved Orchid, Showy Lady's-slipper, and Hooker's Orchid. The spring flora includes an abundance of *Clintonia* and Fringed Polygala, several solomon's-seals, Trailing Arbutus, baneberries, Prince's Pine, and shinleafs. It is suggested that the visitor engage the services of a guide to point out the several attractions of these woods. Follow Highway 26 southeast 6 miles from Collingwood, turn left at intersection at Shell gas station, go east on Byrnes Avenue 1½ miles to the southerly turn on the road. The trail into woods will be found on the north side of the highway.

TAMARACK AND SPRUCE BOG. From Collingwood follow Highway 26 and Byrnes Avenue eastward 16 miles to Wasaga Beach; then follow Highway 92 eastward 2 miles from Wasaga Beach to road leaving Highway 92 on the right; follow this road to Jack's Lake. White Spruce, Tamarack, and White Cedar are predominant trees in this area, with a ground cover of Spaghnum Moss, Red-osier Dogwood and other shrubs. Here Labrador-tea grows abundantly, also the Twinflower, Goldthread, pyrolas, and Showy Lady's-slipper. A colony of Grass-pink is found here together with sundews, Pitcher-plant, Stemless Lady's-slipper, and some twayblades. Nashville and Black-throated Green Warblers and Green Herons nest here. The services of a guide will be helpful in covering the area.

CRAIGLEITH. Craigleith is 4 miles west of Collingwood on the Blue Water Highway 26. Drive to the Ski Club road at Craigleith Station and turn left off the highway. Proceed to the bottom of the first hill and road to the ski hills and park. Here in this area sheltered by a ridge of hills one will find many summer birds. Several species of wintering birds will be found here: Red-breasted and White-breasted Nuthatches, Hairy and Downy Woodpeckers, Slate-colored Junco, Cardinal, Tree Sparrow, Brown Creeper, and Black-capped Chickadee. If one walks through the woods along either side of the roadway, and along the sheltered hillsides, one will find in spring a good representation of spring flowers. This has been and is probably yet the headquarters for a pair of Great Horned Owls. A nest with young was observed during the summer of

1959. When this area has been covered it is suggested that the visitor return to Highway 26, and go west to the Craigleith camping ground maintained by the Department of Lands and Forests. Here one may camp while visiting the surrounding countryside. Opposite the camping ground, on the south side of the highway, is a roadway leading to the Arrow Head Ranch (see sign along highway). Follow this road, crossing the C.N.R. railway track and drive till the roadway reaches the top of a hill. Park along the roadside. Here, on either side of the road, will be found extensive pasture fields, overgrown with Hawthorn and wild rose bushes. A colony of Clay-colored Sparrows has been nesting here for several years and will be found, after some searching of course, on either side of the road among the wild rose and Hawthorn growth. This area also is a favourite nesting area for the Brown Thrasher, Catbird, and Field, Song, Vesper, and Savannah Sparrows.

The visitor may get in touch with one of the following members of the Blue Mountain Field-Naturalists' Club:

Mr. A. J. Mitchener,   Mr. L. A. Holbrook,   Mr. Len Wambold,
127 Robinson St.,      60 Katherine St.,     629 Hurontario St.,
Collingwood, Ont.      Collingwood, Ont.     Collingwood, Ont.
Phone 2218.            Phone 1708.           Phone 673.

A. J. MITCHENER

## ❀ FORT WILLIAM AND PORT ARTHUR

THE CANADIAN LAKEHEAD cities of Fort William and Port Arthur are situated on the Kaministikwia River and Thunder Bay respectively, approximately at Latitude 48° 25′ N and Longitude 89° 15′ W on Lake Superior. A small farming belt lies west of these twin cities. Part of the area lies in the Canadian (Predominantly Forest) Zone of the Boreal (Coniferous) Forest Region, with the characteristic Black Spruce and Jack-Pine, while the area south and west of Fort William is in the Superior extension of the Great Lakes–St. Lawrence (Mixed) Forest Region, with the characteristic Red and White Pine as well as Yellow Birch and Sugar-Maple. White Birch, White Spruce, Balsam-Fir and -Poplar are common to both sections. Geologically, the area is in the Precambrian Shield; many hills are capped by intrusive diabase and evidences of glacial action are noticeable. The area is approached from the west by Highway 17, from the south by Highway 61, and from the east by Highways 11 and 17. Routes described start from the McIntyre River bridge where Memorial Avenue becomes May Street North at the junction of the two cities.

The local natural history organization is the Thunder Bay Field Naturalists' Club whose monthly meetings, on the first Monday from October to April, alternate between the two cities. Visitors can get in touch with officers of the club by contacting the reference desk at either Public Library. Executive members of the club welcome visiting naturalists and will be happy to assist them to reach any of the places mentioned below or to direct them to spots not described where some species of particular interest may be found. For a copy of the news letter of the club please write the Editor, 317 Morse Street, Port Arthur, Ontario.

EMPIRE ELEVATOR. From the McIntyre bridge drive south across the Neebing River, and one block past the stop lights turn left and follow Pacific Avenue over the overhead bridge. Three blocks further on turn right; at the third block turn left and drive through to the elevator. Water and shorebirds are plentiful in migration seasons.

VICKER'S PARK. From the McIntyre bridge drive south on Highway 17 to Arthur Street, turn right and 10 blocks further on the park is on the left side of the highway. A public park of Fort William, this is excellent at times during migrations for warblers, finches, and thrushes.

LAKEHEAD AIRPORT AREA. In this area, 2 miles west from Vicker's Park on Highway 17, Bobolink, Upland Plover, Western Meadowlark, and Clay-colored and LeConte's Sparrows have been seen frequently.

STANLEY. Twelve miles past the airport on Highway 17 turn left to Stanley. At the store turn right. Bur Oak, White Elm, and an unusual variety of plants make this area attractive to the botanist as well as the birdwatcher. The Canada Plum, Hoary Puccoon, and a rare grass, Rough Fescue, occur, and Rough-winged Swallows may be seen.

WHITEFISH LAKE. From the foot of Stanley Hill cross the bridge, turn right, and follow Highway 588 for 30 miles to Whitefish Lake. On the way are breeding grounds for warblers and Rose-breasted Grosbeaks. A great variety of ducks patronize the lake in the fall, attracted by the crop of Wild Rice. Birds which are uncommon at the Lakehead but which nest here include Indigo Bunting, Winter Wren, Pigeon Hawk, and Red-necked Grebe. A tremendous cedar bog at the western end of Whitefish Lake will reward the ardent bog-trotter with the Calypso and other orchids. Bell's Painted Turtle is found in sloughs nearby. Many type specimens of butterflies were collected near Hymers which is passed on the way.

VICKER'S HEIGHTS. From Vicker's Park drive west on Highway 17 to the turn to the airport, turn left and drive past the airport and the Canadian Car and Foundry plant and turn right. A mile on look for a sign "Bus Stop 5" and another on the left "The Rydholm's." The Carl Rydholms extend an invitation to naturalists to walk through their yard and down to the river. Skunk-cabbage, Nodding Trillium, Carrion-flower, Jack-in-the-pulpit, and other spring flowers are the attraction in addition to waterbirds on the oxbow slough. Evening Grosbeaks are seen here in the summer. Nearby is historic Point de Meuron.

CHIPPEWA. Follow Highway 61 from May Street north across the Kaministikwia swing bridge, then turn left and follow the signs to Chippewa Park. This park is in good warbler country; the Black-throated Green and Cape May Warblers nest here. Mission Bay is best scouted in a boat. Brule Bay, nearby, presents Closed Gentian and several species of bur-reeds. During the winter the park superintendent keeps a feeding tray well stocked, and Boreal Chickadees, Gray Jays, and Downy and Hairy Woodpeckers come for regular meals. Pileated Woodpeckers and White-winged Crossbills may be seen.

MOUNT MCKAY. When driving to Chippewa Park a road on the right leads through the Indian village and up to the first

sylvia Hahn

**WHITE-WINGED CROSSBILL**

ledge of the mountain. Common Ravens are usual here in spring and fall. Many liverworts have been collected, and in the spring and early summer several species of rock plants grow in the crevices.

BOULEVARD LAKE. Drive north from the McIntyre River bridge to the lake, turn left, and follow the drive. The woods at the upper end are attractive to thrushes, warblers, and kinglets. The bluffs above the lake provide an excellent view. Jefferson's Salamander has been found here, and interesting algae occur in rock pools at the foot of the bluffs.

ABITIBI SLOUGH. Follow Highway 17 through Port Arthur north 2 miles from the bridge below Current River dam to the Thunder Bay Mill Road near the edge of the city. Between Thunder Bay and the Provincial Paper mills are muddy ponds where many shorebirds are usually to be seen in season. Wilson's Phalarope, Yellowthroat, and Solitary Vireo have been seen near here. Permission to cross through this area must be requested from the Abitibi Power and Paper Company. Three species of sundew are found in this area, including the rare Linear-leaved Sundew. Also in the rock cut just west of the mill is the only Thunder Bay station for Macoun's Gentian.

TROWBRIDGE FALLS. Follow Highway 17 east through Port Arthur to Hodder Avenue Hotel, and from there drive straight ahead 2 miles to the Kin Park. Amethystine quartz occurs in veins while Wilson's Arnica, Hyssop-leaved Fleabane, Bird's-eye Primrose, and many mosses and liverworts are found in the vicinity. A fresh-water sponge grows in Savigny Creek.

SIBLEY PROVINCIAL PARK. See guide for this park.

MCKENZIE RIVER. Go 14 miles from Port Arthur along Highway 17 east. The Stemless Lady's-slipper can be found along the right bank of the river, towards Lake Superior from the highway.

OUIMET CANYON. Follow Highway 17 east to Ouimet where a sign indicates the turnoff to the new Department of Lands and Forests park. A very scenic rugged country provides much of interest to the amateur botanist. Several Arctic species of plants are to be found in the bottom of the gorge.

DORION HATCHERY. This is an unusually good birding area. Parula Warbler, Lincoln's Sparrow (nesting), Eastern Wood Pewee, and many other species occur in summer. The spring-fed pond does not freeze in winter and Black Ducks, Common Mergansers, and Common Goldeneyes swim in its waters while Belted Kingfishers and Rusty Blackbirds may be seen in addition to the usual winter residents. The hatchery is well worth visiting; sometimes "Siamese" Speckled Trout are in the troughs. Follow Highway 17 east to Dorion where the Fish Hatchery signs will lead one to this unique spot 45 miles from Port Arthur. Near the hatchery is the Bat Cave on Cavern Lake. The Smooth Cliff-Brake has been found here. Contact club members regarding visiting this location.

LAKE SUPERIOR PARK. The opening of Highway 17 through this area in September 1960 made the park accessible to motoring birders. The Agawa River and Gamitagama Lake areas are both good for birding; nesting warblers were numerous at the latter in 1960. There are few written observers' records of the park area, but plant collectors should enjoy its almost virgin state. It is in the Algoma extension of the Huron-Ontario forest region; hardwoods gradually give way to conifers as one travels northward through the park.

RAINY RIVER DISTRICT. Good birding can be enjoyed at Emo, One-sided Lake, Nym Lake, and throughout Quetico Park (see guide to Quetico Provincial Park). A new road from Atikokan to Fort Frances will open up new territory for field naturalists.

*Thunder Bay Field Naturalists' Club*

### ❀ GEORGIAN BAY ISLANDS NATIONAL PARK

EASTERN SECTION, BEAUSOLEIL ISLAND AND VICINITY.

The eastern section of the park consists of thirty-eight islands or parts of islands in the southeastern part of the 30,000 island archipelago of Georgian Bay. Beausoleil Island (2,712 acres) is the largest island of the group and is the administrative headquarters of the park (including Flowerpot Island). The remainder of the islands in this section of the park extend along the eastern shore from the southern tip of Beausoleil Island to Moose Deer Point in the north, a distance of approximately 40 miles by water.

Beausoleil Island and the other park islands near it may be reached only by boat from Honey Harbour (3 miles) on Highway 501, Port Severn on Highway 103, or Midland on Highway 26. Lake cruisers use Lake Huron and Georgian Bay to reach the islands. There is no regular service to the islands, but persons not having their own boat may hire water taxis or boats at the villages named. No motor vehicles are allowed on the islands and these must be individually parked by the owners in the villages of the mainland.

This section of the park is open all year but is easily accessible only during the summer season. There are twenty-two campsites, which supply kitchen shelters, stoves, firewood, water, laundry, sanitary facilities, and docks. The largest campsite is on Beausoleil Island near the park office. This is the only location at which public telephone service to the mainland is available. There are no stores or shops of any kind on any of the islands, so food and other necessities have to be brought by each park visitor from the mainland. There are two nature trails of the self-guided type on Beausoleil Island, and in addition 18 miles of hiking trail and 11 miles of fire road.

The islands consist of Precambrian, mostly pinkish-coloured rocks, which in a few places are overlaid by glacial till and soil, but which in other places are exposed in large expanses. These rocks show the effect of glaciation in that they are smoothed, polished, and scratched. The many islands of the archipelago were formed by the rise in water level and consequent invasion of the land by Lake Huron in comparatively recent times.

Very little is known, in detail, of the plants and animals of the park. Records made by competent persons are needed in all fields of natural history.

This section of the park is within the Georgian Bay portion of the Great Lakes–St. Lawrence (Mixed) Forest Region of Canada. It has also been called the Canadian Biotic Province of North America. The presence of trees, plants, and animals which are representative of both a more southern and a more northern biota makes the area an extremely interesting one for the naturalist. Sugar-Maple, Beech, Yellow Birch, Red Oak, Basswood, and White Ash grow to magnificent size where the soil is deep, as on the southern portion of Beausoleil Island. On poorer soils White Spruce, White Pine, Balsam-Fir, Hemlock, White Birch, Trembling Aspen, and White Cedar are some of the common trees. Shrubs and wildflowers are also varied and abundant. Fringed Gentian, Cardinal-flower and Great Lobelia, all very attractive, are plants found here. Published records of birds are scarcer than those for plants; the best reference is *Birds of Simcoe County, Ontario*, by O. E. Devitt, published by the Royal Canadian Institute, Toronto, 1943–44.

WESTERN SECTION, FLOWERPOT ISLAND

The western section of the park consists of Flowerpot Island (495 acres) located in Lake Huron about 3 miles from Tobermory on the northwestern tip of the Bruce Peninsula. It is approximately 100 miles northwest of Beausoleil Island by water, and about 170 miles by road. Tobermory is on Highway 6.

Flowerpot Island is accessible only in the summer months and at that time a caretaker, who lives in Tobermory, is on duty. Because the island can be reached only by small boat, an adequate dock has been built in a small cove on the southeast side. Near the dock is a prepared campsite which is provided with picnic shelter, tables, stoves, and other facilities. There are no supply stores, and food and other necessities must be brought in by the visitor from the mainland. Hotel and motel accommodation and supplies are available at Tobermory.

The geology of this island is very different from that of Beausoleil and the other islands in the eastern section of the park. The rocks here are dolomitic limestone belonging to the Middle Silurian Period of the Palaeozoic Era. They are very much younger than the Precambrian rocks of the eastern section, having been laid down only about 360 million years ago. The island is named for two huge, isolated, pedestal rock formations, one of which is about 50 feet high. These vase-shaped formations of limestone have been fashioned by erosion. The shoreline in many places consists of sheer rock cliffs, some of which are about 200 feet high. At other places there are gravel beaches. In the cliff face are seven fairly large caves which are of great interest although little is known of their natural history.

The island is within the Huron-Ontario section of the Great Lakes–St. Lawrence (Mixed) Forest Region of Canada. It is covered by an attractive mixed forest, much like that on the islands of the eastern section of the park, except that there are more coniferous trees. The vegetation and animal life is also very similar to that of the Bruce Peninsula. As the latter has special ferns and orchids, a good American Woodcock migration, and many nesting sites for various gulls, to mention only a few of its attractions for the naturalist, it is likely that most of these will be found on Flowerpot Island, but no one knows for sure because the natural history of the island has not yet been recorded.

GEORGE M. STIRRETT

 **HAMILTON**

HAMILTON IS situated at the west end of Lake Ontario where the Niagara Escarpment comes close to the lake, swings westward north of Dundas and Ancaster, is broken by the head of the Dundas Valley, appears again south of the city, and continues eastward to Niagara Falls. The escarpment rises approximately 425 feet above Hamilton harbour at the top of the Dundas Mountain and 350 feet above Lake Ontario east of Hamilton. Its edge is broken by small streams which descend in falls or narrow precipitous valleys. Hamilton harbour is separated from Lake Ontario by a sand strip providing interesting areas for shorebirds at migration, and on the harbour side for Snowy Owls in winter. Hamilton lies near the northern boundary of the Carolinian Zone (Deciduous Forest Region) so that in the ravines close to the city one finds plants such as the Rue Anemone which is commonly found farther south, and a few miles northwest of the city the Bunchberry and Twinflower which are familiar farther north.

The local natural history club is the Hamilton Naturalists' Club which holds its meetings in the Lecture Room of the Main

Branch of the Hamilton Public Library, Main Street West, 2.3 miles east of Westdale Collegiate, at 8.00 P.M. on the second Monday of each month from September to May. Visitors to the city can get in touch with officers of the club by telephoning the reference desk at the Main Branch of the Hamilton Public Library.

Routes to points of interest to naturalists start at Westdale Collegiate, at the junction of Highways 2 and 8 at the corner of Longwood Road and Main Street West.

ALBION FALLS AND KING'S FOREST PARK. Go east on Main Street 4.3 miles to King Street East, right on King Street East for 2.3 miles to Albion Road, right for 2.3 miles to Mountain Brow Boulevard, right for 0.4 miles to Albion Falls. The rocky wooded ravine below the falls is spectacular at floodtime. Buttermilk Falls is 0.4 miles farther along Mountain Brow Boulevard.

ROYAL BOTANICAL GARDENS. This includes most of the land surrounding Coote's Paradise Marsh. It is maintained as a public park and conservation area with nature trails and picnic facilities.

(*a*) *Westdale Ravine and Coote's Paradise Marsh*. Go north on Longwood Road one block to Marion Avenue, the first street entering from the left. Follow Marion Avenue to the end at Dromore Crescent. A cinder drive and nature trails lead through the ravine. Wild Rice has been planted in a pond beside the cinder drive. Mallards nest there and Muskrats live in the banks. Along the trails are many native trees, shrubs, flowers, and ferns, and there is excellent shelter for local and migrating birds. Sometimes one sees Red Fox, White-tailed Deer, and Raccoons. Trails end on the shores of the marsh.

(*b*) *Hendrie Park*. Go north on Longwood Road (Highway 2) for 3.2 miles. Cherry Hill Gate is on the left, opposite the Rendezvous Restaurant. Varied trails are interesting at any season.

(*c*) *North Shore of Coote's Paradise Marsh*. Go north on Longwood Road 1.7 miles to Old Guelph Road, follow around the marsh 0.6 miles, turn left to Royal Botanical Gardens Arboretum parking circle. Signs indicate trails to the shore of the marsh through woods with a fine stand of Sassafras. Ducks, shorebirds in migration, herons, hawks, woodland and water plants, and ferns are to be found.

(*d*) *Rock Chapel.* Continue on Old Guelph Road from Arboretum entrance above for one mile to first crossroad. Turn left and go 1.2 miles to York Road. Turn right to the top of the mountain and go left for 0.6 miles to Royal Botanical Gardens parking lot and picnic facilities. Rugged paths lead along the wooded brow and down the mountainside.

(*e*) *Coldspring Valley.* Go west on Main Street (Highway 2) for 1.2 miles to Hollywood Street. Go right one block into Binkley Crescent and ½ block around the crescent to Lakelet Drive. Trails lead into thick damp woods with good shelter for birds and an abundance of moisture-loving plants.

DUNDAS HYDRO STATION. Go west on Main Street for one mile to Highway 102, Dundas cut-off, right on 102 for 1.7 miles, right at East Street one block, right at Hunter Street. Paths lead east through rushes and reeds (*Phragmites*), between mud flats, ponds, and the Desjardins Canal. The area is excellent for shorebirds at migration.

WEBSTERS FALLS. From Westdale Collegiate follow Highway 102 as above and Highway 8 through Dundas and up the mountain 4.2 miles. Turn right at sign for Websters Falls. Steps descend the cliff by the falls. The ravine below can be followed down to Dundas. The area is interesting at any season.

BEVERLY SWAMP. Go west to Websters Falls Road as above and continue on 0.2 miles to Bullock's Corners. Leave Highway 8, which turns left, and continue straight ahead on Brock Road 8.5 miles to Concession 8, Beverly Township. Go left 4 miles into the swamp. Access is by permission of local farmers and owners. This large "island" of wet land is inaccessible in spring. It is botanically rich (many ferns and orchids) and is a haven for birds and other animals as there are few roads into the swamp.

RATTLESNAKE POINT. Go north on Highway 2 (Longwood Road) 5.1 miles to Aldershot stop light, left 3 miles on Waterdown Road to Highway 5. Turn left on Highway 5 and go one block, then turn right on road to Carlisle 6.3 miles. Go right at Carlisle for 7 miles to Appleby Line, then left up the mountain. Paths lead from the roadside to a lookout. Watch for ferns.

LA SALLE PARK. Take Highway 2 north to Aldershot stop light as above, turn right 0.3 miles to park entrance. Wooded areas overlook Burlington Bay. Good for ducks, geese, and swans in early spring, and for local birds at any time.

GAGE PARK. Go 4 miles east on Main Street to Gage Avenue, turn right on Gage and go around to the entrance to the parking lot at the back of the park. A public park in the city of Hamilton, it includes native and introduced trees and gardens. Local and migrating birds are to be found in season, especially in early morning and in the evening.

SULPHUR SPRINGS ROAD. Go west on Highway 2 for 5 miles into Ancaster, turn right at Church Street, Sulphur Springs Road. The road leads through hilly, partly wooded country where native birds are to be found at all seasons.

JERSEYVILLE ROAD. Go west on Highway 2 for 5.6 miles through Ancaster, turn right. This road likewise leads through hilly wooded country.

YORK ROAD. Go west on Main Street one mile to Highway 102 and 2 miles on Highway 102 to York Street. Turn right and follow to York Road. Turn right. Access to woods along the road is by permission of local farmers and owners.

MOUNTAIN SIDE (within the city). Go east on Main Street 0.7 miles to Dundurn Street. Turn right and follow to the end of the street at the foot of the mountain. A path leads west along the wooded face of the escarpment.

Miss A. E. Le Warne
*Hamilton Naturalists' Club*

## ✿ HUDSON BAY LOWLANDS

THE HUDSON BAY LOWLANDS are a vast peatland wilderness, extending from the foot of James Bay, near Rupert's House just inside the Quebec boundary, to the west coast of Hudson Bay at Churchill, Manitoba, a distance of nearly 800 miles. Inland, the area includes the entire basin of Palaeozoic sedimentary bedrock to the edge of the Precambrian Shield between 40 and 240 miles from the coast. Most of the "Great Muskeg" is in Ontario, and naturalists are often surprised to realize that it comprises one-quarter of the land surface of the province.

A small population of Indian trappers seasonally disperses over this area on their traditional hunting grounds. Beaver pelts were and are the mainstay of the fur trade in this part of Canada. Hunting pressure nearly wiped out the Beaver but their numbers have risen again in the last quarter century in response to modern game management. Summer gatherings of the several Cree bands occur at the scattered trading posts and missions, all of which are at river mouths on the coast. The only inland post is Ogoki where the people are Ojibway. The non-Indian population is confined to small settlements at Moose Factory and Moosonee with a few persons serving the outlying stations at Albany, Ogoki, Attawapiskat, Winisk, and Severn.

This area is a plain that slopes gently towards James and Hudson bays. The bedrock, which outcrops only infrequently in deep cuttings of the chief rivers, is generally overlaid by a succession of unconsolidated deposits well displayed on the steep banks of nearly all rivers. First, there is an over-all mantle of glacial drift. Then, most of this is covered by marine clay deposits of the saltwater Tyrrell Sea, the highest levels of which are now 400 to 500 feet above sea level and date from 7,000 to 8,000 years before the present. Following release of pressure from the weight of the last glacial ice and the subsequent rise of the land, sand and gravel coastal deposits have been stranded successively; these strand lines are conspicuous from the air near the coast and can be traced far inland where they are the uppermost inorganic deposits. Deep peat, made up of the incompletely decomposed remains of growing mire vegetation, covers nearly all the land surface, and this growth continues. The rivers erode all these layers with great force during the spring run-off. River banks are flooded annually, and in years of very high water the overflow drops silt and forms natural levees where ice also assists by pushing up the tops of the banks. Finally, a great load of silt is carried out the river mouths. The coast is miserable for travellers because of silted, shallow water and extensive tidal flats.

The Ontario portion of the Hudson Bay Lowlands lies in the east central part of the Boreal (Coniferous) Forest Region, which has a remarkably uniform cover of spruce forest with wide-ranging species of plants and animals. The Hudson Bay Lowlands Forest (Forest and Barren) section of this larger region is characterized by dwarfed Black Spruce and Tamarack on peat, reflecting poor drainage, cool climate, and other interrelated factors. The forest is but the wooded portion of the mire vegetation which also includes much open fen and bog. As you move away from the river drainage, the closed, boggy Black Spruce forest gradually thins out to open bog with hummocks of stunted Black Spruce and ericaceous shrubs and hollows of sedges and cottongrasses. Sphagnum Moss carpets the ground. Peat long remains frozen under this insulating cover so that spring and early summer conditions are very wet. The tops of the hummocks, however, dry quickly, and a striking growth of lichens has developed. Sub-Arctic lichen-spruce forest occurs on low sandy ridges and in the few areas of upland country where drainage is not held up by underlying clay. Fen forest of Tamarack and Dwarf Birch is replaced by open wet meadows. Unlike bogs, fens receive some water from mineral soils (here high in lime) by percolation, and fen vegetation is richer in species, many of which are absent from bogs. However, there are many forms of fen including poor patches where the supply of mineral soil water is not sufficient to stop the acid bog condition. Yellowlegs are the noisiest avian denizens of the lonely open mire. Pools are frequent, and in some areas there are extensive small-lake-lands which provide important breeding grounds for Canada Geese. Very striking are the string bogs—alternating low vegetated ridges and long narrow pools oriented transversely to the slight slope of the land surface. "Islands" of boggy Black Spruce forest sometimes stand out sharply from the surrounding open mire. The whole complex is an intricate mosaic pattern of intermixed forms of bog and fen. The sub-Arctic woodlands decrease northward until you reach tundra at Cape Henrietta Maria (see the guide for that area).

Travel conditions are highly seasonal. In winter, trappers with dog teams move easily over the frozen mire. During spring break-up and fall freeze-up even aircraft have to stop for lack of landing places. Cross-country travel on the mire is very hard going in summer and beset with hordes of mosquitoes and black flies. In the growing season all traffic other than air and railway is on the rivers and along the coast. River banks are the most frequented places, and likewise are the most common haunts of the visitor. They thus require a special paragraph.

Active erosion of the steep banks of our main rivers leaves these places barren. On moderately disturbed open shores there is a great variety of showy and interesting plants down to low summer water levels. Here, too, are important pathways for mammals and food and water for many birds. On more stable shores willow and alder thickets provide dense cover with more open Balsam-Poplar groves above them but still below the spring flood level. The best alluvial sites are remarkably rich in more temperate species. For example, at the abandoned Mammamattawa post on the Pagwa-Kenogami-Albany river route there is an elm-ash woods with Ostrich-Fern, Nodding Trillium, Smooth Yellow Violet, and Wild Ginger on the floor. The zone of tall White Spruce on the tops of the banks affords ideal habitat for crossbills. Also at this highest level Trembling Aspen and White Birch often mark interesting communities. The front edge of the high "hedge" of tall trees is rich in plant and animal species. The peatland begins close behind the exposed mineral soil of the riverbank zones.

Naturalists visiting this remote region should prepare their trip with more than usual care. Good advice may be obtained from the Ontario Northland Railway, North Bay, from the regional and district offices of the Ontario Department of Lands and Forests, Cochrane, who maintain a local station at Moosonee, and from the Hudson's Bay Company at Moosonee or other posts. Maps and air photos are obtainable from the provincial and Dominion governments. Some notes on this area with a check-list of vascular plants and references to the literature are given in the guide book of the *Botanical Excursion to the Boreal Forest Region in Northern Quebec and Ontario* published in 1959 by the National Museum of Canada, Ottawa.

TRAIN TRIPS: COCHRANE TO MOOSONEE. From the railway junction and road centre of Cochrane the Ontario Northland Railway has a thrice-weekly service 186 miles north to James Bay tidewater at Moosonee. This line transects the southern part of our region. You enter the Hudson Bay Lowlands abruptly at Coral Rapids, mile 96, where the Abitibi River descends over the Precambrian-Palaeozoic contact. This point also marks the highest levels of the marine submergence. The railway tracks parallel the river. From the train you see mostly boggy Black Spruce forest, some patches of old brules, occasional open bog and fen complexes, and fen forest of Tamarack and Dwarf Birch. At Moose River Crossing, mile 142, note the sedimentary bedrock, the river bank exposures of unconsolidated deposits, and the rich river forest on exposed mineral soil with good drainage. At Renison, mile 156, you pass a former lumber camp where fine White Spruce lumber and Black Spruce pulpwood were cut. You reach railhead after a 6½ hour journey.

MOOSONEE. This settlement, at the railway terminus on the left bank of the Moose River, is surounded by boggy Black Spruce forest and fenny Tamarack–Dwarf Birch woods. There is a good outlook over the tidal estuary but the river-bank frontage is disturbed by the transportation business of this transshipment point. Accommodation is limited so you should make reservations in advance of your visit.

MOOSE FACTORY ISLAND. This island is about 2 miles southeast of Moosonee station in mid-river. Canoes are frequently crossing to the older settlement and can be hired, or you may join an O.N.R. excursion party. The Hudson's Bay Company's first trading post was Rupert's House established as Charles Fort two years before the company was incorporated in 1670. In 1673 Moose Factory was established on Hayes Island, but because of repeated flooding the fort was moved to nearby Factory Island. This post is the oldest continuous settlement in Ontario. A few relics of the old fur trade are preserved, and the old Anglican mission church still stands, but the modern development of hospital, schools, Indian housing, and new H.B.C. buildings has completely changed the appearance of this historic place. Naturalists should walk beyond the settlement into the best forest and along the rich river-bank habitats.

SHIPSANDS ISLAND. This island is about 12 miles northeast of Moosonee at the mouth of the Moose River estuary. The O.N.R. arranges trips for tourist parties; or you may hire an Indian guide with canoe and outboard motor. On the shore of the island you will see marine strand plants not occurring elsewhere in Ontario. Salt marshes, tidal pools, and willow thickets are accessible. This is an excellent place for bird-watching. There is a lookout tower which serves as a beacon for James Bay.

OTHER TRIPS FROM MOOSONEE. You may be able to arrange various trips from this jump-off place. When water levels permit, tourist parties are taken to the Indian Reservation at head-of-tide about 10 miles south of Moosonee. Depending on weather, wind, tide, and a good Indian guide you can make a canoe trip out into James Bay landing at Nattabisha Point about 14 miles east of Shipsands. In the goose hunting season parties are arranged to meet the migratory concentrations on the marshes around the foot of James Bay. Aircraft frequently call at the Moosonee depot. It is sometimes possible to arrange unscheduled flights with commercial pilots, or by pre-arrangement with the air service operators, to such places as Albany or Attawapiskat. It is more difficult to get to Winisk and Severn although there has been a scheduled air service directly from Ottawa to Winisk and on to Churchill with terminations at Montreal and Winnipeg. Small coastal vessels serve the posts and missions on James Bay and it is occasionally possible to arrange a passage.

CANOE TRIPS. The old river routes of the fur trade freighting make interesting trips for experienced paddlers. Every year a few canoes come down the Moose River from the tributary Abitibi, Mattagami, and Missinaibi Rivers starting from rail and road points of the Clay Belt. More rarely, parties make the longer Albany trip starting from Pagwa. Prospective "voyageurs" are strongly urged to get good advice beforehand because travel conditions differ greatly from the familiar resort country of the Great Lakes–St. Lawrence (Mixed) Forest Region.

W. K. W. BALDWIN

## ❁ KINGSTON AND GANANOQUE

KINGSTON AND GANANOQUE are located in the northernmost outlier of the southern Oak-Hickory forest, and about 30 miles to the north are surrounded by the Great Lakes–St. Lawrence (Mixed) Forest Region. This is the only place where oak-hickory forests grow on the Canadian Shield. Kingston and Gananoque both have the advantage of being near large bodies of water, Kingston at the eastern end of Lake Ontario as well as at the beginning of the St. Lawrence River and on the mouth of the Cataraqui River, which is the start of the Rideau Canal system; and Gananoque on the St. Lawrence River in the heart of the Thousand Islands region.

The area comprises two physiographic regions: the Napanee Plain, and the Leeds Knobs and Clay Flats. The Napanee Plain includes the centres of Bath, Odessa, Cataraqui, Kingston, Sydenham, Yarker, and Camden East. It has a bedrock of limestone which in those areas represented by prosperous farms with woodlots on rocky outcropping has a reasonably thick soil covering. In other places where the soil is only a few inches deep, the resulting arid condition makes the land unsuitable for farming and easily abused by over-grazing.

The bedrock of the Leeds Knobs and Clay Flats region is Precambrian and forms the Frontenac Axis extending from Algonquin Park, through the Thousand Islands to the Adirondack Mountains in New York State. Only the clay flats are suitable for farming because most of the rest of the region is covered by numerous small lakes and by a forest which has been cut over twice. There are numerous pine ridges and hardwood groves, and also many marshes between ridges and along the edges of the shallower lakes.

Most of the Lake Ontario shore is rocky with either low cliffs or pebbly beaches. The islands of the region are of two sorts: those of the limestone plain, Wolfe, Amherst, Simcoe, and Howe, are flat with open fields and some woodlots, and those of Precambrian bedrock consist of granite outcroppings wooded with conifers and deciduous trees and used mostly for summer residences. A dozen of these islands are in the St. Lawrence Islands National Park (see the guide for this park).

The habitat for birds and mammals in the Kingston-Gananoque area thus ranges through deep woods, scrub, fields, marshes, and shoreline.

The Kingston Field Naturalists hold their meetings on the third Thursday of every month from September through April at 8.00 P.M. at the Agricultural Boardroom, Ontario Building, Barrie Street. Application to the Chamber of Commerce will provide interested visitors with the names of club officers.

KINGSTON AREA

Kingston is reached from the west and east by Highway 2 and bypassed by Highway 401, from the southwest by Highway 33, from the northwest by Highway 38, and from the northeast by Highway 15. Several county roads lead north from Kingston. Routes of interest to naturalists in this area start at Old Fort Henry at the junction of Highways 2 and 15 just east of the city.

CITY DUMP. From Old Fort Henry proceed west on Highway 2 turning right at Montreal Street, the fourth traffic light. Continue north along Montreal Street across the single railway track and then right into the city dump (closed on Sundays). Glaucous, Iceland, and Great Black-backed Gulls are regular visitors in December, late February, and early March along with thousands of Herring and Ring-billed Gulls.

SQUAW POINT. From Old Fort Henry proceed west on Highway 2 to the traffic circle. Follow Highway 33 for 1.4 miles to a single railway track. Park near the bridge that crosses the Little Cataraqui River and walk south on the seldom-used railway line. The track goes through marsh and also through a wooded section of higher ground, Squaw Point. The woods are good during spring and autumn migration for warblers, thrushes, and sparrows, and the mud flats for shorebirds depending on water levels. During the summer there is an excellent breeding population of marsh birds.

BAY VIEW BOG. Continue west along Highway 33 to the village of Collins Bay, and go 3 miles further to an unpaved county road which turns north and after 1.6 miles crosses the main railway line. Inquire for permission to visit the area from the last farmhouse on the left before reaching the railway line. Park on the north side of the railway tracks at the transformer hut and follow the hydro line east across the field to a wooded swamp. Skirt this swamp for about ¾ mile and then turn left. After walking 100 yards, you should have reached the lake in the Tamarack bog, but if you miss it come out to the edge of the swamp again and start in in another place. It is the only bog of this type in the region and in it will be found Labrador-tea, Lambkill, One-flowered Wintergreen, various types of orchids, Pitcher-plants, and a rich moss and liverwort flora.

AMHERST ISLAND. Continue west on Highway 33 to the village of Millhaven where a car ferry may be taken to Amherst Island. In 1963 the fare for car with driver was $1.50 return, and for a passenger 50¢ return. A ferry schedule may be secured from the Chamber of Commerce, Kingston, or by calling the telephone operator at Stella on Amherst Island. Four large swamps at the heads of bays with sand beaches are located on the southwest side of the island and may be reached by the numerous roads crossing and circling the island. Bird life here is rich in spring and autumn with large rafts of ducks off shore. The gravel beaches of the east end are good for shorebirds and gulls, and in late autumn Water Pipits and Snow Buntings. Bonaparte's Gulls are regular in April and October on the southwest tip of the island, accessible only on foot.

CATARAQUI RIVER. During March and April there are large concentrations of ducks on the river, as many as sixteen species having been seen here in a day. Because conditions in the river and Rideau Canal system differ from year to year, try any of the following vantage points starting from Old Fort Henry and driving northeast on Highway 15 through the village of Barriefield. (1) Stop about ½ mile from Barriefield, opposite the Military Hospital, and look out over the Cataraqui River. (2) Continue one mile to a road marked "Rideau Marina." Go down this road to the marina. Pond ducks often stay close to shore. A clear view north up the river may require a short walk along the shore. (3) Continue north on Highway 15, about 4 miles beyond Highway 401 to Hughes Point Road, and drive down this road to the canal. (4) Return to Highway 15 and continue north almost 6½ miles to the Washburn Road. The Washburn Road crosses the Rideau Canal within ¼ mile.

MARSH ON HIGHWAY 401. From Old Fort Henry take Highway 15 northeast until it joins Highway 401, about 5 miles. Turn west onto Highway 401 which, in about a mile, crosses the Cataraqui River, and after another mile a marshy section will be reached. Park on the shoulder of the highway and without leaving the car study the marsh which here has many open patches of water. During the summer Black-crowned Night Herons, Green Herons, American Bitterns, Black Terns, Long-billed Marsh Wrens, Common Gallinules, Black Ducks, Blue-winged Teal, and Common Snipe will be seen, and Virginia Rails, Soras, and Least Bitterns, if one is lucky. On the stretches of water on the south side look for rafts of ducks in the winter, for there is often open water here when there is none elsewhere in the vicinity of Kingston.

BELL'S SWAMP. From Old Fort Henry go west on Highway 2 to Division Street, the seventh traffic light. Turn north onto Division and continue north past Highway 401 (note that this point is Interchange 102 on Highway 401). Turn off Division Street at the second right, at Kemp's Garage. This road leads through Bell's Swamp, a low lying piece of land characterized by small ridges with small ponds and marshy areas between, the result of moraines formed as crevice filling under the calving glacier. From the road there are paths and tracks along the ridges which may be explored. This is a good spot during spring and fall migration and for breeding birds in summer. On the northeast side of the wood will be found extensive beaver workings. Beech-drops, Rattlesnake-plaintain, ferns, and a large variety of club-mosses can be found here.

WOLFE ISLAND. A day's trip to Wolfe Island at almost any season can be most rewarding. The extensive fields make it a good hunting ground for hawks and, in some years, Short-eared Owls. Savannah, Vesper, and Grasshopper Sparrows, Bobo-links, Upland Plover, and in late autumn Water Pipits, Snow Buntings, and Lapland Longspurs are found. The many bays, pebbly beaches, sand beaches, rock ledges, and gravel bars are good places for shorebirds and gulls. Off shore large rafts of ducks congregate in spring and autumn. In March and early April, Canada Geese feed in cornfields at the south-western corner of the island. A paved road crosses the island to Horne's ferry which connects with the mainland in New York State (from June to October only), and this is also a good place for concentrations of ducks. Many unpaved roads lead around and through the island. Access to many of the bays and the shore is by permission of the local farmers. To find the Wolfe Island ferry, go west into the city from Old Fort Henry over the causeway, along Ontario Street to Brock Street, and turn east to the waterfront. Ferry schedules are posted on the Brock Street dock or can be obtained from the Chamber of Commerce. In 1963, the fare for car with driver was $1.50 return, and for a passenger 40¢ return. Eventually, the ferry dock will be moved to a new location. From Old Fort Henry drive east on Highway 2 past the army camp to Rogers Side Road. The new entrance road for the ferry will be made somewhere in this vicinity. There are to be two end-loading free ferries at 15-minute intervals to Wolfe Island.

ABBEY DAWN AND MADOMA MARSH. From Old Fort Henry go east along Highway 2 about 4 miles. An extensive marsh will be seen on both sides of the road and an unpaved road marked "Madoma Marsh" leads north. Wildflowers in spring are par-ticularly good here and bird life is abundant. This unpaved road continues north through a dry habitat of cedar woods, access to which may be had from almost anywhere along the road.

RIDEAU LAKES. Five roads lead north either from the city or from Highway 401 into the Rideau Lakes District. Go west from Old Fort Henry and Highway 2 along Princess Street and then north on either Montreal Street or Division Street, the fourth or seventh traffic light respectively. Interchanges 104–100 on Highway 401 lead to all five roads north, from east to west, Highway 15, Montreal Street, Division Street, Syden-ham Road, and Highway 38.

A set of topographical maps (1:50,000) or Map 31C (1:250,000) can be secured from R. W. Alford and Company, 121 Princess Street. If this region is to be explored thoroughly and if one is to avoid getting lost, the purchase of at least the

Map 31C is recommended because most of the roads leading from the five main roads are unmarked.

Here is a suggested day's round-trip tour through this area. Go north on Highway 38 to the village of Hartington (about 12 miles north of Highway 401), turn right (east) for 1.1 miles, then left (north) onto a dirt road for 0.8 miles, then right (east) again. The famous Holleford meteor crater is crossed by this road. The centre of the crater is about ¼ mile north of the road, and is filled with a wooded swamp. The road passes twice through the raised southern rim of the crater. Turn left (north) at a white church and continue north past Holleford Lake. After 5 miles there is a T-junction. Turn right (east) through the "village" of Desert Lake, located between Desert and Holleford lakes. Watch for Green Herons and American Bitterns in the marsh, and Cliff Swallows near the village. The road continues northeast. About a mile past the bridge at Desert Lake, there is a junction with a sideroad leading southward.

A side trip to the Otter Lake Sanctuary may be made by turning right (south) along this road for about 1½ miles to Otter Lake. The sanctuary (44° 30′ N, 76° 35′ W) is a tract of 210 acres recently acquired by the Kingston Field Naturalists. The property has within its boundaries a part of Otter Lake and Sucker Lake. The area is typical of much of the country of the Rideau Lakes—mixed woods, swamps, marshes, Beaver ponds, and rocky outcroppings. Several trails lead to a Beaver pond and lookout point from which Red-shouldered Hawks, Turkey Vultures, and Osprey may sometimes be seen. Ruffed Grouse, Pileated, Hairy, and Downy Woodpeckers, Yellow-bellied Sapsuckers, Red-eyed and Warbling Vireos, Black-and-white and Black-throated Green Warblers are among the many nesting species. Wildflowers in the spring are found in great profusion, and in late summer Cardinal-flowers and Pipewort surround the lakes.

Returning to the junction (a mile past the bridge at Desert Lake), continue on the "main" road north again. This road passes through thick woods east of Desert Lake. About 4 miles north of the sanctuary turnoff, there is a road leading off to the west. (This road goes between Desert and Canoe lakes, eventually reaching the town of Godfrey on Highway 38.) Stop at this corner, where Golden-winged Warblers may often be seen and heard. Do not turn left, but continue north stopping occasionally to look and listen for Cerulean Warblers. About 1½ miles along this road, there is a possible right turn. Do not turn, but stop at this corner and walk or drive west along a trail whose start is just a few feet from this junction. This trail leads into a series of wood-cutters' trails, passing through an area where Golden-winged Warblers nest. About ¼ mile from the road is a good place to start looking. Take a compass with you if you plan to go far from the car.

Return to the road and continue north past the east shore of Canoe Lake. Ospreys are regularly seen here. About 1½ miles north of the end of Canoe Lake this dirt road ends at a paved road. Turn right onto this paved road through the tiny village of Fermoy, past the south shore of Wolfe Lake, and on into Westport.

There are two ways of returning to Kingston. (Before returning, however, the swamp and bog near Portland might be visited, see below.) For the first which is a little longer but faster because you may not be tempted to stop as many times, go east from Westport on Highway 42 to Highway 15 at Crosby and straight south to Kingston. For the second shorter but more interesting route, follow the paved road which leads south about halfway between Fermoy and Westport. At Bedford Mills the road crosses a small lake and marsh, and then continues paved south all the way to Kingston, becoming an extension of Division Street. It passes close to the shores of Devil and Buck lakes.

STINSON'S SWAMP NEAR PORTLAND. From Old Fort Henry drive northeast on Highway 15 about 40 miles to Portland. After leaving the village turn to the right when you reach the shore of Rideau Lake. Leave the car at the railway station ½ mile southeast of Highway 15 and walk south-southeast for a few hundred yards. The swamp forest surrounding Stinson's Lake is very narrow on the west side and the floating margin with northern bog plants is easily reached. For a longer hike skirt the lake clockwise over Beaver dams into a dense zone of Dwarf Birch and through a Tamarack bog with beautiful orchids onto the open, floating sedge meadow in the northeast corner of the lake.

PORTLAND BOG FOREST. Three and a half miles northeast of Portland along Highway 15 take a gravel road to the left. Always turning right at the crossroads one can stop the car one mile from the highway. Walking a few hundred yards northeastwards, one cannot miss the beautiful little bog lake which is surrounded by a Tamarack forest with rare orchids and a cranberry marsh on the east side. The Seaside Arrow-grass has a relic occurrence there. Returning to the car, drive on, always turning right. Highway 15 will be reached again after 2 miles of skirting the south shore of Otter Lake (not to be confused with Otter Lake above).

RIDEAU CANAL. For those travelling by boat up the Rideau Canal from Kingston towards Ottawa, there are many excellent birding opportunities all through the Rideau Lakes. In the drowned land just north of Kingston Mills there are many Common Terns and some Caspian Terns in late summer. Shore visits at Kingston Mills, Jones Falls, Chaffeys Locks, and Westport are recommended. Osprey are usually seen on Upper Rideau Lake.

HELL HOLES NEAR ROBLIN. Go west on Highway 401 to Napanee. Take Highway 41 north for 9 miles and park the car at the railway crossing. Walk northeast along the railway for about one mile and 10 telegraph poles after the milepost "67." Turn south and follow any of the ridges and gorges until you are at the edge of the deepest gully. Descend into the gully and walk southwestwards until you reach the railway again. The Hell Holes can also be approached from the south.

The criss-crossing gorges are lined with grottoes, overhangs, caves, and mushroom-rocks like the famous Flowerpot Island of the Bruce Peninsula. The limestone strata are of varying hardness, and harder layers remained over the weathering lower layers until the roofs caved in. The limestone walls are coated with rare plants, among them a great number of ferns, especially Slender Cliff-Brake and Walking Fern. Take ropes and headlamps along if you intend to explore the caves.

GANANOQUE AREA

Gananoque is approached from the west and east by Highways 2 and 401, and from the north by Highway 32 and county roads. Routes of interest to naturalists in this area begin at the cloverleaf junction of Highways 2 and 401 east of the town.

ST. LAWRENCE RIVER MARSHES. Proceed eastward from Gananoque along the scenic route, Highway 401. For some 8 miles along this highway there are several excellent marshes. Many species of marsh birds may be easily observed during the breeding season, and during the spring and early fall the duck flights are excellent at sunrise and sunset. The Department of Highways park near the twin highway bridges is a good place from which to watch the Canada Goose migration about the first week in May and in October.

IVY LEA. About 9 miles east of Gananoque on Highway 401, and, when within sight of the Thousand Islands Bridge, take the unpaved road to the right along the river through the small community of Ivy Lea. As the river is open here through the winter it is an excellent location from which to observe many species of winter ducks or early spring migrants: Canvasback, Scaup, Oldsquaw, Redhead, Goldeneye. Bald Eagles may often be seen hunting over the area during the winter. The sheltered places along the road also provide good habitat for many of the smaller winter birds.

On any stop at Ivy Lea a visit to Hill and Wellesley islands should be included. Cross the first span of the International Bridge; toll is $1.00 return for the first span (or $1.50 return for both spans, leading to United States). Stop at Canadian Customs and look for Turkeys. One hundred Turkey chicks (*Meleagris gallapavo*) were introduced into the area in 1960. They have nested successfully in the wild, and a small flock is often seen in the vicinity of the Canadian and American customs houses where food is put out for them. There is also a number of ducks to be seen from the small bridge between the two customs houses.

THE NORTHERN LAKES. Turn north from Highway 401 at the Ontario Tourist Information Bureau near the entrance to the Thousand Islands Bridge and proceed on the country road

**WILD TURKEY AND PITCH-PINE**

through Lansdowne, Black Rapids, and Outlet. The country around Lansdowne is fairly flat and many species of field birds may be seen here. About 3 miles north of Lansdowne the land changes abruptly and the road becomes winding and hilly through the lakes and wooded hills of the Precambrian Shield. In October the autumn colours are particularly good here. Continue to Lyndhurst and from there to Highway 32 or 15.

SOUTH LAKE AREA. Drive north from Gananoque for some 8 miles on Highway 32. The wooded area to the north of the lakes is good for many species of migrant warblers and other land birds. Pileated Woodpeckers, Broad-winged Hawks, and Cerulean Warblers have been known to nest here. Those interested in spring wildflowers will find the area a good one.

THE THOUSAND ISLANDS. Turn south at the Gananoque Post Office corner on Highway 2 and proceed along Stone Street to the public dock on the river. Thousands of early migrating ducks may be seen here in the very early spring after the ice has left this part of the river. During the summer months there are boat tours from Gananoque through the islands. A few of the small uninhabited islands provide nesting grounds for gulls and terns.

MRS. HELEN QUILLIAM
*Kingston Field Naturalists*

## KIRKLAND LAKE

KIRKLAND LAKE, about 375 miles north of Toronto, is on the Precambrian Shield. From Matachewan on the scenic Montreal River, at the west, to Virginiatown on Larder Lake, at the east, lies one of Canada's large gold producing areas. Virginiatown is the home of Canada's largest gold mine, while Kirkland Lake speaks of its "Mile of Gold." In the southern part of the district under consideration is New Liskeard, a partially industrial and agricultural town situated in the smaller of two clay belts. To the north, a distance the equivalent of from Toronto to Huntsville, is Cochrane, in the greater clay belt. Within this vast area there is good farming land on the north and south while the mid-section is dominated by rocks, spruce forests, and lakes. The rugged beauty and tourist attractions are familiar to many. The open lands attract many field birds, while the woodlands, bogs, lakes, and rocky islands provide homes for many other species. Bear and Moose are also common. Timber, fur, and minerals were responsible for making many routes and towns well known, but, because of the relatively large area with its sparse population, there is much new to be found in its flora and fauna.

CASEY TOWNSHIP. New Liskeard is on Highway 11, 110 miles north of North Bay. Judge is 13 miles northeast of New Liskeard near the intersection of Highway 65 and the Ontario-Quebec border. See *National Topographic Map*, New Liskeard sheet. In mid-April hundreds of Canada Geese feed in the fields south of Judge on both sides of the Blanche River. Later in April ducks stop over to feed.

MOUNTAIN LAKE. One by 2½ miles in size, this lake is an enlargement of the Montreal River, downstream from the town of Elk Lake. From Elk Lake, take Highway 65 over the railroad crossing 8 miles from Elk Lake bridge, opposite a gravel pit and close by railroad marker no. 21. Take first right, at which point the lake is visible. Shallow and weedy, with extensive reed beds, this is a good feeding area for ducks and geese, and numerous varieties of shorebirds may be observed when the water level is low and the beach exposed during migration seasons. It is also game country, and Moose and Black Bear are commonly seen on shore during summer. Land birds are plentiful along the north and east margins.

MATACHEWAN AREA. Several spots may prove interesting in this area. Crossing Highway 66, within sight of Highway 65, Whiskey Jack Creek has a gravel pit on one side and boggy ground with spruce woods on the other side. It is about 3 miles from the village. About ¾ mile from the village on the east side of the highway and about ¼ mile in, is the town dump, which is patronized by a number of birds and the occasional Black Bear. In Matachewan village, below the bridge, ducks have been seen throughout the winter in the swift water of the Montreal River.

ROUND LAKE. From Kirkland Lake go 3 miles west to the junction of Highways 66 and 112. Turn south onto Highway 112 and go 8 miles to the Legion Road which runs along the north side of Round Lake. There are several roads leading off this road which you can follow to the lakeshore. Water and shore-birds are common here in migration. When you reach the Blanche River, you are in good owl country.

Another interesting road is about 2 miles south from the Legion Road along Highway 112. Turn right at the Clover Valley service station (Esso). Watch for Red Foxes in the fields. Follow this road to the bridge which crosses the Blanche River to Highway 11, or instead of turning to the bridge go straight to Karlsons' farm which is near the outlet of Round Lake. There are many interesting birds to be seen here, especially during migration.

LAKESHORE SLIMES. An extensive area of marsh and mine tailings which borders the community of Kirkland Lake on the north-west can be reached through the Teck-Hughes Mine property on the western outskirts of Kirkland Lake. To reach the best vantage point, a railroad bridge, drive or walk straight north from the main gate, among the mine buildings, taking a slight jog to the right where necessary. Past the last buildings along this road there is another gate, often locked to vehicular traf-fic, but within easy walking distance of the railroad bridge, which is visible from this point. Permission has been granted by the mine to use their property as an access route. Extreme caution should be used in walking on the slimes, which are often deceptively treacherous. Rails, Common Snipe, and other marsh birds breed here, and shorebirds and waterfowl, particularly surface-feeding ducks, stop during migration.

KIRKLAND LAKE DUMP. Bordering on Gami Lake on Goodfish Road about 3 miles north of town there is an area set apart by the municipality as a disposal area. This area attracts such birds as Common Crows, Common Ravens, gulls, Common Grackles, and Starlings, which feed on the waste during the summer season, and some of these species remain close by during much of the colder season.

WRIGHT HARGREAVES SLIMES. On the Wright-Hargreaves Mine property some 2½ miles north on Goodfish Road and ½ mile east of this road there lies a body of water some ten acres or more in area. It is probably much smaller now than formerly because the mine slimes have been poured into this area. Many migrant water birds make this water hole a place of call in spring and fall for rest and feeding. Such birds as sandpiper, plover, Ruddy Turnstone, and yellowlegs are commonly observed.

LARDER LAKE STATION ROAD. Off Highway 66, one mile east of Larder Lake village (15 miles east of Kirkland Lake) are the Omega slimes and the town dump about ½ mile from highway. The latter is well patronized by birds during winter, and shorebirds visit the slimes during migration.

VIRGINIATOWN. This village is 24 miles east of Kirkland Lake on Highway 66.

(*a*) *Town Dump.* This is ¾ mile west of town, and is an active area for wildlife in winter and summer. A no trespassing sign is posted.

(*b*) *Marsh.* This is across from dump on highway. Beaver are seen occasionally.

(*c*) *Town.* The Beach Road just past post office, as well as the beach and footpath to the corner of Waite and Connell avenues are usually good for small birds.

(*d*) *Kearns.* One mile east of Virginiatown on Highway 66, take first turn right on going east, then turn right again to the beach. This area is good for marsh and land birds.

(*e*) *Chemins Mountain.* To the south of Highway 66 on the Ontario-Quebec border is a dome shaped outcropping of rock about 600 feet high. It can be climbed by a fair trail, and provides an excellent view of the countryside. A travel permit is required in season (because of fire).

CULVER PARK. Proceed west 5 miles from Kirkland Lake on Highway 66 to Swastika. As you reach the farther end of Swastika (where the houses end), you can see Otto Lake, with a good gravel road leading down to it. This clearing is Culver Park. The combination here of field, shrubbery, river, lake, beach, and forest encourages a good variety of bird life at all seasons. The gravel road continues on the other side of the clearing and leads across a floating winter bridge to a spruce swamp which provides good shelter for small birds in winter.

SHARP-TAILED GROUSE MUSKEG. This is located in Beatty Township, 10 miles east of Matheson station on the north side of Highway 101, or approximately ½ mile west of the Johns-Manville Mine turn. Sharp-tailed Grouse are observed in this area during late fall and occasionally during February and March. The timber is mostly scrub spruce and willow. A small creek flows along the east side of the muskeg, and Beaver and shorebirds are abundant.

MOOSE LAKE. Located in Bond Township, this lake is 3 miles west of Shillington or 13 miles west of Matheson station on Highway 101 to Timmins. Little Driftwood Creek flows across and south of Highway 101 approximately 2 miles to the lake, the west side of which is accessible by car. The marshes along the west shore and the river at the south end of the lake are ideal for ducks and shorebirds, especially during spring and fall migration. There is mixed timber around the lake: poplar, White Birch, spruce, and Balsam-Fir. Aquatic plants as well as Moose, Muskrat, and Beaver are in abundance.

CONNECTICUT WARBLER SWAMP. On Highway 11 in Hanna and St. John townships, 5 to 8 miles north of Potter or 11 to 14 miles south of Cochrane, is an extensive stand of tall spruce interrupted by a high tension power line and several wet patches of scrub spruce and Labrador-tea. Many warblers and boreal birds breed among the tall spruce, and White-winged Crossbills are often seen here. The wetter, more open areas with stunted trees have produced Connecticut and Palm Warblers during several summers. June is the best month.

LILLABELLE LAKE. For directions to Lillabelle Lake consult the Department of Lands and Forests district office at the south entrance to Cochrane. It is a shallow lake a few miles north of Cochrane and has a decidedly western flavour to its bird life. Summering water birds include Red-necked Grebe, Shoveler, teal, American Widgeon, and Bonaparte's Gull. This is considered one of the most interesting lakes in the entire region; further study may produce even more rewarding finds.

F. HELLEINER
*Kirkland Lake Nature Club*

### ❀ KITCHENER AND WATERLOO

KITCHENER AND WATERLOO, at the junction of Highways 85 (from the north), 7 (from the west), and 8 (from the southeast), are in the centre of southwestern Ontario, surrounded by some of the richest farmland in the province. Through this country, land of the Mennonites in the north and Scottish settlers in the south, flows the Grand River, joined by its tributaries, the Nith, Speed, and Conestogo. In spite of extensive farming and a high population (Waterloo County is the only county in Ontario in which there are three cities), there are still many largely unspoiled woods, streams, and marshes of interest to the nature lover. The two life zones of southern Ontario, the Carolinian (Deciduous Forest) and the Alleghenian (Mixed Forest), meet a few miles south of Kitchener, the division being most apparent in the plant life. The whole area was glaciated, and such post-glacial geological features as eskers (the best example is along Highway 7 on the western outskirts of Guelph), drumlins (east of Guelph), and kames (the Baden "sandhills" on Highway 7) are still evident.

The Kitchener-Waterloo Field Naturalists, the area's nature club, meet at 7.30 P.M. on the fourth Monday of every month from September to April (inclusive) except December, in the Children's Department of the Kitchener Public Library, 58 Queen Street North. A hike is usually held on the following Saturday. The library will be glad to give the names of club directors and dates of club hikes.

VICTORIA PARK, KITCHENER. These fifty-four acres of parkland surround an artificial lake, with playgrounds, picnic sites, canoeing, trailer camp, and ornamental game and water birds. The main entrance is on Courtland Avenue West.

WATERLOO PARK, WATERLOO. This park has some natural woodland, an antificial lake, recreational areas, picnic sites, and swimming pool. The main entrance is on Young Street West.

BREITHAUPT PARK, KITCHENER. Here are natural woods, playground facilities, and picnic site. The main entrance is on Margaret Avenue.

VICTORIA PARK, GALT. Formerly called Dickson's Woods, this park has a deer herd and ornamental birds in a large enclosure. The main entrance is on Highway 97.

HOMER WATSON MEMORIAL PARK (Cressman's Woods). This park consists of a fine stand of Alleghenian (Mixed) forest (huge Hemlocks), scenic bluffs overlooking the Grand River, and picnic and camping areas. Go south out of Kitchener on Mill Street, off on to Waterloo Township Road 27 to the first woods on the right.

BRIDGEPORT DAM. This is a good spot for shore and water birds, particularly in late summer. Go north out of Kitchener on Lancaster Street to the village of Bridgeport.

STECKLE'S WOODS. These wildflower woods are noted for the May display of Large-flowered Trilliums (the owner asks you to enjoy them but not destroy them). Take Waterloo Township Road 6 off Mill Street, Kitchener (watch for signs at entrance).

SPHAGNUM BOG. A peat formation with heaths and Gray Birch, this is the first swamp on the right on Waterloo Township Road 23 off the Sheldon Street Extension (Township Road 30), Kitchener.

DOON SEWAGE DISPOSAL AND REFORESTATION AREA. This area is best in colder months when there are usually many birds and smaller mammals in the brush and evergreen. Ducks and gulls are seen on the river and shorebirds about sewage beds in the fall. Get permission to enter from the City Engineer, City Hall, Kitchener, or the plant superintendent. It is on Waterloo Township Road 27 on the left side before entering the village of Doon.

BLOOMINGDALE. Deer are often seen in the general locality, and there is a heronry in the swamp. The village is on Waterloo Township Road C13 off Highway 7 out of Kitchener or off Township Road C12 out of Bridgeport.

PUSLINCH LAKE. This lake offers summer boating and swimming with beach and picnic sites. There are many ducks in early spring and late fall and a large swamp at nearby Killean. Permission to enter private properties should be secured from owners. Take Waterloo Township Road C21 out of Preston to the Waterloo-Wellington county line, then turn either left or right and follow signs.

DOON PINNACLE. This point offers a scenic view of surrounding country, and many forest birds can be seen and heard (Great Horned Owl, Pileated Woodpecker, thrushes). Go south of the village of Doon on Waterloo Township Road 27.

CRUICKSTON PARK FARM (Wilke's Bush, private). Wooded river flats and limestone formations with Prickly Ash and ferns are located along Blair Road (C14) between Blair and Galt (signs on gates).

ROSEVILLE SWAMP. This large tract of swamp and bog has many interesting plants (orchids, ferns, and Trailing Arbutus), and in the summer waterthrushes and several other warblers. It extends along both sides of Highway 97 between Galt and Roseville and along Waterloo Township Road 27A off Highway 97.

ORR'S LAKE (BARRIE LAKE) AND ALTRIEVE LAKE. This area changes from marshy lake to bog to swampy woods with the associated plants. It is 1½ miles west of Galt on the left of Highway 97.

ALPS ROAD. This road provides a scenic drive through wooded hills including Carolinian (Deciduous Forest) trees (oaks, hickories, Sassafras) and plants. Cerulean Warbler, Blue-gray Gnatcatcher, Yellow-throated Vireo, thrushes, and other forest birds are summer residents. Take the first road to right off Highway 24A after leaving Galt (woods are about one mile past first crossroad on this road).

CAUSEWAY. This narrow road crosses a swamp with pond life, birds (Northern Waterthrushes and other warblers), and plants (orchids and ferns). Take the third road to left (just before Bannister's) off Highway 24A out of Galt.

BANNISTER'S MARSH. This is an excellent spot to watch marsh birds right from the road—particularly ducks (some nesting), American Coot, Common Gallinule, rails, herons (one or two Common Egrets visit the marsh almost every summer), Pied-billed Grebe, Long-billed Marsh Wren, Common Snipe, and a nesting colony of Black Terns. Many Muskrats (houses can be seen in fall and winter), turtles, frogs, Water Snakes, and other aquatic animals and plants are here. Take Highway 24A southwest out of Galt and turn right at Wrigley Corners (marsh on both sides of road).

GLEN MORRIS AND SPOTTISWOOD. A scenic drive follows wooded river bluffs from Glen Morris to Galt (on Highway 24 part of the way). Two lakes surrounded by heavy woods are at Spottiswood. Blue-gray Gnatcatcher, Gray Partridge, Blue-winged and Golden-winged Warblers nest in the general vicinity, and Turkey Vultures and Bald Eagles can usually be seen soaring overhead. Glen Morris is on the third road on the right off Highway 24 out of Galt, and Spottiswood on the fifth road to the left (turn right at first fork in this road) off the same highway.

PINEHURST PARK. Take Highway 24A out of Galt past Wrigley Corners (follow sign). For details of park, see guide for Brantford.

BEVERLY SWAMP. It is on both sides of Highway 97 between Galt and Freelton in Beverly Township, Wentworth County. See guide for Hamilton.

*Kitchener-Waterloo Field Naturalists*

## ❀ LONDON

LONDON IS SITUATED in the midst of farming country in southwestern Ontario and has at its centre the confluence of the north and south branches of the Thames River. From this point the Thames flows westward to Lake St. Clair. Consequently there are in and around London wooded river banks and river flats. The city is at the northern limits of the Carolinian Zone (Deciduous Forest Region) which includes in its fauna and flora several birds, mammals, insects, and plants found over much of the eastern United States but found in Canada only in extreme southern Ontario. London is approached from the west by provincial Highways 2 and 22, from the north and south by Highway 4, and from the east by Highways 2 and 401. Routes to points of interest to naturalists, in the following account, start at the war memorial (cenotaph) in the southwest corner of Victoria Park at the corner of Wellington Street and Dufferin Avenue in the heart of the city. Victoria Park is at the junction of Highways 2, 4, and 22 and is bounded by Clarence Street, Wellington Street, Central Avenue, and Dufferin Avenue.

The local natural history club is the McIlwraith Ornithological Club which holds its meeting at 8.00 P.M. in the auditorium of the Williams Memorial Library on Queens Avenue, 2 blocks from the cenotaph, on the third Monday of the month, January to May, October and November. Visitors to the city can get in touch with officers of the club by phoning the reference desk at the Williams Memorial Library.

VICTORIA PARK. This public park of the city of London includes many native and introduced trees, formal gardens, and lily ponds. It is inhabited by Gray Squirrels, mainly the black phase. Many species of birds are to be found, particularly during the spring migration.

GIBBONS PARK. From the northwest corner of Victoria Park go north on Richmond Street 7 blocks (counting on the east side) to Grosvenor Street, west one block to St. George Street and the entrance to Gibbons Park. It is a public park of the city and has playgrounds and a swimming pool. A considerable growth of trees and the banks of the Thames River which traverses the park provide shelter for birds.

SPRINGBANK PARK. From the cenotaph go south on Wellington Street 2 blocks to Dundas Street, west on Dundas 8 blocks (crossing the Thames River) to Wharncliffe Road, south on Wharncliffe 7 blocks (crossing the Thames River) to Springbank Drive, west on Springbank Drive 3 miles to Springbank Park. The park extends for about a mile along the south bank of the Thames River. It is well wooded and includes playgrounds, a zoo, and "Storybook Gardens." Native birds may be seen any time of the year, wading and water birds and other migrants in spring and fall.

WALKER PONDS. From the cenotaph go south on Wellington Street and Wellington Road 3½ miles to a crossing with the Dearness Home for Senior Citizens at the northeast corner. Walker Ponds are three ponds northeast of the corner and mainly on property of the federal government. Access is by permission of local farmers and owners. The ponds are surrounded by woods. Many native birds nest here, and wading and water birds are particularly evident in spring and fall.

POND MILLS. Continue east 1½ miles from front of Dearness Home (see Walker Ponds) to Pond Mills. Two ponds are visible from the road and adjacent fields. Access is by permission of local farmers and owners. Wading and water birds are particularly evident in spring and fall.

BYRON BOG. From the northwest corner of Victoria Park go north on Richmond Street 4 blocks (counting on the east) to Oxford Street, west on Oxford 3¾ miles to Hyde Park Sideroad. The Byron Bog is in a hollow southwest of the corner of Oxford Street and Hyde Park Sideroad. Access is by permission of local farmers and owners. It is the only Black Spruce–Tamarack–Sphagnum floating bog in the vicinity of London and includes several orchids, heath plants, cranberries, Pitcher-plants, and sundews. Water birds, warblers, and finches are particularly evident in spring and fall migration.

WONNACOTT'S FARM. From Victoria Park follow Highway 2 south and west 12 miles to the village of Delaware, go north from Delaware 2 miles to the Thames River, north from the river bridge ¾ mile to the first east-west road (south of Komoka), 1¾ miles west along this east-west road to the lane leading to Wonnacott's Farm, south of the road. The farm is marked by Wonnacott's mail box. Access is by permission of the owner or tenant. A broad flood plain of the Thames River is surrounded by wooded slopes. It is an excellent site for bird study at all times of the year; water birds, waders, swamp and marsh birds, and warblers are particularly evident in spring and fall migration. There is a nest of Bald Eagles on the flood plain.

DORCHESTER SWAMP. From the cenotaph follow Wellington Road south 4 miles to Highway 401 and go east on Highway 401 for 10½ miles to Highway 73. Dorchester Swamp is about 4 square miles in area and surrounds the junction of Highways 73 and 401. Access is from parking spots on the highways and by permission of local farmers and owners. The swamp is heavily wooded, mainly with poplars and conifers, and gives shelter for many birds including hawks, owls, and Ruffed Grouse.

FANSHAWE PARK. This is a public park, recreation area, and conservation project under the jurisdiction of the Upper Thames Valley Conservation Authority. The building of Fanshawe Dam has created Fanshawe Lake, about 4 miles long, surrounded by flood plains, wooded slopes, woodlots, and fields. The park may be approached by several routes to excellent vantage points for observing birds. (1) From the cenotaph go south 2 blocks to Dundas Street, east 2¼ miles to Highbury Avenue, north on Highbury 2½ miles to Concession 4 of London Township, east 2½ miles following signs to Fanshawe Dam. Waders and water birds are particularly evident on the mud flats below the dam in migration. (2) From the corner of Highbury Avenue and Concession 4 continue north ¾ mile to Concession 5, then east on this concession 2½ miles to Cameron Wilson Park and public beach on the lake. (3) From the corner of Highbury Avenue and Concession 5 go north on Highbury Avenue ¾ mile to Concession 6, then east on this concession to high banks overlooking the lake. This is an excellent vantage point from which to see migrating ducks, grebes, mergansers, Common Loons, and Whistling Swans in spring and fall migration. (4) From the corner of Highbury Avenue and Concession 6 go north on Highbury Avenue ¾ mile to Concession 7, east 3 miles on this concession to a north-south road (blind end), then south ½ mile to the lake. Here is the upper end of Fanshawe Lake with wooded slopes on the north and flood plains on the south. Water birds and waders are seen to good advantage in spring and fall.

BANK OF THE THAMES RIVER. In and around London, access to the river is by parking at approaches to bridges crossing the river by Highbury Avenue (north and south), Adelaide Street (north and south), Richmond Street (north and south), University Drive, Wharncliffe Road, Ridout Street, and Egerton Street. Location of these streets and bridges are on maps of the city available from the Chamber of Commerce, City Hall, library, and travel agencies.

Mrs. C. A. Cline
W. W. Judd
*McIlwraith Ornithological Club*

### 🏵 LONG POINT

LONG POINT can be reached from the village of Courtland on Highway 3 midway between Tillsonburg and Delhi. Drive south from Courtland 20 miles to the village of Port Rowan. The road leading west and south from Port Rowan extends 5 miles to the base of Long Point. The point extends for 20 miles from its base eastward into Lake Erie, forming the south shore of Long Point Bay. The north shore of the bay is formed by the mainland shore of Lake Erie extending eastward. The "Inner Bay" is protected at its eastern end by Turkey Point jutting southward from the mainland and by Pottohawk Point jutting northward from Long Point. The "Outer Bay" opens out into Lake Erie.

Most of Long Point is the property of the Long Point Company. The numbers of waterfowl taken annually are slight and the point remains essentially a waterfowl preserve. At the base of the point is Long Point Provincial Park with facilities for parking and camping. Many cottages have been built surrounding this park area.

The marshes of Long Point and Long Point Bay are important as places in which tremendous numbers of waterfowl concentrate in spring and fall. Thousands of ducks of many species find resting and feeding areas here during migration, and many remain to nest. Thus Long Point is one of the best areas in Ontario for viewing ducks, geese, swans, wading birds, and marsh-dwelling birds. Whistling Swans concentrate here in spring migration, first appearing about the middle of March. The beaches and marshes at the base of the point can be reached by driving from Port Rowan along the causeway to Long Point Park. The marshes lie close against the causeway, and there is an excellent opportunity for seeing birds by parking on the causeway and scanning the marshes with binoculars.

The outer end of Long Point is still a wilderness of forests, swamps, and beaches, and arrangements to visit it by boat must be made in Port Rowan. White-tailed Deer are present in the woods, and there is an abundant fauna of reptiles and amphibians

Sylvia Hahn

**WHISTLING SWAN**

as well as a varied population of nesting birds. The animal population of this area has been described by L. L. Snyder and E. B. S. Logier (1931) in the *Transactions of the Royal Canadian Institute*, vol. XVIII, pt. 1, pp. 117–236, under the title "A Faunal Investigation of Long Point and Vicinity, Norfolk County, Ontario."

K. BEEMER

## ❀ MANITOULIN ISLAND

MANITOULIN ISLAND, situated in northern Lake Huron, is separated from the north shore of the lake by the North Channel and the northwest corner of Georgian Bay. The island, mainly a limestone tableland, is slightly tilted from north to south or southwest, forming nearly perpendicular limestone cliffs overlooking the North Channel. These cliffs form part of the Niagara Escarpment. The tableland slopes gently towards Lake Huron on the south shore.

Extensive rock plains, flat and thinly covered with soil, characterize much of Manitoulin Island's topography. As a result of Pleistocene glaciation, glacial striae appear on some of the exposed limestone, and glacial boulders are abundant. In certain areas there are post-glacial beach levels well above the present lake level. Second growth mixed hardwood-conifer forest covers extensive areas. Approaching Manitoulin Island from the north, one notices a rather abrupt transition from Precambrian Shield granite to Palaeozoic limestone (between Whitefish Falls and Little Current). A point of interest on this road is the plaque marking the route of the early voyageurs.

There are two approaches to Manitoulin Island: from the north, Highway 68 from Espanola enters at Little Current over a combined highway-railway bridge; from the south a ferry from Tobermory, at the tip of the Bruce Peninsula, docks at South Baymouth.

SOUTH BAYMOUTH PARK. From the dock in South Baymouth follow Highway 68 (about ¼ mile) to the "Camping and Picnic Area" opposite the Community Hall. A nature trail is marked.

ROGER'S CREEK. From South Baymouth follow Highway 68 for 2 miles to Cedar Park Road. Turn right along Cedar Park Road, following the signs past Cedar Park Lodge, about 3½ miles to a log bridge (it's safe!). This is a marshy creek area with interesting birds and plants. An occasional Bald Eagle is seen.

BLUE JAY CREEK. From South Baymouth follow Highway 68 about 3 miles to the first right-angle turn. Continue straight north on the secondary road towards Tehkummah, about 1¼ miles to fork in the road. American Woodcock perform here nightly in spring. Continue via either left fork or middle fork to bridges over Blue Jay Creek.

MANITOU RIVER AND MICHAEL BAY. Continue across Blue Jay bridge on middle fork (above) for approximately 1¾ miles to first road on left (sign to Providence Bay). Follow Providence Bay road about 4 miles to the concrete bridge over the Manitou River. Directly across the bridge follow a sandy road to the left. The road is often poor, so it is safer to park your car here and walk in. It is about 3 miles to the Lake Huron shore, along a wooded road which often borders the river. Interesting birds and flora are present all the way. Michael Bay is a shallow, sandy bay open to Lake Huron. West of Michael Bay along the Lake Huron shore there are extensive sand dune areas. About ½ mile upstream from the lake there are scenic low falls on the Manitou River. Some 50 years ago the open area in this part was the site of a thriving lumbering community which was destroyed by forest fire.

PROVIDENCE BAY. Continue from the Manitou River bridge (above) for about 9 miles to the village of Providence Bay, or from Mindemoya take Highway 551 to Providence Bay, about 9 miles. An interesting road for a walk begins at McDermid's store and goes west along the Lake Huron shore. East from the dock towards the lighthouse is a rocky shore, where fossils are found. Providence Bay is another sandy bay open to Lake Huron. The Mindemoya River empties into Providence Bay here. There are picnic tables and a fireplace.

DEAN BAY. From Providence Bay follow Highway 551 north (about 1½ miles) to the first sideroad on the left. Follow this sideroad about 1½ miles to Scott McDermid's farm. Obtain permission from Mr. McDermid to enter the road directly opposite his farm buildings. One may drive along the road about 1½ miles to the beach. Bog plants and warblers are present.

PORTAGE BAY AREA. From Little Current take Highway 540 to West Bay, then Highway 551 to Mindemoya, or from South Baymouth take Highway 68 to Highway 542 which goes to Mindemoya. From Mindemoya take Highway 542 to the Poplar Sideroad (about 16 miles). Turn left along the Poplar Sideroad through the hamlet of Poplar about 7 miles to an area of recently reforested sand dunes on the left and a cemetery in a Beech grove area on the right. Continue about ½ mile until the road turns sharply to the right. A trail leads off on the left at this corner over flat rock about one mile through open mixed scrub pine to the Lake Huron shore.

MINDEMOYA LAKE. From Little Current take Highway 540 to West Bay, then Highway 551 to Mindemoya. Follow the Ketchankookem Trail west along Lake Mindemoya about ⅛ mile. There is a stream here surrounded by marshy areas.

WEST BAY BLUFFS. From Little Current, Highway 540 to West Bay passes along the foot of limestone bluffs. High Hill in this area is the highest point on the island. These north-facing cliffs provide habitat for interesting flora.

KAGAWONG RIVER. From Little Current take Highway 540 to Kagawong. The Kagawong River drains Lake Kagawong into the North Channel. The river is crossed by Highway 540 and is an excellent place for those with a canoe or boat to see waterfowl and other marsh birds.

GORE BAY AIRPORT. From Little Current follow Highway 540 and continue west approximately 3¾ miles past the Gore Bay Ontario Provincial Police Detachment building. Then, instead of turning south on the highway, continue straight west approximately 2 miles. The road to the airport turns off to the left. This is one of the dancing grounds for Prairie Chicken in season (March–May). Because the best dancing time is early morning, it is suggested that anyone interested contact Mr. Grant Johnson at the airport the afternoon before a visit in order to obtain permission to enter and to get the detailed location of the dancing ground.

INDIAN POINT BRIDGE. From Little Current follow Highway 540 west to Indian Point Bridge. The narrow channel between Lake Wolsey and Bayfield Sound is crossed by a causeway and bridge at this point. There is a Department of Highways camping ground and picnic area here. During spring, waterfowl and American Woodcock are often abundant in this vicinity. Just west of the bridge is an old Indian burial ground.

YOUNG LAKE WATERFOWL SANCTUARY. From Little Current follow Highway 540 to Meldrum Bay (approximately 80 miles). A federal waterfowl sanctuary has recently been established. For details concerning the sanctuary, inquire in Meldrum Bay.

JAMES L. BAILLIE

 **MUSKOKA**

MUSKOKA IS SITUATED north of the southern edge of the Precambrian Shield, and the whole rocky area abounds in rivers, lakes, and streams. It is heavily wooded with mixed deciduous and coniferous trees, and countless Sphaghnum bogs can be found. Any part of the area is of general interest to lovers of nature.

MEMORIAL PARK, HUNTSVILLE. Turn off Highway 11 in Huntsville to Highway 27, go south 3 blocks, and turn left into park as marked. Follow signs to lookout. Trees, shrubs and ferns, Pitcher-plant, and representative bird life occur. For guide, phone Aubrey May of the Huntsville Nature Club (Phone 346).

PENINSULA LAKE TRILLIUM FIELD. Follow Highway 60 east from Huntsville 3 miles to Canal Resort Area signboard. Follow Deerhurst signs. Inquire from Mr. Bill Waterhouse, Deerhurst

Lodge, for directions to one of the largest displays of Large-flowered Trillium to be found in Ontario in late May. From Huntsville it is about 6 miles.

THREE MILE LAKE. Go south from Huntsville on Highway 11 to Utterson and continue west on Highway 516 to the sign marked "Windermere." Continue one mile, stopping at the top of the hill overlooking Three Mile Lake. At this point a gate on the right and a path lead across fields to Three Mile Creek. This stream is very interesting during early spring run-off when Walleyes are running, usually in mid-April. Information can be obtained from the Department of Lands and Forests official stationed at the stream.

DEE RIVER. Proceed further along Highway 516 through Ufford towards Windermere about 6 miles; make right turn at Dee Bank School, cross the bridge over the Dee River, and take the first turn to the right. There is a picnic area at lake. Buttonbush, Swamp-Loosestrife, Cardinal-flower, Swamp-Milkweed, Royal Fern, and Beaver dams are to be found.

LIMBERLOST. Go east from Huntsville on Highway 60 about 5 miles to Highway 514 and Limberlost turn. Follow signs about 12 miles to Limberlost Lodge. Inquire from Mrs. G. Hill about general flora and fauna characteristic of Muskoka, for example, warblers, Wood Duck, and Peregrine Falcon nests.

LAKE MUSKOKA HERONRY (Great Blue Heron). From Highway 11 at north entrance to Gravenhurst, take first turn to the right (west) after the railway crossing and follow road signs to Muskoka Beach about 3 miles. Inquire locally for location of heronry island.

SCENIC DRIVE (Highway 35). Highway 35 from Dorset to Minden is known as the Scenic Drive. Many lakes will be observed along the way, and any of these will show interesting fauna or flora. About 5 miles south of Dorset at Wren Lake, you will find a Department of Highways picnic area. Cardinal-flower grows in the surrounding district. Continuing on this highway about 2 miles will bring you to large white buildings on the left. This is the Department of Lands and Forests Training School for Foresters which is affiliated with the University of Toronto. Guides are on duty. The buildings and wildlife museum are of interest. About 8 miles from Dorset after

PARULA WARBLER

passing St. Nora's Lake, Ox Narrows, Partridge Lake, and Saskatchewan Lake, you arrive at Aunt Sarah's Lookout and Picnic Area which overlook Hall's Lake, one of the deepest in North America (at the deepest point over 1,000 ft.). Go south another 3 miles to Buttermilk Falls. Here the water drains from Hall's Lake and drops about 150 feet to Boshkung Lake. Go south through Carnarvon and Minden and 2 miles south of Minden to the junction of Highways 35 and 121, where there is a pond at the right side of the highway. At the deep end of this, where the stream flows out of the lake, is a Beaver dam. The Beaver house is located on the west side of the lake.

R. J. RUTTER

## ❀ NIAGARA FALLS (GEOLOGY)

BY NIGHT AND by day, in summer or in winter, the Falls of the Niagara River attract millions of travellers and honeymooners, as well as geologists. But these mighty cataracts are not the only unusual features of this river which begins in a lake and ends in a lake. Its head is wider than its mouth. It carries a tremendous volume of water over the relatively short distance of 35 miles, with no significant tributaries. Seven of these miles follow a picturesque, rock-bound gorge.

The first white man to record his visit to Niagara was Father Louis Hennepin, a Récollet priest. In 1678, he wrote: "Betwixt the Lake Ontario and Erie there is a vast and prodigious column of water which flows down in a surprising and astonishing manner, in as much as the universe does not afford a parallel."

By 1841, the Niagara Falls were famous. They had been visited and studied by such eminent geologists as James Hall of the New York Geological Survey, and, from England, Sir Charles Lyell, who is considered to be the founder of modern geological thought. Sir Charles wrote in his diary on August 27, 1841: "We first came in sight of the Falls of Niagara when they were about three miles distant. The sun was shining full upon them—no building in view—nothing but the green wood, the falling water, the white foam. At that moment they appeared to me to be more beautiful than I had expected, and less grand, but after several days, when I had enjoyed a nearer view of the two cataracts, had listened to their thundering sound . . . and when I had explored the delightful island which divided the Falls, where the solitude of the forest is still unbroken, I had at last learned by degrees to comprehend the wonders of the scene, and to feel its full significance." To Lyell "full significance" included a thorough geological examination of the area. The frontispiece of his diary shows Lewiston and Queenston beneath the escarpment. It also shows the relationship of the Niagara River to the escarpment, and the lay of the major rock units exposed along it and up the Niagara Gorge.

Today, geologists subdivide these rocks into the formations shown in Figure 6. The rocks are all sedimentary in origin, and were deposited in a sea during the Ordovician and Silurian periods of the Palaeozoic Era; they are considered to be in the neighbourhood of 400 million years old. The Ordovician rocks are the Queenston shales, at the bottom of the section; these are the red shales that may be seen at various localities along the base of the escarpment. In this area, they are exposed in the lower part of the gorge walls from the mouth of the Niagara River almost to Niagara Glen. The Silurian rocks can be seen along the entire length of the gorge. They consist of sandstones, shales, limestones, and dolomites. The sandstones and shales were originally deposited as the sands and muds of large deltas that built out into the seas which flooded parts of North America during Silurian time. The source of the sands and muds lay in the ancestral Appalachian Mountains of the northeastern United States.

The formation over which the falls cascade is the Lockport Dolomite, a hard calcium-magnesium-carbonate rock. It can be traced along the rim of the gorge in its entirety and, indeed, all along the rim of the Niagara Escarpment.

Although all these rocks are of extreme significance in the interpretation of Palaeozoic history, they assume even more importance when they are considered in connection with the Niagara River, because it is the particular lithologic succession

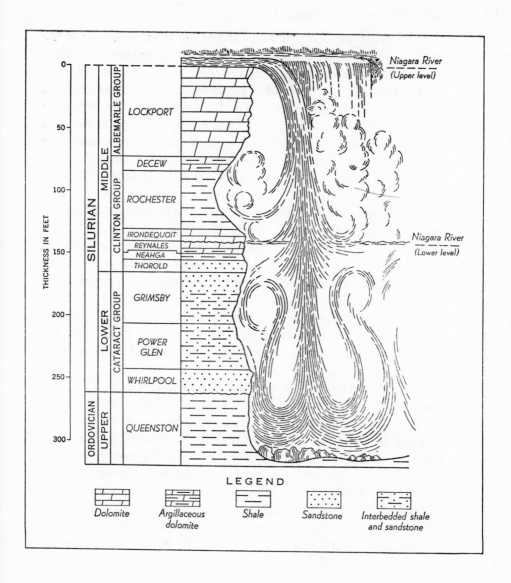

FIGURE 6. THE STRATIGRAPHIC SECTION AT NIAGARA FALLS

The whole section depicted above can be seen at the northern end of the gorge where the red Queenston shales are well exposed, as is their contact with the overlying Whirlpool sandstone. This contact marks the boundary between the Ordovician and Silurian periods. (Diagram courtesy Geological Survey of Canada.)

that accounts for Niagara Falls as we see them today. It is the simple arrangement of the hard dolomite overlying the softer shales and sandstones that controls the type of erosion exercised by the running waters of the Niagara River. The process is plain to see and easy to understand. The hard dolomite over which the river courses at the falls becomes undermined, owing to the ease with which the softer rocks beneath it can be worn away by spray and frost. Cracks develop, and a rock fall occurs. The process, called "sapping," then repeats itself. A vertical face is thereby maintained, allowing the river to erode or cut its way upstream and still maintain a waterfall. The process here also produces a reduction in the width of the river.

In this way the Niagara River has gnawed its way southward into the escarpment, and has left as testimony the magnificent gorge, and, as we shall see, evidence of its earlier channels. The process of sapping, of course, is still going on. It should be noted, however, that it has been slowed down considerably in recent years, because of the decreased flow of water (principally for hydro-electric purposes) and the remedial works that have been undertaken.

Now, let us turn to the origin of the Niagara River. The story begins several thousand years ago, when the glaciers of the Great Ice Age were retreating for the last time. As the ice melted back into the basins of the Great Lakes, the meltwaters became impounded, and formed a succession of transitory ancestral Great Lakes. In the Erie Basin, one of these lakes is known as Lake Whittlesey. With a further retreat of the glacier the Niagara area and the Lake Ontario Basin were uncovered. In this basin the waters of Lake Iroquois accumulated. The shoreline of the western end of the lake was at the base of the Niagara Escarpment.

It is obvious that an ancestral Niagara River could flow between the Erie and Ontario basins as soon as the ice uncovered the area, and indeed, it was at this time that gorge-cutting began. It should be noted here, however, that the ancestral Niagara River did not flow with a constant volume. Drainage changes associated with the de-glaciation of the Great Lakes area caused the volume of water flowing between the Erie and Ontario basins to vary. The seven-mile gorge has been subdivided into segments, and each segment named (Figure 7). The wide portions of the

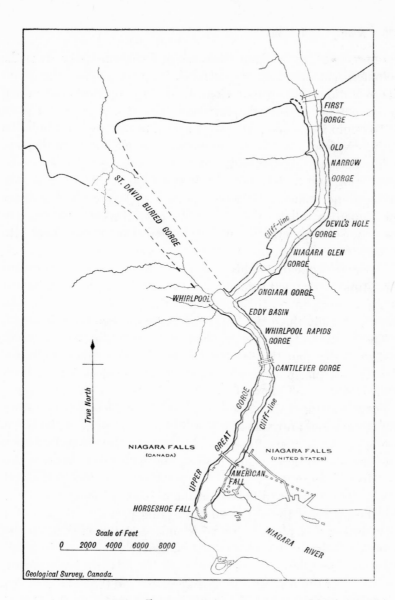

FIGURE 7. THE SUBDIVISIONS OF THE NIAGARA GORGE

These subdivisions have been correlated with major drainage changes in the Great Lakes system over the past 12,000 years. Narrow portions correspond with periods when the volume of water in the Niagara River was low. For example, the Old Narrow Gorge may have been excavated when the ancestral upper Great Lakes drained through Kirkfield and the Trent Valley into ancestral Lake Ontario, that is, Lake Iroquois. (Map courtesy Geological Survey of Canada.)

gorge reflect large volumes of water, and the narrow ones smaller volumes. Some of these changes will be mentioned as we discuss the evolution of the gorge. Good views of various portions of the gorge may be had by following the Niagara Parkway.

To begin this discussion, let us return to the time when the ice withdrew from the immediate vicinity of Niagara Falls; at this point the glacier halted temporarily with an approximately east-west front, and built a moraine—the Niagara Falls Moraine. The high ground immediately west of Table Rock House (just west of the Canadian falls) will identify the central part of this feature for you. Subsequently, the northerly retreat of the ice moved the glacier to the base of the escarpment. Above the escarpment Lake Tonawanda appeared. This lake was somewhat peculiar in that, for a time, it drained through six spillways. The spillway located at the western end of this lake was at the lowest elevation, so that eventually only this—the Lewiston Spillway—remained active.

The Lewiston Spillway was the first phase of the Niagara River, and its waters cut the first 2,000 feet of the present gorge. The shoreline of the spillway was perhaps best developed as the forerunner of the bluff above Table Rock House. This particular bluff is not the original shoreline, but is a modification of it, owing to lateral erosion into the Niagara Falls Moraine by subsequent stages of the Niagara River. In this vicinity, the original bluff of the Lewiston Spillway shoreline was probably somewhere out in the Horseshoe Falls.

The waters of the spillway became reduced in volume, decreasing the width of the river. An interesting part of the river's history during this phase is to be found at Niagara Glen, located about 2½ miles up the river (that is, south) from Brock's Monument at Queenston. Here, a small island, similar to the one at the south end of the American Falls today, divided the river, and thus produced two cataracts. The large, eastern channel on the "American" side cut past the island first, thus capturing the waters of the western channel. The rubble that constitutes the "glen" is made up of the remains of this island, and the shoreline of the river is a little bluff. The flat area at the base of the bluff, known as "Wintergreen Flats," is the bed of the western channel of the old Niagara River.

From the Niagara Glen, the river continued its gorge development southward but when it reached the Whirlpool, it exposed a controversial problem. The Whirlpool occurs at a sharp bend in the river. It can be seen well from the lookout on the Niagara Parkway at Whirlpool House, and even better by riding the cable car from this point. In the deep embayment of the Whirlpool, no bedrock appears in the walls of the gorge. The materials are sands, clays, and till of glacial origin. Drilling has revealed that the Whirlpool area is the beginning of a buried gorge called St. David Gorge, which is known to be over 260 feet deep. It can be traced northwest to the large re-entrant in the escarpment near the village of St. Davids. The significance of this gorge lies in the fact that it is filled with glacial deposits, a fact which indicates that it was formed either prior to the Ice Age, as suggested by Lyell, or during an interglacial period, as suggested by Spencer. We still await the correct interpretation.

The St. David Gorge presents another problem. Immediately upstream from the Whirlpool are the Whirlpool Rapids which occupy the Whirlpool Gorge—the narrowest portion of the present river. Here the sides are very steep, and show signs of undercutting; it is as if the present river were "too big for its britches." It may be observed that the Whirlpool Rapids are in line with the buried St. David Gorge. For access to a walk along the edge of these rapids, enter at Whirlpool House.

Is it possible that the Whirlpool Gorge is a continuation of the St. David Gorge, and that it too was filled with glacial deposits? In other words, has the present river re-excavated this narrow gorge? The answer seems to be "yes," because data obtained from drill holes bored prior to the building of the railway bridges over the Whirlpool Rapids revealed the presence of glacial deposits. The full course and function of the St. David River have yet to be found.

The Whirlpool Gorge passes upstream into the Upper Great Gorge. It is generally assumed that this last segment of the Niagara Gorge has been excavated since the inception of the present Great Lakes and their accompanying drainage pattern, a period of time extending back roughly 4,000 years. The positions of the American Falls and the Canadian Falls at the head of the Upper Great Gorge are, of course, controlled by Goat Island and the bend of the river at the Niagara Falls Moraine.

How long did it take the Niagara River to cut its gorge? The pendulum of the Niagara clock that, until relatively recently, has been used to try to answer this question is the rate of retreat of the present falls. Over the past 250 years, the swing of the pendulum, that is, the rate of retreat, is fairly easily obtained by using information from Father Hennepin's drawing and description, other old drawings, and data from several precise surveys. A plot of these results shows the tremendous amount of material—about 1,000 feet maximum, or an annual "bite" of between 3 and 4 feet, from 1678 to 1927—that has been removed from the area of the Canadian falls, and the small amount removed from the American falls. This is because 94 per cent of the river's flow passes over the Horseshoe Falls.

On the assumption that the above rate of retreat applied over the whole history of the river from the time of the Lewiston Spillway, a period of around 12,000 years would be required to excavate the present gorge.

This figure was considered too low by most who used this method to estimate the age of the falls, because of known variations in the hardness of the rocks and in the volume of water that passed down the Niagara River, and the complications at the Whirlpool Gorge. But the rate of erosion was the only pendulum available for gauging the speed of the work of the Niagara River up until a dozen or so years ago, when new techniques were developed for solving the ages of relatively recent geological events. These techniques are based on the use of a radio-active isotope of Carbon—Carbon 14. The use of Carbon 14, in so far as it applies to the Niagara problem, is dependent upon finding organic material (wood, or peat) in the deposits of the glacial lakes know to be most closely associated with the origin of the Niagara River. The dates so far obtained which bracket the age of the gorge are: 12,800 years ago for Lake Whittlesey in the Erie Basin, and between 12,660 and 12,080 years for Lake Iroquois in the Ontario Basin. These figures suggest, then, that gorge-cutting began between 12,000 and 13,000 years ago, and that it has required this length of time for the Niagara River to have excavated its gorge. This figure corresponds with the minimum figure obtained by using the data from the measured rate of erosion.

The contents of this paper have been based mainly on the observations and deductions of some of the noted geologists who have contributed so greatly to our knowledge of the Niagara River and its history. Beginning with James Hall and Sir Charles Lyell, men such as G. K. Gilbert, A. P. Coleman, J. W. W. Spencer, F. B. Taylor, F. Leverett, and E. Antevs have devoted their talents to interpreting this spectacular area. Since 1928, when Johnston presented the evidence for the re-excavation of the Whirlpool Gorge, nothing has appeared in the literature which would allow us to answer some of the tantalizing problems such as the significance of the St. David Gorge, or the pre-glacial Great Lakes drainage. Therefore, in some ways, Niagara Falls presents as big a challenge to a geologist today as it did 125 years ago.

WALTER M. TOVELL
P. F. KARROW

## ❀ NIAGARA PENINSULA

THE NIAGARA PENINSULA is bounded on the south by Lake Erie, on the north by Lake Ontario, and on the east by the Niagara River which extends for 30 miles between the two Lakes. Westward the peninsula extends to Hamilton and Hamilton Bay on the north and Dunnville and the mouth of the Grand River on the south. Halfway along its length the Niagara River tumbles over Niagara Falls, one of the most famous natural phenomena in the world and a major tourist attraction. The Niagara River above the falls is broad and swift, and in spring and fall it is a gathering place for flocks of ducks, geese, and swans. Below the falls the river flows through a deep gorge, the Niagara Gorge, which still retains many of its original features of rock walls, jumbled rock slides, and wooded ravines.

The most striking feature of the peninsula as a whole is the Niagara Escarpment extending for 50 miles from Queenston on the east to Hamilton on the west. Its face of exposed rock strata is some 200 feet high and separates the lower plains along Lake Ontario from the upper part of the peninsula extending south to Lake Erie. At Queenston the escarpment is 6 miles from Lake Ontario. Westward from Queenston it approaches more closely to the lake, and at Grimsby it is one mile from Lake Ontario. Westward from Grimsby it swings gradually backward from the lake, and at Hamilton is 3 miles from the lake.

Because the Niagara Peninsula is bounded on three sides by water there is ample opportunity at all times of the year to see water birds. It lies within the Carolinian Zone (Deciduous Forest Region) and thus affords an opportunity to see plants and trees representative of this zone. Niagara Falls is approached from the west by the Queen Elizabeth Way and Highways 3, 8, and 20, and from the east by United States highways terminating at Buffalo and Niagara Falls, New York. Routes to places of interest in this account begin at the Rainbow Bridge in Niagara Falls. The boulevard along the west bank of the Niagara River is under the supervision of the Niagara Parks Commission.

QUEENSTON. From the Rainbow Bridge follow the boulevard north 7 miles to Queenston. Along the way there are several paths by which one can descend on foot into the Niagara Gorge. At Queenston is Queenston Heights Park where, on a clear day, one can look out over the plains below and over Lake Ontario. The wooded slopes of the escarpment here are a habitat for many local species of birds.

NIAGARA-ON-THE-LAKE. From Queenston continue north along the boulevard 8 miles to Niagara-on-the-Lake. Here, at the mouth of the Niagara River, ducks and other water birds are to be seen in abundance in spring and fall.

BOULEVARD SOUTH OF NIAGARA FALLS. From the Rainbow Bridge drive south along the boulevard. It follows the bank of the river closely, and the traveller can stop and scan the river with binoculars. Look for rare waterfowl, gulls, and Bald Eagles during the cooler months.

USSHER'S CREEK. Five miles south of Niagara Falls Ussher's Creek flows into the Niagara River at the boulevard. In the creek grows the Green Arrow-Arum (*Peltandra virginica*).

BAYER'S CREEK. Continue for 4 miles along the boulevard from Ussher's Creek to the mouth of Bayer's Creek. Here there are stands of the Flowering Rush along the shores of the creek.

FORT ERIE. Continue for 10 miles along the boulevard from Bayer's Creek to Fort Erie. One mile south of Fort Erie is the restored Old Fort Erie. The beaches here afford an opportunity to see wading birds. There are small stands of Wild Licorice (*Glycyrrhiza lepidota*).

CRYSTAL BEACH. Follow Highway 3C from Fort Erie for 10 miles to Crystal Beach.

PORT COLBORNE. Follow Highway 3 for 10 miles from Crystal Beach to Port Colborne where water birds can be seen in the harbour.

WAINFLEET SWAMP. Four miles west of Port Colborne and just north of Highway 3, Wainfleet Swamp is visible from the highway. It is a peat bog eight miles square and contains an assemblage of plants characteristic of bog areas. It is inhabited by the Swamp Rattlesnake or Massasauga. Lincoln's Sparrows have summered here, far south of their normal breeding range.

DUNNVILLE. Follow Highway 3 for 25 miles west from Port Colborne to Dunnville. At this town there are extensive cat-tail marshes along the Grand River inhabited by Redwinged Blackbirds, Black Tern, bitterns, and other marsh-dwelling birds. These marshes extend along the Grand River to its mouth 5 miles downstream at Port Maitland.

PORT WELLER. From Niagara-on-the-Lake follow the lakeshore road (along the south shore of Lake Ontario) west 8 miles to Port Weller where the Welland Canal enters Lake Ontario.

PORT DALHOUSIE. From Port Weller follow the lakeshore road west 3 miles to Port Dalhousie.

JORDAN HARBOUR. From Port Dalhousie follow the lakeshore road west 6 miles to Jordan Harbour at the mouth of Twenty Mile Creek.

GRIMSBY AND GRIMSBY BEACH. From Jordan Harbour follow the lakeshore road west 10 miles to Grimsby Beach and Grimsby at the mouth of Forty Mile Creek.

STONEY CREEK. From Grimsby follow the lakeshore road west 12 miles to the mouth of Stoney Creek.

WATERFALLS OF THE NIAGARA ESCARPMENT. Between the Niagara River and Hamilton there are several creeks that tumble over the escarpment on their way to Lake Ontario, thus producing a series of small waterfalls that are picturesque features of the Niagara Peninsula. Below the falls the creeks pass through deep ravines which, because of their relative inaccessibility, retain many of their original features such as rock-strewn walls, forested banks, and vegetation of moss, ferns, and wildflowers. Interesting ferns growing in the crevices in the rocks are Purple Cliff-Brake, Maidenhair-Fern, Walking Fern, and Maidenhair Spleenwort. Flowering plants in the ravines include Wild Ginger, Poke Milkweed, and green Trilliums.

*Decew Falls.* From the Rainbow Bridge follow Highway 20 west 9 miles to Allanburg. Cross the Welland Canal at Allanburg and follow Highway 20 for 3 miles to Highway 3A. Follow Highway 3A north 4 miles to Lake Gibson. Cross Lake Gibson and immediately turn left and follow the road along the north shore of Lake Gibson one mile to Decew Falls on Twelve Mile Creek.

*Rockway Falls.* From Decew Falls follow the road passing above the falls west 3 miles to Rockway Falls on Fifteen Mile Creek.

*Balls Falls.* From Rockway Falls follow the road passing above the falls west for ¼ mile. Turn right onto the road leading south down the escarpment. Follow this road for 2 miles to Highway 8. Turn left onto Highway 8 and follow it for 3 miles to the village of Jordan and Twenty Mile Creek. Follow the road that leaves Jordan and passes south along the east bank of Twenty Mile Creek up the escarpment. Two miles from Jordan this road passes above Balls Falls.

*Beamers Falls.* From Balls Falls return to Jordan and Highway 8. Follow Highway 8 west for 12 miles to the village of Grimsby and Forty Mile Creek. Take the road leading south out of Grimsby and up the escarpment for one mile. Turn right onto the first road on the brow of the escarpment and follow it for ½ mile to Beamers Falls.

*Stoney Creek Falls.* From Beamers Falls follow the road passing above the falls and west along the brow of the escarpment for 12 miles to Stoney Creek Falls on Stoney Creek.

*Others.* Routes to other falls on the escarpment are described in the guide to the Hamilton region.

*Peninsula Field Naturalists*

## ❀ OTTAWA

THE CITY OF Ottawa, situated on the south shore of the Ottawa River, has in its environs many features of significant interest to naturalists. The region surrounding Ottawa as well as its sister city of Hull, Quebec, on the opposite shore, is part of the St. Lawrence Lowlands. Northward, only a short distance beyond the outskirts of Hull, these lowlands are abruptly interrupted by the rise of the Laurentian Hills which are a part of the great Canadian Shield. That section of the Laurentians which is north of Ottawa is referred to locally as the Gatineau Hills. The high elevation conspicuous in the northwest when viewed from the city is King Mountain (named after Dr. W. F. King, First Director of the Geodetic Survey of Canada) which is less than 10 miles from the National War Memorial. The altitude of King Mountain is 1,125 feet while the Ottawa River at Ottawa is 131 feet above mean sea level.

This northern boundary between the St. Lawrence Lowlands and the Laurentian Hills is doubly significant because it is also an accepted boundary, in this section of the Ottawa Valley, between two important life zones. The lowlands (south of the hills) are considered to be in the Transition Life Zone (Mixed Forest Region) while the hills are strongly representative of the Canadian Life Zone (Coniferous Forest Region). For example, birds such as Swainson's Thrush, Hermit Thrush, Red-breasted Nuthatch, Olive-sided Flycatcher, Common Raven, and in recent years Evening Grosbeak have been observed as summer residents in the northern limits of the Ottawa district (defined by the Otawa Field-Naturalists' Club as the area included within a 30-mile radius of the city of Ottawa).

At Ottawa two important rivers which drain dissimilar watersheds flow into the Ottawa River. The gently rolling agricultural lowlands to the south are principally drained by the Rideau River system while from the Laurentian highlands the waters of the Gatineau River join the Ottawa River opposite the city.

The Rideau River bisects Ottawa, flowing in a south to north direction. At the Hog's Back (3 miles inside the south boundary) the Rideau Canal separates from the river to continue an independent man-made course through central Ottawa, finally descending in a flight of eight locks to enter the Ottawa River immediately north of the site of the National War Memorial. The Rideau River winds through east central Ottawa to join the Ottawa River at Green Island, site of the City Hall. Here the Rideau waters form a twin falls by falling over a 35-foot ridge of limestone into the Ottawa River. Champlain first approached these falls via the Ottawa River in 1613 but it was several years later that French explorers first used the name Rideau, which in French means "curtain," to describe what was in those days a roaring pair of falls of sustained volume. Opposite the Rideau Falls on the Quebec side, Brewery Creek joins the Ottawa. That area is described in charming detail in *The Birds of Brewery Creek* by Malcolm MacDonald.

The contrasting Gatineau River is a non-navigable rapid stream which drains a vast area of Archaean Formation. Its shores are often rocky and precipitous. Within 30 miles of Ottawa a series of three large dams have been built across its course with accompanying hydro-electric generating plants. In addition, this river floats millions of logs from remote timber limits to several pulp and paper mills. In the elevated valleys of the Gatineau Hills there are numerous lakes of glacial origin.

The National War Memorial, on Confederation Square, located at the junction of Wellington, Sparks and Elgin streets, the Driveway, Rideau Street, and Mackenzie Avenue, is considered to be the centre, or hub, of the Ottawa district. Ontario provincial highways terminate at the Ottawa city limits but are directed via through streets or scenic driveways to the war memorial with the one exception of Highway 17, Trans-Canada Highway Ottawa Valley Route, which crosses Ottawa through its longest, west to east, dimension and continues to the Quebec boundary at Point Fortune (47 miles west of Montreal). Highway 15 begins at

Kingston (130.8 miles southwest), enters Ottawa at the junction of Highway 17 and Richmond Road, the latter leading directly to the war memorial. Highway 16 begins at Johnstown which is 58.9 miles south of Ottawa. At this point there is direct access into New York State by the Highway Skyway Toll Bridge opened in 1960. This highway crosses the Rideau River (and canal) 3 miles north of Kemptville and then follows the watercourse into Ottawa via the Experimental Farm and scenic Driveway to the war memorial. Highway 31, the shortest route to the Seaway, begins at Morrisburg (48.4 miles southeast) and enters Ottawa via Bronson Avenue or Bank Street, both of which lead into the centre of the city. Quebec provincial highways are accessible by a choice of three toll-free bridges which cross the river at Ottawa.

An up-to-date road map of Ottawa and district is essential for efficient guidance. Construction of the Queensway, a limited access expressway which crosses the city, is in progress at this writing, and some sections are already carrying traffic. Completion and full use of the Queensway, expected by 1965, will radically alter by stages most of the highway approaches to Ottawa.

The local natural history club is the Ottawa Field-Naturalists' Club. Although the club includes all of Canada in its field of activity and research, a local Excursions and Lectures Committee is active in arranging meetings from October to April, usually held in the National Museum, and a series of field excursions each spring and autumn. Visitors may obtain information about club officers and current activities by phoning or visiting the National Museum located at the south end of Metcalfe Street, at McLeod Street.

Information pertinent to the elaboration of this general guide is available at: Canadian Wildlife Service, Norlite Building, Wellington Street; National Capital Commission, Information Division, Daly Building, Rideau Street; City Tourist and Convention Bureau, 70 Nicholas Street.

THE DRIVEWAY. The Driveway system is clearly indicated on recent maps and when entered by car is easily followed to any of its expanded park areas (some of which are discussed below). Ottawa has 45 miles of Driveway which connect about 4,000 acres of parkland. It is not permissible to stop cars or park on the Driveway but parking areas are provided.

There are many footpaths in the system and walking on the
sward is permitted. There is an entrance to the Rideau Canal
section of the Driveway in front of the war memorial. This
leads through the oldest and most mature stretch of Driveway tree planting, notable in which are the large willows and
hybrid poplars.

CENTRAL OTTAWA. Within walking distance of the war memorial
is the Ottawa River bank behind the Parliament Buildings. It
has retained much of its natural plant cover, thus affording
shelter, food, and nesting sites for bird species. There are
occasional rustic footpaths up, down, and along this rather
precipitous slope.

Major's Hill Park and Nepean Point, directly behind the
Chateau Laurier, provide delightful walks. For the naturalist
with only an hour to spare in Ottawa this is the area to see.
The panorama is magnificent and an aid to orientation. The
history of the pre-Bytown period, as indicated by the Champlain Monument on Nepean Point, is worthy of note.

ROCKCLIFFE PARK AND EASTERN SECTION OF THE CITY. Mackenzie
Avenue, which starts at the east side of the Chateau Laurier,
leads by scenic Lady Grey Drive to Government House gate
and thence into Rockcliffe Park. This is a large parkland
which has excellent facilities for picnics but not for camping.
Wooded ravines, high bluffs and promontories, interesting
communities of White Pine, White Spruce, White Cedar,
Hemlock, and a variety of broad-leaved trees provide habitat
for birds, small mammals, and an interesting herbaceous plant
cover. The park has several commanding "lookouts" and there
are walking trails in the wooded sections.

SOUTH AND WEST IN THE CITY. Follow the Driveway in front of the
war memorial and go along the west bank of the canal for 3
miles to an artificial expansion of the canal called Dow's Lake.
Here the lawns are extensive and have a rising background of
huge flower beds which form a spectacular display of annual
plants throughout summer and early autumn. This show of
summer bloom is preceded each spring, usually during the
second and third week in May, by the Annual Tulip Festival
when several millions of tulips and narcissi, planted in beds
and borders along the entire Driveway system, burst into
bloom. The greatest concentration of mass plantings of tulips

is at Dow's Lake and tens of thousands of visitors to the city pause here to admire and take snapshots.

Although given over to intense aquatic activities by man in summer, Dow's Lake continues to attract large numbers of migrating ducks, gulls, and occasional waders during spring and fall. Wintering birds are often attracted in considerable numbers to the fruit of mountain-ash trees which are planted along Dow's Lake shore and the Driveway.

CENTRAL EXPERIMENTAL FARM. This is located adjacent to, and southwest of Dow's Lake. The Driveway and Highway 16 coincide up a straight incline to a traffic circle in the Experimental Farm. Here, the main Driveway turns westward (leaving Highway 16) into the region where the horticultural gardens, greenhouses, orchards, administration buildings, stock barns, dairy and poultry plants, as well as various experimental plots are located. Turning eastward (towards canal) at the traffic circle, one finds the Arboretum and Botanic Garden where ample parking areas are provided for visitors. The Arboretum has a large collection of native and introduced trees, shrubs, and herbaceous plants. Many of the tree specimens were planted prior to 1900. The Arboretum is one of the best areas within city limits for the observation of birds. Here for many years the Ottawa Field-Naturalists' Club has conducted a series of early morning bird walks during the spring migration season.

CARLETON UNIVERSITY CAMPUS, AND HOG'S BACK PARK AND PICNIC AREA. These are located across the Rideau Canal directly east of the Experimental Farm. They are reached by crossing the canal at Bronson Avenue or on Highway 16 at the Hog's Back Bridge. The Rideau River, which separates the university grounds from the park and picnic area, has mature mixed woods over its high banks while at the shoreline are stretches of marsh land interspersed with rocky beaches. This is excellent territory for observing bird life. There are good walking trails. Geologists are especially interested in the Hog's Back formation where spectacular faults in the sedimentary rock permit comprehensive inspection.

CHAMPLAIN BRIDGES. These are probably the most scenic of Ottawa's bridge crossings to the Quebec shore. The Driveway, on leaving the west boundary of the Experimental Farm,

turns northward to follow a 2-mile section known as Island
Park Drive onto the Champlain Bridges which connect a
series of three islands to cross the Remic Rapids of the Ottawa
River 2 miles above the Chaudière Falls. The largest island
(Bate) has parking areas overlooking expansive water surfaces as well as long shorelines both up and down the river.
This is one of the few easily accessible areas in the district
which attract waterfowl and sometime shorebirds. A varying
population, principally of diving ducks, feed in the open
waters of the rapids throughout the winter months.

GREENBELT. Briefly, the Greenbelt is a semicircular belt of land
averaging more than 2¼ miles in width, extending around the
entire land boundary of the city of Ottawa. It starts on the
west shore of Lac des Chenes (expansion of Ottawa River),
includes Uplands Airport on the extreme south and, continues
east and north to join the Ottawa River again in the vicinity
of Green's Creek. The area consists of 32,000 acres, most of
which has already been purchased or optioned by the federal
government. It has several undeveloped areas which may be
of great interest to naturalists. The most important is the Mer
Bleue (east side of Ottawa), a Black Spruce–Sphagnum bog
which covers several thousand acres. Some of the rare plants
and birds of this district were recorded from the Mer Bleue
prior to 1939. During the World War II this bog was used as
a practice bombing range and very little investigation has
been conducted in the bog since. The perimeter of the bog is
easily accessible by going to Blackburn Station, via Cyrville,
and continuing south across the western tips of three finger-
like areas of the receding bog. Other accesses to the bog can
be gained at Carlsbad Springs and Navan at its extreme eastern limits. It is not possible at this stage of its development
to direct naturalists into other areas of the Greenbelt.

GATINEAU PARK. This is a federal (not national) park, wholly in
Quebec. It stretches for 35 miles within the Laurentian
Shield. Paved driveways climb to 1,100 feet to allow magnificent views of the Ottawa Valley. Flora and fauna are suggestive of the Canadian Life Zone (Coniferous Forest Region). Walking trails are well marked and some remote areas
can be reached by these trails. There are picnic areas, and

some camping and fishing privileges are available. The National Capital Commission offices gladly supply full details.

AREA OUTLYING THE GREENBELT. Ottawa district is not considered to be on a recognized migration flyway and large concentrations of bird species are not regularly observed. However, many species do go through this area and quite large numbers of certain species remain as summer residents. Characteristic of the district is the close proximity of surprisingly diverse types of habitat, so that the keen observer can easily identify, from dawn to dusk on a May or June day, at least 100 species of birds.

The most rewarding areas for the observer are, in general, in the vicinity of the larger watercourses of the district. On the north side of Highway 17 (west of Ottawa particularly) there are frequent sideroads that lead to the deeply wooded shores of the Ottawa River. A particularly choice area is that of an ancient Ottawa River course, a wide wooded valley now occupied by a small stream known as Constance Creek (20 miles west of Ottawa—leave Highway 17 at first turn after passing South March) which joins a shallow lake (Constance Lake) by a meandering course of about 6 miles through marshy margins to the Ottawa River at Constance Bay. There are sandhills at Constance Bay which support a relic flora of particular interest to botanists. Amongst the birds of the region, such species as Field Sparrow and Rufous-sided Towhee, not commonly found in the Ottawa district, are likely to be observed.

SOUTH OF OTTAWA. The Rideau River system and adjacent territory provide habitat for a wide variety of bird and mammal species. Each side of the river has excellent secondary connecting roads. It is easy to cross and recross from one side to the other by means of bridges at Hog's Back, Manotick, Kars, and Kemptville. Exceptionally attractive to the naturalist are the areas around the massive masonry dams which are accompanied by canal locks. There are several of these sites along the river within the Ottawa district, and they have the added advantage of being public domain. There are also several level ancient lake-bottom areas of varying extent. One of these plains, suggestive of Manitoba prairie, is crossed near Richmond about 15 miles southwest of Ottawa. Another similar area is to the southeast where the flood plain of the South Nation River watershed intrudes into the Ottawa district near Winchester. These areas attract birds of the wet grass-lands such as Horned Lark, Lapland Longspur, Water Pipit, Short-billed Marsh Wren, Marsh Hawk, Killdeer, and Common Snipe. Gray Partridge seem to meet their northern boundary on these plains.

REFERENCES

In addition to the *Canadian Field-Naturalist* and its precursors, and the publications of the Ottawa Field-Naturalists' Club from 1879 to date, see the following for information concerning the natural history of the Ottawa district.

CODY, W. J., Ferns of the Ottawa District (Canada, Dept. of Agriculture, 1956), 94 pp., 42 figs., 1 map, $1.00.
DORE, WILLIAM G., Grasses of the Ottawa District (Canada, Dept. of Agriculture, 1959), 73 pp., 123 figs., $1.00.
GILLET, JOHN M., comp., Checklist of Plants of the Ottawa District (Canada, Dept. of Agriculture, 1958), 89 pp., 1 map.
LEGGET, ROBERT F., Rideau Waterway (University of Toronto Press, 1955), 230 pp.
LLOYD, HOYES, The Birds of Ottawa, Canadian Field-Naturalist, LVIII, 5 (1944), pp. 143–75.
MACDONALD, MALCOLM, The Birds of Brewery Creek (Oxford University Press, 1955).
RAND, A. L., Mammals of the Ottawa District, Canadian Field-Naturalist, LIX, 4 (1945), pp. 111–32.
WILSON, ALICE E., A Guide to the Geology of the Ottawa District, monograph issue of Canadian Field-Naturalist, LXX, 1 (1956), 68 pp., 5 maps, $1.00.

*Ottawa Field-Naturalists' Club*

✿ OWEN SOUND

THE NORTHERN PARTS of Grey and Bruce counties are bounded by Nottawasaga Bay on the east and Lake Huron on the west, extending northward into the Bruce Peninsula. The city of Owen

Sound lies in the geographic centre of the area, and can be approached by Highway 26 from Collingwood on the east, by Highway 10 from Orangeville and Highway 6 from Guelph on the south. From Detroit and Windsor, access to the Bruce Peninsula can be made by the Blue Water Highway 21 along Lake Huron.

The Grey-Bruce Nature Club meets on the second Thursday of every month at the Y.M.C.A. in Owen Sound at 8.00 P.M., January to April, October and November. The Y.M.C.A. is at the corner of Tenth Street and Third Avenue East. Visitors may get in touch with club officials by phoning FR 6-3076, 6-0962, 6-7753, or 6-4675. Field trips are held during summer months.

The Great Lakes shoreline and the Niagara Escarpment form the arch motifs of the region. Their combined influences have created an area of outstanding beauty and a naturalist's paradise. The escarpment extends west from the Blue Mountains, curving northward to form the backbone of the Bruce Peninsula. This spectacular limestone wall is cut by the re-entrant valleys of several river systems, the Beaver, the Bighead, and the Sydenham, and by Colpoys Bay in the Bruce Peninsula.

In this rugged terrain the hand of agricultural man has been partly frustrated. The farmlands are interspersed by a network of cliffs, wooded slopes, and swamps favourable to the existence of native plants and wildlife. The extensive maple woodlots, far from urban centres, still support a natural garden of spring flowers, and most of the rarer rock ferns can be found on the limestone cliffs. On the wet sands of the Lake Huron shore many rarer orchids and other plants flourish, although they are fast disappearing under the summer-resort bulldozer. The cliffs, the abandoned fields, and the swamps encourage a good population of hawks, wading birds, and wildfowl, and the Lake Huron coast is a busy migration route for shorebirds, geese, and swans. The many underground sources of water, characteristic of limestone country, have maintained clear cool streams despite the changes brought about by agriculture.

In the Grey-Bruce region the distribution of features that interest a naturalist are more diffuse than in more thickly settled areas to the south. Hence the points of interest noted below are merely highlights. Many excellent localities for studying birds, rocks,

SHOWY ORCHIS

and plants are not mentioned by reason of their abundance. The following account proceeds from east to west as nearly as possible.

REDWING CAVES. Proceed 8 miles south from Thornbury on the county road to the village of Redwing. On the southeast side of the village there are cracks on the limestone bluffs where elk antlers and bones have been found. The owner does not object to entry. Another interesting crevasse is on the farm of Ray Mitchell nearby. This area merits exploration.

KOLAPORE CREEK AREA. Go south from Redwing to the first section road, and thence east 2 miles to the next corner. Go south 2 miles to the hamlet of Kolapore which is in the centre of a 15,000-acre area of near-wilderness, containing extensive hard-wood bush, a very large bog (to the east of Kolapore), and a few old pasture farms. The wealth of bird and plant life is enhanced by the fact that there is nobody around to throw you out.

BEAVER VALLEY. This is one of the scenic features of southern Ontario. Proceed on Highway 10 to Flesherton, thence east on the county road a distance of one mile to the gravel road leading north through the valley to Thornbury. The well-defined fan-shaped valley, lined by dolomite cliffs, can be seen extending north to the blue waters of Georgian Bay. The view from the edge embraces a 70-square-mile patchwork of farm, forest, and stream. The valley road follows the stream, but a panoramic view is best obtained by going west up the gravel road about one mile north of the Eugenia power station. Look for hawks and vultures and many species of rock ferns and carry a copy of Chapman and Putnam's *Physiography of Southern Ontario* with you for a fascinating explanation of the valley's origins.

BIGHEAD VALLEY. According to one geography text, Bighead Valley contains the finest show of drumlins in North America. A panoramic view of the valley and these drumlins "like a flock of sheep" can be best seen by going south 6 miles on the county road from Meaford, and proceeding west on the township road just north of Griersville. From the top of the hill beside the road there is a good view of this lovely valley.

Another excellent view can be seen by continuing to the next corner and driving south 2 miles.

MEAFORD TANK RANGE. Proceed 4 miles west from Meaford on Highway 26 to the road (indicated by National Defence sign) north to the Tank Range. This extensive promontory of land bordering Georgian Bay was taken over by the Army in 1942. The abandoned farms and orchards are rich in wildlife, particularly hawks which favour the mouse-ridden fields of long grass. A study of plant and animal succession after 20 years of abandonment can be made here. Bald Eagles nest at the west end of Mountain Lake and are considered the mascots of the range. A bog at the west end of the lake once supported Calypso, but this has been flooded out by Beaver dams. Permission to enter the range depends on whether it is being used for firing at the time. Applicants must be escorted by Bill Linn, R. R. 3, Woodford (Franklin 6-2159) who is the range game warden and naturalist. The next road leading north, to the west of the main road to the range, leads past a high escarpment 3 miles north of Highway 26. Here Turkey Vultures have been nesting in past years. This is outside the range boundaries.

BOGNOR WILDFOWL SANCTUARY. Proceed south on Highway 10 from Owen Sound 2 miles to Rockford, and thence east 7 miles to the road leading north to the sanctuary, marked by the Conservation Authority sign. This 100-acre marsh is a year-round sanctuary run by the North Grey Region Conservation Authority. No boats are allowed without the Conservation Authority's permission (office in Owen Sound County Building), but a good population of nesting ducks, grebes, herons, and bitterns can be observed. Wood Duck and Eastern Bluebird houses have been set out recently. Migrant Blue and Canada Geese now use this marsh in the autumn. The adjacent lands, part of the Conservation Authority Forest, can be entered. These are rich in perching birds and hawks, particularly along the escarpment to the north.

BOGNOR–WALTERS FALLS. Continue from Bognor Sanctuary east and south through Bognor to Walters Falls, a distance of 6 miles. A spendid mill and waterfall are located there. Just east of the village one can get a superb view of the Bighead Valley which is south of the upstream mill pond just to the west of the village. Continue south to the second road running west and proceed west on the township road 11 miles to Highway 10, passing through Massie. This road is a remaining bit of unspoiled Ontario—before the days when hydro, telephone, weed killers, and bulldozed improvements laid waste the natural beauty. In May the spring flowers and migrant birds will be at your car window. Some fine unspoiled woodlots are worth exploration. Another unspoiled area is east of Walters Falls. Here, a 20-acre virgin forest borders the Bruce Trail between Blantyre and Walters Falls below the rock ledge. It is a fine study area for primeval maple, Beech, elm, and Hemlock, and on the north-facing talus slope are possibly the oldest living things in Ontario, cedars up to 40 inches in diameter.

HARRISON PARK–INGLIS FALLS CONSERVATION AREA. Proceed south from the Owen Sound City Hall on Second Avenue east for one mile to Harrison Park. The forested ravine slopes and conifer plantings bordering the Sydenham River, the absence of wind, and a well-stocked bird feeder have created a good habitat for perching birds, particularly in winter. A rough trail from the park through the forested gorge of the Sydenham River to Inglis Falls will take the courageous through a primitive wilderness of escarpment, rock "chimneys," and cascades, an area preserved by its very inaccessibility. The botanist will find an abundance of rock ferns, but we urge that they be left growing. This land and the falls is a conservation area open to the public. Inglis Falls can also be approached from above via the county road extending 2 miles south from the entrance to Harrison Park. The falls tumble 100 feet into the wooded gorge, and during spring and early summer the volume of water makes this cataract one of the finest views in Ontario.

LONG SWAMP HERONRY. This lies 3 miles west of Owen Sound on the Southampton Road, Highway 21. Proceed to the farm of Carman Sword on the south side and ask permission to visit the heronry, about ¼ mile south of the buildings beside the Pottawatami River. This fine forty-nest colony is situated in the tops of several enormous elm trees and is guarded by Mr. Sword's son. Extensive stands of Ostrich-Fern beneath the large open-grown elms create a tropical impression during summer. Look for the Nodding Trillium in spring.

MCNAB LAKE. Proceed 7 miles along the Owen Sound–Wiarton road to Shallow Lake village. Drive north from the village one mile to the first sideroad bearing west and later the road to McNab Lake as directed by a sign. This lake, recently restored by the Sauble Valley Conservation Authority, now supports a large population of resident and migrant wildfowl, clearly visible from the hill beside the lake. The west shore beside the hill often is visited by shorebirds and waders. The adjacent land is Conservation Authority Forest, managed by the Department of Lands and Forests. Some dozen species of ferns can be observed in the 50-yard stretch where the road runs through the woods.

SAUBLE BEACH. Proceed west from Owen Sound through Hepworth to Sauble Beach, a distance of 17 miles. On the sand dunes and in the bogs behind the dunes there was once the finest natural garden of rarer orchids and other wildflowers in Ontario. Summer cottage development and flower pickers have destroyed much of this garden but many interesting littoral and bog plants still remain. During August several species of migrant shorebirds feed on the sands. At the north end of the beach where the Sauble River enters Lake Huron a clear view can be had of many water birds, such as Whistling Swans, geese, ducks, and the Caspian Tern which is resident on offshore islands to the north.

OLIPHANT–RED BAY SHORELINE. This section of the Lake Huron shore can be approached by driving north from Sauble Beach, or directly west from the town of Wiarton, a distance of 7 miles. The flora is similar to that of Sauble Beach, but, though fast disappearing, has been less destroyed by summer resorts. From May until October the wet sands beside the lake show a continual colourful display, starting with Primula, Dwarf Iris, and Yellow Lady's-slipper in spring, changing to Pitcher-plant, Pogonia, Grass-pink, and Bladderwort in summer, with a finale of Fringed Gentian, Grass-of-Parnassus, and Swamp Aster (*Aster puniceus*) in autumn. The offshore islands are good for seeing aquatic birds during the spring and fall.

THE SAUBLE ELM. Proceed west from Hepworth on the Sauble
Beach road across the Sauble River bridge to Zion Church on
the northeast corner of the second road past the bridge. Go
north to the Sauble River and walk up the north bank a distance of ½ mile to what is believed to be the largest White
Elm in Ontario. Three feet from the ground, this stout specimen measures 24 feet, 9 inches in circumference, and is estimated to be 260 years old. All landowners concerned permit
the public to visit the elm.

*Grey-Bruce Nature Club*

❀  PERTH

THE TOWN OF Perth is situated in Lanark County about 60 miles
south of Ottawa and about the same distance north of Kingston.
The town is on the Tay River which rises in Bobs Lake, flows
through Christie Lake, and empties into Rideau Lake. It is a
district of good farms, many lovely lakes, happy rivers, and fine
deep swamps. Thus, the birds and flowers are varied and abundant. Perth was founded in 1816, and many descendants of the
original settlers still live in Perth and on the farms surrounding
the town. There is an active historical society named the Alexander Morris Society.

STEWART PARK. In the centre of Perth is this lovely park through
which a branch of the Tay flows. The centre of the town is an
island.

SILVER LAKE PROVINCIAL PARK. West on Highway 7 about 20 miles,
this park has camping facilities.

TAY RIVER. This river flows from Perth towards the Rideau and
has been converted into a canal as a part of the Rideau Waterway. On its stretches are areas of slow water, marsh, and cat-
tails. There is an abundance of waterfowl. It can be approached by water from Perth, or one can walk for quite a
distance along the canal bank.

LONG SWAMP. Extending along the second line of Drummond Township on the south side of Highway 7, this swamp contains Pitcher-plant, Skunk-cabbage, and wild orchids. In winter, there are Bohemian and Cedar Waxwings together with many other winter birds, and in summer a host of warblers and finches.

CRANBERRY MARSH. Go about 3 miles west along the Scotch Line and then walk about a mile through the fields. Here is found the Ground Cranberry.

BLUEBERRY MARSH. This marsh extends from Perth to Drummond Centre, along Highway 7 north of the road. In this area is found the Ground Cranberry and the Pitcher-plant.

OTTY LAKE. Part of the Rideau system, this lake is 4 miles south of Perth. There are Beaver here and an excellent Osprey nest. Cedar swamp areas around this lake are inhabited by warblers and Veeries, swallows, and woodpeckers. There is also an Osprey nest at Mud Lake, near Otty. North of Otty Lake, east of the town line of Elmsley and Burgess, there is an interesting hardwood bush on Ray Poole's farm.

GRANT'S CREEK. This creek, which flows out of Pike Lake 10 miles southwest of Perth, has a Beaver dam.

CHRISTIE LAKE. Twelve miles west of Perth is Christie Lake. Bald Eagles nest here, and there are good cedar swamps for warblers.

MISSISSIPPI RIVER. This river is about 25 miles north of Perth. There are Beaver here, also a Great Blue heronry.

LETT'S GROVE. Here, 14 miles northeast of Lanark Village, there are a few large White Pine left.

*Tay Naturalists' Club*

 **PETERBOROUGH**

PETERBOROUGH, the "Gateway to the Kawartha Lakes," is situated approximately 80 miles east of Toronto and 30 miles north of Lake Ontario in the south-central region of Ontario. The city is approached from the north and south by Highway 28, from the east and northwest by Highway 7, and from the west by Highways 401, 115, and 28.

The local natural history club, the Peterborough Nature Club, holds regular monthly indoor meetings from October through April and outdoor field trips during the remaining months of the year. Programme schedules, giving full information on the date, time, and place of meetings and a list of club officers, are available from the Public Library situated next door to the City Hall (see next paragraph).

Routes to points of natural history interest commence at the City Hall, located at the corner of George and Murray streets, and all directions and estimated distances are calculated from this starting point.

The entire county of Peterborough, stretching from Rice Lake (15 miles south of the city) to north of Apsley (40 miles north of the city), shows evidence of the Wisconsin Glaciation which left a mantle of till over the southern part of the county and formed large eskers (one of which may be seen along the north side of Highway 7 at the eastern outskirts of the village of Norwood 18 miles east of Peterborough), extensive drumlin fields, and moraines (visible also along Highway 7 east of the city). The igneous and metamorphic rocks (Grenville series) of the Precambrian Shield underlie the whole area and outcrop north of a line which passes approximately through Buckhorn and Burleigh Falls (20 miles north of the city). South of this line sandstones and limestones of the Black River and Trenton Age (Middle Ordovician period) rest unconformably on the Precambrian rocks.

SHORT TRIPS

LITTLE LAKE CEMETERY (about 5 minutes drive from the City Hall). Go south on George Street through the main business section until opposite the Market Plaza (you will see Little Lake on your left here). Proceed to the first cross street, turn left one block, then right and follow Crescent Street around the southern edge of the lake to the cemetery gate. This cemetery is a park-like, landscaped, and treed point of land which juts out into the lake and along the edge of the Otonabee River. It is an ideal place for observing both land and water birds, especially during the migration period.

RIVER ROAD DRIVE (with a side-trip to an old quarry—about one hour round trip). Go east on Murray Street one block, turn north (left) on Water Street (one-way street), and go 6 blocks to Parkhill Road (stop light). Turn right and drive east across a cement bridge over the Otonabee River to the top of a hill (Nichols Oval Park on right). Turn left (north) at first intersection (Armour Road) and proceed north out of the city, passing the Peterborough Golf and Country Club course (on your right at the city limits). Follow the paved road north and slightly east (across a bridge over the Trent Canal) to Nassau 4 miles from the city. Continue north following the edge of the river to the village of Lakefield (about 9 miles).

As you enter the village of Lakefield you will see a large cement building on the right side of the road. Immediately south of this building a narrow gravel road leads off to the right (east). If you follow this road to the end (just over the slope) you will come to an abandoned quarry with interesting fossil specimens.

Returning to the paved River Road proceed north into Lakefield, past the large cement building, and you will come to the junction with Highway 28 at the cement bridge (on your left) crossing the Otonabee River and the Trent Canal. Turn left and follow Highway 28 back to Peterborough and the City Hall via Water and George streets.

Besides being a beautiful drive this route has many excellent birding places and interesting plant habitats to explore along the roadsides.

JACKSON PARK AND LILY LAKE AREA (about 2 hours round trip). Go east on Murray Street one block, then north on Water Street 6 blocks (stop light), turn left (west) and drive west on Parkhill Road over a steep hill, pass one stop light, and continue west several blocks to gate of Jackson's Park. Drive into the park and follow the winding road to the right, down a slope across a small cement bridge, and park just to the left (near the C.N.R. railway tracks). You may either wander in a westerly direction along the edge of the creek or follow the railway tracks in the same direction and find quite good birding any time of the year. About 2 miles west (on the north side) you will come to Lily Lake (a marl pit really) which is also an excellent birding area. Return east on Parkhill Road and south on George Street to City Hall.

LONGER TRIPS

BURLEIGH FALLS AND WARSAW CAVE AREAS (at least a half-day jaunt, 3 or 4 hours). From City Hall go east (left) one block, then north (left) on Water Street past the stop light at Parkhill Road, and continue north on Highway 28 past the filtration plant to the village of Lakefield (about 9 miles). Go through the village and continue north, staying on Highway 28, through Young's Point to Burleigh Falls (20 miles). Cross bridge and park car beside the Park Hotel. A few yards to the southeast of the hotel you will see a good outcropping of gneiss rocks. There are good birding areas on both sides of the bridge here and lovely picnic sites as well. For interesting points north of Burleigh Falls, see guide for Bancroft area.

On leaving Burleigh Falls drive 9 miles south back along Highway 28 to the Nephton Road corner (Melody Inn Motel), turn left (east), and drive 2.8 miles to where a side-road enters (on the right) at the top of a long hill. Here look for an excellent example of unconformity between Palaeozoic and Precambrian in the mounds beside the road.

Proceed east on Nephton Road another 2.7 miles to junction of Warsaw Road (red brick church on left side at corner), turn right (south) and drive 1.3 miles to Warminster Road (this is 1.5 miles north of village of Warsaw); turn left (east) and drive one mile on dirt road to a bridge across the Indian River. Park here, and unless you have a guide you should ask for direction of the path leading to the mouth of the Warsaw caves from the persons living in one of the houses here. You are strongly advised to watch for Poison Ivy along the path and also not to enter the caves further than the entrance unless properly dressed and equipped with ropes and flashlight as the rocks are very slippery and steep in places. Return to your car and cross over the bridge, turn right (south), and drive about 0.3 miles to the end of a long left curve in the road. There is a break in the trees and a path across a grassy field on the right side of the road here. Follow this path a short way through the woods and observe the pot-holes (on your right). On the rocky ridges near the pot-holes grows the Walking Fern (a rare species here). Returning to your car, you may continue to drive southeast on this road to the first intersection, turn sharp right, and follow this road into the village of Warsaw, returning to Peterborough via the Warsaw Road, Parkhill Road, and George Street to City Hall.

CAVAN SWAMP AREA (about 2–3 hours). This is an interesting area, especially for botanists. From the City Hall proceed south 5 blocks on George Street to main intersection (Charlotte Street), turn right (west) and follow Charlotte Street west to Clonsilla Avenue (flashing light and Medical Centre building at corner), then south on Clonsilla and Highway 28 and west out of the city to the junction of Highway 133 (about 5 miles). *Cross over* Highway 133 and follow the dirt road leading west for 0.3 miles to the *old highway*. If you follow the old highway north (right) from this intersection, several trails lead west into the Cavan Swamp, any one of which will prove interesting to explore. A diligent search by an experienced botanist will turn up a varied list of flora including sundew, Pitcher-plant, and other bog-living species. Birds seen in this area include Golden-winged Warbler, Traill's Flycatcher, and many other species, especially during the migration periods. All visitors are urged to leave plants and shrubs unmolested for others to enjoy and to take care not to disturb nesting birds or other wildlife found here.

OTHER TRIPS

Contact Nature Club officers for detailed instructions:

EEL'S CREEK PARK. This small roadside park is located about 25 miles north of the city in a Crown game preserve. Watch for the sign on Highway 28 north of Burleigh Falls.

SCOTT'S MILLS. This rocky, wooded terrain with a small river flowing through it is about 2 miles north of Buckhorn in the Bald Lake area. Cardinal-flower grows here.

CROWE LAKE. This lake is off Highway 7, about 35 miles east of Peterborough (one mile *west* of Marmora). The Dominion Entomological Laboratory is located here, and Dr. Hammond, a keen naturalist, knows ferns, fossils, birds, and insects. It is a good region for the all-round naturalist to explore.

MT. NEBO. This abandoned railway right-of-way runs south of Highway 7 at west end of the village of Omemee (16 miles northwest of Peterborough). It is an interesting trip at any time of year.

OTONABEE RIVER. A 15-mile boat trip to Rice Lake skirts swamps and marshes, wildlife habitats.

BURNHAM PARK. This 100-acre woodlot is 2 miles east on Highway 7 at eastern outskirts of city. There are wildflowers, nature trail, birds and mammals, and picnic facilities.

SERPENT MOUNDS PARK. South off Highway 7, this park is 6 miles east of city on north shore of Rice Lake.

FRANK PAMMETT *et al.*
*Peterborough Nature Club*

## ❀ POINT PELEE NATIONAL PARK

POINT PELEE NATIONAL PARK is one of the best places in Canada for the study and observation of birds. It is equally good for the pursuit of other branches of natural history. There are plants and animals here not found elsewhere in Canada, and a few of them are restricted to the park and a small sandy soil area surrounding it.

The park is a narrow, V-shaped peninsula of Eastport sand, jutting into Lake Erie near the western end of the lake about 6 miles south of Leamington. Located in Mersea Township, Essex

County, it is the most southerly mainland in Canada. It is accessible by road from Leamington on Highway 3 or Highway 18. Leamington may be reached by bus either from the east or west or from Windsor, and air or train service is available to Windsor.

The park has all the usual facilities for receiving visitors, including excellent camping areas. Hotel and motel accommodation, however, must be sought outside the park, usually in the vicinity of Leamington.

A park naturalist is present during the summer months to answer questions and to provide organized illustrated talks, field trips, and other interpretive activities. The Woodland Nature Trail is of the self-guiding type. Some of the plants on the trail are labelled, and a self-guiding trail pamphlet is available. There is a nature reserve which is not open to the public but part of it is available for study from the Woodland Nature Trail.

Natural history publications of interest to the park visitor are readily available from the park office. Among these are: *Spring Birds of Point Pelee National Park, Plants of the Woodland Nature Trail,* and *Provisional Check-List of Birds.*

Point Pelee is in the true Deciduous Forest Region of North America, or Carolinian Biotic Province as it has also been called, and therefore has plants and animals which have their centre of distribution south of the Canadian border, and which are at or near their northern limit at Pelee. It also has plants and animals that are more characteristic of a western or southwestern life zone. The evergreen or coniferous forest trees of the north and their associated plants and animals, more familiar to most Canadians, are absent or represented by a few relics.

There is a surprisingly large number of habitats within the small space of the 3,500 acres comprising the park, for example, sand beaches, open lake, and several forest associations such as Elm–Black Ash–Red Maple swamp forest, Oak–Hickory forest, Hackberry-Blue Ash forest (this latter tree is now very scarce), and Red Cedar parkland. One of the most attractive areas of the park for natural history pursuits is the 2,000-acre, deep freshwater marsh. This particular type of marsh makes up only about 3 per cent of the marshes left in the United States, and in Canada they are much scarcer.

PRICKLY PEAR

There are about 600 species of plants reported from Point Pelee. Many of them are of special interest because they are rare in Canada or grow more profusely here than elsewhere in Canada. Black Walnut, Hackberry, Red Mulberry, Cottonwood, Sycamore, Red Cedar, Sassafras, Blue Ash, and Chestnut-Oak grow well. Other plants of note to be seen are Spicebush, Hop-tree, Drummond's Dogwood, Prickly Pear, Flowering Spurge, Wild Potato-vine, Swamp-Mallow, Appendaged Waterleaf, Sweet Cicely, Tall Bellflower, and Many-mouthed Earth Star.

The fauna of the area likewise include several special attractions: Seaside Grasshopper, Northern Katydid, Giant Swallow-tailed Butterfly, Blue-tailed Skink, Fox Snake, Blanding's Turtle, Map Turtle, Spiny Soft-shelled Turtle, Fowler's Toad, Cricket Frog, Eastern Mole, and Raccoon.

Point Pelee National Park probably attracts more birdwatchers and ornithologists than any other small area in Canada. About 280 species of birds have been noted here since recording began in 1879. The park is on the spring and autumn migration route of many birds, some of which are rarely seen in other parts of Canada. Some of the less common birds Prothonotary Warbler, Carolina Wren, Bewick's Wren, Blue-gray Gnatcatcher, Orchard Oriole, Cardinal, and Yellow-breasted Chat, even remain to nest in the park.

The spring migration between March 15 and June 1 is a spectacular event. At the height of the season in May well over 100 kinds may be tallied in one day by one observer. Reverse migration may also be seen in the spring. In this case birds that are migrating northward, having arrived at the park, rest, reverse their direction, and fly southward again. The autumn migration southward is also an extremely interesting event at the park, beginning in August but reaching its height during September and October. The hawk migration during the latter part of September affords the spectacular sight of many hawks of several kinds all in the air at one time. Many migrating birds, such as the various swallows, Redwinged Blackbirds, and Blue Jays, form large aggregations of flocks and these are worth seeing at Pelee.

GEORGE M. STIRRETT

## ❀ PORT HOPE AND COBOURG

THIS AREA includes the southern part of Durham and Northumberland counties, bounded on the south by Lake Ontario and extending inland about 10 miles. The southern part is good farming land and the northern part is the Oak Ridge Moraine. Highways 2 and 401 pass west to east through this area. Highway 28 runs north from Port Hope, past the western end of Rice Lake to Peterborough, and Highway 45 goes northeast from Cobourg.

Regular meetings of the Willow Beach Field Naturalists are held on the last Saturday evening of each month, except during the summer months, when outdoor activities are usually planned. For information phone Mr. and Mrs. H. Reeve, R. R. 3, Port Hope (Phone Clarke 17-14), or Mr. and Mrs. J. A. B. Wilson, R. R. 5, Cobourg (Phone Cobourg FR2-3971).

PORT HOPE HARBOUR. Turn south at John Street to the public beach and picnic grounds. The harbour may be explored from both the north and south sides. Water birds and shorebirds can be seen in migration.

WILLOW BEACH. Four miles west of Port Hope, by Highway 2, on the lakeshore, there are marshes, woods, sand beaches, and open fields. This is a good area for botanizing and for watching birds migrating. Of special interest are the Whimbrels during the week of May 24 and Red-necked Grebes from September 1 to November 15.

GANARASKA CONSERVATION AREA. This area is northwest of Port Hope. Use a road map to get to Elizabethville. From there go west ½ mile to the bend in the road, then go north for several miles to Glamorgan. Go west for several miles to the forester's headquarters which is on the left side and is painted white. Inquire about the road through the forest to Kendal, then go south to Newtonville and Highway 2. If there is no information at the forester's, proceed west to McCrae's church and turn south to Highway 2. This is the moraine area and has tobacco farms, Christmas tree farms, and reforestation in various stages. The area is dry and sandy and the plants are of interest to botanists. This is a good nesting district for birds. For several years past there have been spots in this area of an acre or more infested by stick insects.

COBOURG HARBOUR. Go south on Highway 45 along Division Street, Cobourg, to east dock of Cobourg harbour. Migrating shorebirds are most likely to be seen at the west end of the harbour, also west of this and at the foot of D'Arcy Street in the east end of Cobourg. Flat rocks along the shore of Lake Ontario, particularly accessible at the foot of D'Arcy Street, contain fossils of the Ordovician period.

LAKESHORE EAST FROM WICKLOW. From Cobourg go east 8 miles on Highway 2 to Grafton, then 2 miles further to Wicklow, and turn south. This will bring you to the lake where the road turns east close to the water, then north back to Highway 2. This road passes some small ponds.

NORTHUMBERLAND FOREST. This is a reforested area belonging to Northumberland County and extends along Highway 45 from 9 to 12 miles northeast from Cobourg. An occasional Brush Wolf is seen, also some White-tailed Deer, and in the creeks Beavers have built dams.

HAROLD REEVE
*Willow Beach Field Naturalists*

&#x273f;  **PORCUPINE DISTRICT**

THE PORCUPINE DISTRICT, in the heart of northern Ontario, is 435 miles north of Toronto on excellent paved highways. The area is easily accessible by Ontario Northland Railway and scheduled Trans-Canada Viscount service from Toronto. Five modern communities are situated in the Porcupine—Timmins, Schumacher, Mountjoy, South Porcupine, and Whitney. The fabulous Porcupine district is the largest gold mining region in the Americas. Each year hundreds of persons, from near and far, are visitors at the mines and see something of the operations either on the surface or a mile underground. The forest is distinguished by extensive stands of Black Spruce which are most abundant on poorly drained and boggy flats. Bog lakes are numerous. Various mixtures of spruce, fir, aspen, poplar, and White Birch occur on better drained sites. Precambrian rock outcrops, small lakes, and rather sluggish streams further distinguish the area. Wildlife is abundant, and Moose, Black Bear, fur-bearing animals, and northern birds and wildflowers make the Porcupine particularly attractive to the naturalist.

The Porcupine Chamber of Commerce, 167 Pine Street South, Timmins, is pleased to offer visiting naturalists its services. The officers of the Ontario Department of Lands and Forests, Timmins, will furnish directions to areas of particular interest, such as the nesting sites of the Bonaparte's Gulls in the trees of the spruce bogs. Detailed maps are available from the local office of the Ontario Department of Lands and Forests.

PORCUPINE LAKE. This lake is 6 miles east of Timmins, on Highway 101. Birds here include ducks and shorebirds during spring and fall migrations, and northern-nesting warblers.

CONIAURUM LAKE. This lake is 1½ miles east of Timmins, ½ mile north of Highway 101 on Coniaurum Mine property. This is cat-tail marsh habitat with nesting ducks, grebes, rails, warblers, thrushes, kingbirds, kinglets, bitterns, Chimney Swifts, and Muskrats and Beavers.

PEARL LAKE AND MCINTYRE PARK. At Schumacher, one mile east of Timmins, go to McIntyre Porcupine Mines property. Birds include migrating and nesting ducks, migrating shorebirds and rails, grebes and bitterns. Common Terns and Bonaparte's Gulls are here during spring and fall.

MOUNTJOY TOWNSHIP. This is a farmland district adjacent to Timmins on the west. Birds include Eastern Bluebirds, Bobolinks, meadowlarks, swallows, Marsh Hawks, Hawk Owls, and Barred Owls, and in winter redpolls, Snow Buntings, Northern Shrikes, and Snowy Owls.

TIMMINS TO FOLEYET. Sixty miles of recently completed wilderness highway extending west from Timmins, traverses all the
forest types of the area. Streams, lakes, and bogs are readily
accessible.

*Sudbury Field Naturalists' Club*

❁   PRESQU'ILE PROVINCIAL PARK

PRESQU'ILE PARK is three miles south of Brighton on Highway 2,
halfway between Cobourg and Belleville. During the summer,
from May to September, Provincial Park signs on Highway 2
mark the road to the park. A permanent highway sign also indicates the way to "Presqu'ile Point." Department of Lands and
Forests staff are always available at the park office to provide
information as well as adequate directions to each point of interest. Mimeographed maps are also available here. No restrictions
are placed on travel in the park other than on the two islands.
These are set aside as "wilderness areas," and permission to enter
must be first obtained from the park superintendent or the park
naturalist.

A naturalist programme is conducted at Presqu'ile during July
and August. There are conducted hikes and campfire programmes
as well as a permanent nature museum with exhibits of park wildlife. A park naturalist is present at Presqu'ile for most of the year.
Any inquiries should be directed to the District Forester, Department of Lands and Forests, Lindsay, or the Department of Lands
and Forests, Presqu'ile Provincial Park, Brighton, Ontario.

The park is a foot-shaped peninsula extending into Lake
Ontario, almost 4 miles long and ½ mile wide. Although embracing
only 2,150 acres the park environment includes a wide variety of
habitats. The extensive marsh in Presqu'ile Bay covers 583 acres
or one-quarter of the park area, providing for an abundance of
bird and mammal life. Seven miles of shoreline provide an excellent
stop-over for shorebirds during the spring and fall migrations.
There are extensive open fields with a variety of birds and plants.

To date over 300 species of plants have been recorded in this park. The woodland is of the Beech-Maple type of the Transition Zone (Mixed Forest Region), attracting many species of nesting birds as well as migrants. Over 225 species of birds are now recorded in Presqu'ile, at least 100 of which nest in the park. The smaller of the two islands adjacent to the park is a nesting site for Ring-billed Gulls and Common Terns. At least 10,000 gulls and terns nest here in a summer season.

*Ontario Department of Lands and Forests*

## ❀ QUETICO PROVINCIAL PARK

SINCE 1909 when Quetico Provincial Park was established, it has been preserved as a wilderness area in its natural state. It has the reputation of being the finest unspoiled canoe country on the North American continent. Such groups as the Chambers of Commerce of Northwestern Ontario, the Quetico Foundation, the Ontario Department of Lands and Forests, and countless numbers of canoe-trippers and fishermen have become increasingly aware of Quetico's magnetic recreational and wilderness potential. Ranger stations and lookout towers have been erected as strategic points in the park for the safety and protection of both forests and campers. Wildlife is plentiful, fishing is excellent, and scenic beauty predominates. Quetico Provincial Park covers approximately 1,800 square miles. It is centrally located in mid-continent and within easy driving distance of about fifty million people.

There are no roads in Quetico, but in order that more Canadians can reach the area, the first of two access points has been established at Dawson Trail Campgrounds (French Lake) on the northern boundary of the park. French Lake is 100 miles from Fort William on Highways 17 and 11; Highway 11 touches the north boundary of Quetico. Many people also enter Quetico from Minnesota and the Superior National Forest. Tourist camps and canoe-trip outfitters operate at both northern and southern boundaries of Quetico, supplying visitors with a complete line of necessary camping equipment and groceries.

The Ontario Department of Lands and Forests operates a nature programme at the Dawson Trail Campgrounds, and during the summer months experienced naturalists are on duty in the park. A natural history museum, located centrally in the day-use area at French Lake (plans call for a modern permanent structure to replace the present temporary building) is open to the public from June to September. Evening nature talks are held during July and August with special emphasis placed on the flora and fauna of Quetico. Labelled nature trails represent the third phase of the nature programme. Five nature trails (three labelled) are maintained during the summer, and two of the labelled trails have clearly marked entrances on Highway 11. During the summer months, these cleared trails are used for conducted hikes but visitors are invited to use them on their own at any time.

As yet, the local town of Atikokan (27 miles from French Lake) is not known to have an active natural history club. The closest affiliated F.O.N. group is the Thunder Bay Field Naturalists' Club (Fort William and Port Arthur) with both junior and senior sections. During the summer months, natural history information on Quetico may be obtained from the naturalists on duty at the park museum.

The Dawson Road Nature Trail (from French to Windigoostigwan lakes) starts directly at the rear of the present museum and is about 2½ miles in length. It is rich in historical value, being the route used by Colonel Wolseley's troops in their effort to stamp out the Red River Rebellion (1869). The French Lake Nature Trail, now five years old, is located on Highway 11, ¼ mile west of the park entrance. It is 1¼ miles long and has a halfway stop on the shores of French Lake before winding back to the highway. The French Falls Nature Trail is located 1¼ miles east of the Park entrance on Highway 11. It proceeds about one mile in a southerly direction along the banks of the French River before ending abruptly at French Falls, a six-step cataract of about 40 feet. The shortest trail of the group, the Lookout Nature Trail (100 yards along the campsite road from Campsite 25), is much used by occupants of the adjacent campsites. Only ¼ mile in length, it rises steeply to overlook French Lake. The Mink Lake Nature Trail (rarely used) starts from the Department of Highways camp across the road from the park entrance, and runs approximately 2 miles in a northerly direction to end on the shores of Mink Lake (beyond park boundary).

As is the rule in such forest areas, visitors must obtain a travel permit before entering the interior of Quetico. These permits may be obtained without charge from the ranger on duty at the gatehouse at the Dawson Trail Campgrounds. Individuals using the campsites are not required to obtain travel permits during their stay at French Lake.

Almost the entire area of Quetico Provincial Park is included in Map 52B of the *National Topographic Series*; the western end of the park is continued on map 52C. A complete map (56A) of Quetico Provincial Park (Department of Lands and Forests, Division of Surveys and Engineering, 1956), may be obtained at any of the park stations.

*Ontario Department of Lands and Forests*

## ✿ RONDEAU PROVINCIAL PARK

PROCLAIMED IN 1894, Rondeau is Ontario's second oldest provincial park. Of the total area of 11,450 acres, 5,000 acres are a triangular sand spit whose apex is joined to the mainland at the north end. Recently, the boundaries were extended to include the surface of Rondeau Bay.

From Windsor the fastest route is via Highway 401 to interchange 12, thence by hard-surfaced road to the park, a total distance of about 75 miles. From the London area, Rondeau is 70 miles via Highways 2 to Thamesville and 21 to Morpeth, then along the shore road; shorter ways are by Highway 401 or by Highways 2 and 4 to Talbotville, thence by Highway 3 to Morpeth. The park is open to visitors the year round. The postal address is Department of Lands and Forests, R.R. 1, Morpeth, Ontario.

Moulded by currents from the east, Rondeau Park is characterized by low ridges of sand and gravel which run north and south and are separated by shallow troughs or sloughs. The latter may vary from damp to wet with several feet of water, depending on time of the year, location in the park, and the prevailing lake level. It is doubtful if any part of the park is more than 10 to 12 feet above mean lake level. Soils found in the park are entirely sand or gravel, waterborne, with a high water table. A thin layer of humus supports a very fine example of southern hardwood forest. About half of the area, bordering Rondeau Bay on the inner side of the spit, is an open marsh.

The forested portion is of three main types. The highest part, bordering the eastern shore, supports a mixed growth of White Pine with oak and other broad-leaved species. Three-quarters of the forest is of pure hardwood character which may be divided into ridge and swamp types. The pine reappears, though on a minor scale, along the margin of the open marsh. White Pine is a vanishing component of the Rondeau forest, owing to its intolerance of heavy shade and to the fact that deer seek it out for food.

The greater part of the hardwood forest is a mature stand and a climax forest, containing a majority of species that will maintain themselves under existing conditions. A significant change now under way is the dying of much White Elm owing to Dutch Elm Disease. Although the bulk of the stand is made up of Beech, Sugar-Maple, Basswood, White Elm, and White Ash, there is a good representation of other Carolinian (Deciduous Forest) species. Tulip-tree is fairly common, found in sizes up to 40 inches diameter or better, and reproduces well. Sassafras is also common, occasionally reaching 24 inches in diameter, and Chestnut-Oak and Red Mulberry are found in fair numbers. Black Walnut, Butternut, Black Oak, Shagbark- and Bitternut Hickory, and Sycamore are other Carolinian trees well represented in the Rondeau Park forest.

Bartlett (1958) found trees which were probably seedlings at the time the first known European explorers, Galinee and de Casson, saw Rondeau in 1669. Although no doubt the forest was plundered of pine, walnut, and other valuable trees in the 1800's, it was never systematically logged, and since 1894 little but salvage cutting has been permitted. Trees of four feet in diameter and more are not uncommon. In all, 124 species of trees, shrubs, and woody vines are recorded as native or established in the park. Ferns and their allies, and herbaceous plants number about 500. Spicebush and Fragrant Sumac are very common, while many sloughs in the marsh and also in the woods are full of Buttonbush.

The marsh, with a fair interspersion of ponds, is characterized by stands of cat-tail (both species), reed (*Phragmites*), bulrush, and considerable Wild Rice. Black Tern, Long-billed Marsh Wren, and Redwinged Blackbird are common breeders in this area. Least Bittern, Common Gallinule, and Virginia Rails and Soras also nest here, and there are sight records of King Rail and Louisiana Heron. Old records, with specimens, exist for Sandhill Crane and White Pelican.

Among naturalists, Rondeau has long been famous as the main breeding place, in Canada, of Prothonotary Warbler and Acadian Flycatcher. The former was much more common before the clean-up undertaken in the depression years of the 1930's. Louisiana Waterthrush and Piping Plover once nested here but have not been recorded in recent years. Carolina Wren, Cerulean Warbler, Blue-gray Gnatcatcher, Orchard Oriole, and Yellow-breasted Chat are southern birds of regular occurrence, and there are a number of records of Hooded Warbler, Summer Tanager, Mockingbird, and Red-bellied Woodpecker, as well as one or two of Dickcissel and Tufted Titmouse. Bald Eagles are year-round residents and nest, although with irregular success. No woodland hawks are known to breed. Whistling Swans make the Eau (Rondeau Bay) a regular resting place in spring. They may be seen here and on the marsh ponds from mid-March and sometimes a few linger until mid-May. They occur again, less regularly, in late fall. The sandbar running west to Erieau and, in years of low water, the bay shore are good spots for the shorebirds in migration. The present list of birds, including 30 hypotheticals, numbers 284, 82 of which are known to breed in the Park while another 25 probably do so.

White-tailed Deer have played a prominent part in the recent life of the park. There was a serious overpopulation between 1912 and 1942 when tree seedlings of most species and indeed most of the undergrowth were destroyed by deer browsing. For this

Sylvia Hahn

**CERULEAN WARBLER**

reason about 1,800 deer were shot during this period. They use the marsh as cover extensively in both winter and summer. The recent policy of the Department of Lands and Forests is to restrict the herd to around 100 head, by an annual shoot in January (carried out by the department).

Muskrat and Mink occur commonly and are now trapped in Rondeau Marsh under department regulations. Small numbers of Beaver maintain a precarious existence in the almost complete absence of aspen and White Birch. Sassafras is their favourite substitute food. Opossum and Gray Fox have both been seen once in the park. Red Foxes are not uncommon, and Coyote have been seen on several occasions. Twenty-five mammals have been collected within Rondeau and another eight are known from reliable sight records.

Perhaps the most interesting reptile in the park is Ontario's only lizard, the Blue-tailed Skink, quite common in open areas and woodland. In all, seventeen reptiles are of known occurrence including Fox Snake and Spiny Soft-shelled Turtle. Among the amphibians, thirteen species have been seen or collected. Fowler's Toad is found here, as elsewhere along the Lake Erie shore.

The Department of Lands and Forests maintains a park museum of natural history and human history, open daily in July and August, and on weekends in late May and June. A park naturalist is permanently stationed here. There are extensive camping and picnic facilities, and a complete naturalist programme with conducted nature walks, labelled trails, and illustrated talks is available in the summer. The museum has published check-lists of birds, of trees, shrubs, and woody vines, and of ferns, fern allies, and herbaceous flowering plants.

A mimeographed annotated check-list of birds with migration dates, and a mimeographed flowering calendar are also available. *A Study of Some Deer and Forest Relationships in Rondeau Provincial Park*, by Charles O. Bartlett (1958), is published by the Department of Lands and Forests and may be obtained from the department's office in the Parliament Buildings, Toronto.

R. D. Ussher
*Ontario Department of Lands and Forests*

## ❀ ST. LAWRENCE ISLANDS NATIONAL PARK

ST. LAWRENCE ISLANDS National Park is made up of twelve small islands scattered in the Thousand Islands section of the St. Lawrence River between Kingston and Brockville, a distance of about 50 miles. In addition to the islands there is a mainland area at Mallorytown Landing, on Highway 401, about 13 miles west of Brockville. This is the park office and headquarters area. The park is open all year but the islands are used only in the open water season between April and November.

Each island is supplied with complete camping facilities and good docks capable of handling large cruisers as well as small boats. Food and other necessities have to be taken to the islands by the visitor as there are no supply houses in the park. Hotels, motels, supply stores, and other services are plentiful in the towns and cities and along the highways on the mainland. A boat is necessary to reach any of the islands in the park. If you do not have your own, water taxis or boats as well as guides may be secured on the mainland.

The park headquarters, at Mallorytown Landing, offers campsites for tenting, nature trails, swimming, car parks, and dockage, but no overnight accommodation or boats. It is not necessary to report to the headquarters before visiting any particular island, but it may be reached from any mainland city or village.

The most westerly island is Cedar Island (23 acres) at Kingston, on the edge of the harbour. The largest group of islands consisting of Mermaid, Aubrey, Beau Rivage, Camelot, Endymion, and Gordon are nearest to and reached best from Gananoque. Georgina and Constance islands are near the village of Ivy Lea and the Thousand Islands International Bridge. In fact, the piers of one section of the bridge arise from these islands. Grenadier Island, only a small part of which is included in the national park, and Adelaide Island are reached from Mallorytown Landing. Stovin Island, the most easterly part of the park is 2 miles west of Brockville.

The narrow Frontenac Axis of Precambrian rocks crosses the St. Lawrence River between Brockville and Gananoque. It is bordered on either side by sedimentary rocks of the Palaeozoic Era. The boundaries are very irregular, so that you may be in limestone country at one point and in the next ¼ mile be on igneous rock formations. Most of the islands are of Precambrian igneous rock but Stovin Island near Brockville shows outcrops of sedimentary rock. The islands are the tops of old hills, formed when the water level of the St. Lawrence River rose and flooded the intervening valleys.

The trees and other plants of the park belong to the Great Lakes–St. Lawrence (Mixed) Forest Region of Canada. It has also been described as part of the Canadian Biotic Province of North America. There is an extensive mixture of southern and northern plants and animals in this transitional area. The most interesting tree of the national park is Pitch-Pine because in Canada it grows only in this area along the St. Lawrence River between Brockville and Gananoque. The best place to find it is between Ivy Lea and Brockville either on the islands or mainland. It does not occur near Kingston but is known to be present at Mallorytown Landing, and on Grenadier, Georgina, and Stovin islands. Among the other common trees of the park are Shagbark-Hickory, Sugar-Maple, White Oak, Beech, White Pine, Yellow Birch, Red Oak, Pin-Cherry, and Black Cherry. Gray Birch should occur but has not yet been identified.

No studies have been made of the natural history of the park and records in this field are greatly needed. Botanists claim that there are a number of rare and relict species of plants in the area but so far none have been identified in the park. Ebony-Spleenwort, New Jersey Tea, Flowering Rush, and Hairy Bush-Clover are known from the park. Among its interesting animals are European Praying Mantis and the fish Muskellunge. The members of both the Kingston Field Naturalists and the Brockville Nature Club should be referred to for information on the natural history of the general area. The Kingston club has prepared a check-list of birds for its area that should be useful in the park. Black Ant Island, which is not part of the park but is near Gananoque, and Mermaid, Aubrey, and Beau Rivage islands, support a large nesting colony of Ring-billed Gull and a small colony of Black-crowned Night Heron. Double-crested Cormorant, Herring Gull, Common Tern, Caspian Tern, and Black Duck are known to nest on other nearby islands.

GEORGE M. STIRRETT

## ✿ ST. THOMAS

ST. THOMAS is situated in the heart of Elgin County, and is reached from the east or west by Highway 3 and from the north and south by Highway 4. Central and eastern Elgin County is drained by the Kettle, Catfish, and other creeks. Routes to points of interest begin at the Elgin County Museum at the west end of St. Thomas at the top of the hill on Highway 3 on Talbot Street.

The local natural history club is the St. Thomas Field Naturalist Club, which holds meetings at 8.00 P.M. in the St. Thomas Public Library (corner of Mondamin and Curtis Streets) behind the City Hall on the first Friday of each month from October until May. Visitors can reach the officers of the club by phoning or contacting the attendants at the museum.

PINAFORE PARK. From the museum go west to Highway 4 approximately ¼ mile, then south on Highway 4 to the first railway crossing, turn left (east), and go about ½ mile to the park entrance. This natural public park includes an area of natural woodlot which is frequented by many species of birds during the migration seasons. The small lake on the northwest boundary of the park attracts many species of waterfowl which are fed and protected during the fall months.

P.U.C. RESERVOIR AND REFORESTED AREA. From the museum go 1½ miles east on Talbot Street to Balaclava Street, then north to the park. The area has the contained waters of Kettle Creek which attracts considerable numbers of ducks, geese, and swans during migration.

WHITE'S WOODS. Go east from the museum on Highway 3 about 10 miles to the town of Orwell, south on the gravel road 2 miles to Springwater Pond and White's Woods on your left. This is a large natural stand of mixed deciduous and coniferous trees with a good understory of second growth hardwoods which provide cover for several species of interesting birds. The most uncommon is the Hooded Warbler. Thrushes, Scarlet Tanagers, Eastern Wood Pewees, and Rose-breasted Grosbeaks are found in reasonable numbers. Wood Ducks frequently use the old workings of Pileated Woodpeckers for nesting purposes. Plant life includes some of the rare orchids and other interesting varieties.

HAWKCLIFF. Proceed as indicated for Pinafore Park, then go east on Elm Street past the St. Thomas–Elgin General Hospital to the first county road, then south to the Lake Erie waterfront. Excellent vantage point for watching diurnal migrants, especially hawks in mid-September.

PORT STANLEY, PORT BRUCE, PORT BURWELL. From museum go south along Highway 4 to Port Stanley. Follow lake road east to Port Bruce and Port Burwell. Each of these ports provides harbour facilities which attract numerous gulls, ducks, and shorebirds. The high sandy cliffs provide nesting sites for Bank Swallows. The west beach at Port Burwell is good for shorebirds during migration. Although greatly reduced in numbers, there are still a few active Bald Eagle nests to be seen along the north shore of Lake Erie in Elgin County.

> F. Lewis *et al.*
> *St. Thomas Field Naturalist Club*

❁　**SARNIA**

FROM THE WEST, visitors enter Sarnia by the strikingly symmetrical Blue Water International Bridge, 210 feet above the St. Clair River. The approach from the east is by Highway 7, a delightful

drive. Most pleasant and impressive is Highway 40 to Chatham
and Windsor on which within a few feet of the river, one meets
or passes ships of the Great Lakes and the oceans. In the following account routes to points of interest to naturalists start at the
Tourist Reception Centre which is at the foot of the Blue Water
Bridge where Highways 40, 402, and 7 meet.

The Blue Water Audubon Society of Port Huron, Michigan,
meets monthly on the first Monday of October to May in the
Y.M.C.A. at the foot of Glenwood Avenue, Port Huron. The
society's officers are listed with the Chamber of Commerce, 920
Pine Grove Avenue, Port Huron.

VILLAGE OF POINT EDWARD. Take Highway 7 to Front Street, turn
left to Michigan Avenue, turn left again to business section
and the St. Clair River. Here one can see Herring Gulls. Also
this part of the river is noted for minnows. In the summer at
dusk one may see Black-crowned Night Herons. In the fall
one can see hawks migrating underneath the bridge.

CANATARA PARK. This park is on Lake Huron and is owned by
Sarnia. It can be reached from Point Edward by going
towards the lake or by taking Highway 40 east to Christina
Street and turning left and going north until you see the park
sign. First one comes to Lake Chipican which is a haven for
Redwinged Blackbirds and shorebirds. Water lilies are plentiful on the little lake. Going further into the park one finds
picnic tables and a public beach. This park has many varieties
of evergreen and shade trees, and there are shrubs and flowers
along the park roads. Small mammals can be seen in the park.

SCENIC RIVERSIDE DRIVE. From the Tourist Reception Centre take
Highway 40 through Sarnia. Beyond the city limits the road
goes along the St. Clair River. There are several roadside
parks along the highway where one can stop and eat or watch
for birds. In the winter northern ducks may be seen swimming on the open water. In the summer various species of
gulls and terns can be seen along the river. If a person is
interested in rocks they can be found along the shore of the
river.

BEAR CREEK. This creek crosses roads where one can find birds that live inland. One good spot is north of Petrolia on Highway 21. Go north on Highway 21 by overhead bridge to next corner, turn right on gravel road on first road north of bridge. This will lead you to Bear Creek again. Here the creek is lined with trees and the birds have a haven.

*Lambton County Nature Club*
*Blue Water Audubon Society*

❀ **SAULT STE. MARIE**

SAULT STE. MARIE, ONTARIO

BELLEVIEW PARK. This park is located east along Queen Street about 2 miles from the centre of town, (Brock and Queen streets). Just east of the deer pens, turn towards the river which is an excellent area for shore and marsh birds, and, at certain times, migrants.

CANADIAN LOCKS. Go west along Queen Street about 2 miles from centre of town, and south along Hudson Street to the lock area. Although the wilder parts are closed to the public, the area is still good for water birds.

FOREST GLEN WOODS. Go east along Queen to Pine Street, north on Pine to the wooded area above McNabb Street. This fast disappearing area of mixed hardwoods is excellent for spring and summer flowers and warblers.

WEST OF SAULT STE. MARIE, ONTARIO

GROS CAP. Take Queen Street west to Gore Street, turn north to Wellington and then west to Wallace Terrace. Follow to Second line, then go west for 12 miles to the loop at Lake Superior. The high rocky promontory north of the road, although of limited interest geologically, has many interesting

orchids and other plants. Birds are found at all seasons. Along
the road many of the old glacial beaches may be seen.

FOURTH LINE. Follow the Second line to the Carpin Beach Road
and turn north. Proceed two concessions. The mixed woods
are good for birds and woodland flowers.

OLD GOULAIS ROAD. Go north on the People's Road to the Fourth
line, east one block, and then north. This winding road goes
through some excellent fern country on the high granite hills,
and passes some Beaver meadows which are active at times.
There are marsh and woodland birds here.

## NORTH OF SAULT STE. MARIE, ONTARIO

HIAWATHA PARK. Follow Highway 17 to the first railway crossing
north of the city. Take the first sideroad east and follow to the
lodge. This is a large area from which cars are excluded.
Paths take visitors through mixed woods to high waterfalls
cutting through moist deep granite gorges. Ferns, wildflowers,
and birds are here in abundance.

BELLEVIEW QUARRY. Follow Highway 17 north for 13 miles to the
Searchmount Road. Proceed along Searchmount Road 4 miles.
The quarry, located on the west side of the road about halfway up Belleview Ridge, is almost pure quartzite with some
narrow veins of hematite and a large exposure of serpentine-
like rock.

BUTTERMILK HILL. Go north on Highway 17 for about 18 miles.
Take the first sideroad to the east after passing the Goulais
River turnoff. Follow sideroad to top of hill. On the granite
ramparts Common Ravens nest and *Woodsia* ferns are found.
In the surrounding hardwood forests are warblers, Scarlet
Tanagers, and Indigo Buntings.

CRANBERRY CREEK. Follow Highway 17 north to Goulais River
turnoff. Turn west and cross river. Keep to the south shore of
river. On the south side of the road is a large swamp excellent
for swamp orchids, Moose, and the usual birds with webbed
feet. This area is at the north end of the Old Goulais Road and
the return trip can be made this way when the road is passable
(check road conditions before attempting!).

EAST OF SAULT STE. MARIE, ONTARIO

VICTORIA (JARDUN) MINE. Follow Highway 17 east to Garden River village, turn north and follow road for 10 miles. The last 1½ miles will probably have to be made on foot. The old mine tailings have a fair number of samples of galena, fluorite, and pyrites. The road in is excellent for early morning birding.

ECHO BAY FLATS. Follow Highway 17 east to the bridge at Echo Bay. Here the broad expanse of marsh affords a good chance to see marsh birds, gulls, ducks, and migrant shorebirds.

ST. JOSEPH'S ISLAND. Follow highway 17 east for about 25 miles to the ferry turnoff. Proceed to landing and take ferry across to the island. This is a limestone island, continuing the Manitoulin Chain. There are several Leray-Rockland outcrops accessible, with good fossils. Ferns, flowers, and birds, not common on the mainland, are here. At the west end of the "D" Line the Sault Naturalists' Club holds its annual spring outing for migratory birds. A little-known bird sanctuary exists at the south end of the island near the remains of the old fort.

RIPPLE ROCKS. Along Highway 17 east 27 miles from the Sault the rock cuts, especially on the north side of the highway, exhibit some excellent ripple marks preserved and severely tilted in the Archaean Quartzite formations. Although these are perhaps the best examples to be found, other smaller occurrences are to be seen in the area through the various quartzites.

BRUCE MINES. This village is 37 miles east of the Sault. There are a trap-rock quarry at the southeast edge of town and a copper mine at the north edge, both of which hold many interesting sights of old mining ventures. Neither mine is working now, and although the tailings are few those near the trap-rock quarry do bear some samples. Double-crested Cormorants and other shore-inhabiting birds are present here.

ROCK LAKE. Take the first road north at the east end of Bruce Mines and follow to Rydal Bank. Go east, then north again to the village of Rock Lake. A lane along the north side of the graveyard leads directly to the old Rock Lake Copper Mine shafts and tailing dumps. Good samples of bornite, malachite, and chalcopyrite are available, but some are weathered.

SAULT STE. MARIE, MICHIGAN

RIVER FRONT. The area anywhere along the river affords good spots to see spring migrant ducks, Bald Eagles, and gulls. Whistling Swans are seen occasionally.

DUNBAR EXPERIMENTAL STATION. Seventeen miles south and east of town, this station, run by the Michigan State University for forest research, is full of interest. There are nature trails and plentiful birding opportunities, including the occasional glimpse of Sandhill Cranes.

STALWART RIDGE. Twenty-five miles south of Sault Ste. Marie, east of U.S. Highway 129, and south of Pickford, this high limestone ridge of Niagara-Clinton formation bears Silurian fossils such as brachiopods and corals.

VARVED CLAYS. Six miles southwest of town, on the road south from Algonquin, these interesting clays deposited by former glacial lakes show typical exfoliation into thin layers when dried.

OAK MEADOWS. Southeast of Rudyard which is 15 miles south of Sault Ste. Marie on U.S. Highway 2, the south slope of the Niagara-Clinton limestone has a small meadow developed from a dried-up lake. Nearby is a flat cut-over area of Bur Oak which is somewhat unusual in the eastern part of the Upper Peninsula.

*Sault Naturalists' Club*

### ❁   SIBLEY PROVINCIAL PARK

SIBLEY PROVINCIAL PARK is reached by driving east from Port Arthur along Highway 17 for 24 miles to Highway 587 then driving south along Highway 587 into the park. Check at the park gate for information and a map. Tent and trailer sites are available, and a park naturalist is on duty.

The park is 58 square miles in area and occupies a large peninsula extending into Lake Superior 24 miles east of Port Arthur. A dominant feature is the "Sleeping Giant" at Thunder Cape. This represents the reclining figure of a man and is actually the hard capping of diabase sills which protect the underlying strata. The west side of the peninsula reaches an altitude of 1,805 feet above sea level and plunges steeply 800 feet to Thunder Bay. These cliffs are the highest in Ontario. The peninsula slopes off to the east to Black Bay 602 feet above sea level. Many rock exposures of the Sibley and Animikie series are apparent, and glacial drift is evident everywhere. There are many lakes in the interior and the drainage is by several small creeks. Lake Marie Louise is the largest lake.

The entire peninsula is forested with a dominant growth of Balsam-Fir. White Cedar is very common. White Birch and Trembling Aspen are common in the southern portion of the peninsula. There are several Black Spruce and White Cedar swamps in the park. Of particular interest is a tract of White Pine, 2,000 acres in area. Botanists will enjoy the many ravines in the west side of the park, where protection and shelter have provided a special environment for many species of ferns and orchids, including the rare Bog-Adder's-mouth. At Tee Harbour the typical tundra biome along Lake Superior is readily accessible and the liverwort flora is exciting. Here, you will find such Arctic alpines as Bistort and False Asphodel, also Butterwort, two species of *Primula*, Creeping Juniper, and Wild Chives. Beard Moss (*Usnea*) hangs from the trees.

Animals often seen in the park are Moose, White-tailed Deer, Snowshoe Hare, and Red Fox.

The birds present a northern fauna with nesting records for Common Loon, Gray Jay, Black-backed Three-toed Woodpecker, and Common Goldeneye. A southern aspect is provided, however, by records of Red-headed Woodpecker. Parula Warblers should be looked for in their favoured Beard Moss habitat. Historic Silver Islet, Middlebrun Bay, and the rugged slopes of the Sleeping Giant afford good birding. Bald Eagles are frequently observed.

*Ontario Department of Lands and Forests*

THE TORONTO REGION is covered by the topographic map sheets for Toronto, Markham, Bolton, and Brampton, and consists roughly of the area north of Lake Ontario from Pickering on the east to Milton on the west and north to Aurora. It is bordered on the west by the Niagara Escarpment, which here reaches a height of 300–400 feet, and on the north by a hilly moraine with an altitude of about 1,000 feet above sea level. One area of bog just to the north of the moraine has been included (Pottageville Swamp). The land enclosed by the escarpment and the moraine consists of gently rolling plain which falls fairly evenly to Lake Ontario. There are no large lakes or bogs in this region, but several small rivers and streams which have their sources above the escarpment and in the moraine cut deep valleys on their way to Lake Ontario, and the remnants of once extensive marshes are to be found at the mouths of most of these rivers. The area along the lake is one continuous urban sprawl. To the north of this is open farmland and then some wooded areas along the escarpment and on the moraine.

POTTAGEVILLE SWAMP. Drive north from Toronto on Highway 400 to the Aurora cloverleaf. Go west on the Aurora sideroad to the first crossing (Concession 6). Follow this paved road north for 2 miles until you reach low ground and see a wooded swamp to the west across a field. Two square miles in area, it is privately owned but visited by naturalists. For birdwatching it is best in early mornings in June. Common nesters are Black-and-white, Nashville, and Canada Warblers, Northern Waterthrush, Yellowthroat, Veery, White-throated Sparrow, Winter Wren, and Brown Creeper. There are many typical bog plants such as Pitcher-plant, Labrador-tea, and Showy, Pink, and Yellow Lady's-slipper. Much of the area is covered with pure stands of Tamarack. The terrain is very rough with low growth and windfalls. Take rubber boots and a compass.

RATTRAY'S MARSH. Take the Lakeshore Road (Highway 2) west

from Toronto past Port Credit about 2 miles to Bexhill Road. Drive south to the foot of Bexhill. Rattray's Marsh is to the south and west. The area is about 200 acres and is made up of pond, marsh, stream, brush, fields, and woods. Many native wildflowers and ferns are still found, including trillium and Interrupted Fern. Mammals include Cottontail, Raccoon, Red Fox, Muskrat, and Striped Skunk. However, the bird population attracts the largest number of naturalists. Here during spring and fall migration it is possible to list over 100 species of birds in one day. In the summer Black Terns, Green Herons, Long-billed Marsh Wrens, rails, and Wood Ducks nest here.

GLEN WILLIAMS. Follow Highway 401 west from Yonge Street, Toronto, approximately 30 miles to Highway 10, then northwest past Brampton to Highway 7, then southwest to Norval. Proceed north for 2½ miles to the first turn left beyond the railway (no. 17 sideroad); after ¾ mile, at a T-intersection turn right for 300 yards, then turn left and carry on about ½ mile until a steep curving hill reaches a bridge over the road and an obvious path leads west to the pond and beyond. This area is privately owned, but frequented by the public. An old pond with a marshy upper end runs into a wooded area. Beyond the pond the side of the valley is steep and tree-covered. There is a good stand of Ostrich-Fern on a wooded island in the river, and there is a good colony of Beech-drops on the slope of the valley. The river flats, between the path and the river, have some interesting plants, for example, Purple Loosestrife and Flowering Rush.

CALEDON HILLS FARM. Go northwest on Highway 10 and turn southwest at Victoria; turn right at the third concession and carry on through Cheltenham until you reach the entrance to the farm, where there is a sign "Caledon Hills Farm." One and a half miles from Cheltenham there is a curve in the road to avoid a conspicuous area of eroded red clay–Queenston Shale, the upper level of the Ordovician Age rock. The farm is owned by the University of Toronto and permission to enter may be had from Mr. Walter Snider at the farm. The farm extends from the third to the second line, dropping over the edge of the cuesta (Niagara Escarpment) on the way. On the upper level is a thin till over dolomitic limestone (Lockport formation), which forms the cliffs. Below the cliffs is a well-developed talus slope richly covered with vegetation of all sizes; below this slope are the Medina sandstones, much worked for flagstones and the like. In a small willow swamp north of the farm road Traill's Flycatchers have occurred, and in the meadow at the parking place, Henslow's Sparrows, Pileated Woodpeckers, Turkey Vultures, and Cedar Waxwings. The dense cover below the cliffs is well suited to some warblers, while the tall trees attract others. The talus slope and the cliffs afford habitats for many interesting plants, among them Slender Cliff-Brake, Walking Fern, and Hart's-tongue Fern. Shining Club-moss occurs on the lower parts of the talus. When leaving the farm, turn right (north). This road, up to the next sideroad, is also of great interest to naturalists, particularly a wet spot on the west side of the road.

FRENCHMAN'S BAY. Take Highway 401 east from Yonge Street, Toronto, for approximately 19 miles to the Liverpool Road cloverleaf. Jog south to the first easterly bearing road (Concession 1, Pickering). Go east ½ mile and turn right. Go south to the bridge over the marsh. Watch fields and roadsides for open-country birds. After checking the marsh, continue south to the lakefront. You can walk west along the lakefront towards Frenchman's Bay, watching the lake for loons, grebes, and ducks, the beach for shorebirds, and the marsh to the north for American Coots, Common Gallinules, and rails.

PICKERING MARSH. Proceed as above (Frenchman's Bay) but turn left about 300 yards before you reach the lakefront. Go east 1½ miles to the point where the road turns south. This point offers the best view of the marsh which is one of the best places in the area to see pond ducks and herons. When the water level is low enough to expose mud flats hundreds of shorebirds congregate. The lake directly to the south is worth checking for migrating ducks, Red-necked Grebes, and loons.

HUMBER RIVER. The Humber River in the west end of Toronto is bordered by parkland along much of its course through the metropolitan area, and it provides excellent habitat for many species of birds. The river itself is attractive to ducks and shorebirds, particularly in fall, and thickets along the river banks with the wooded slopes bounding the flood plain are attractive to a wide variety of land birds, especially during migration. A series of marshes bound the river in its southern section, providing habitat for many birds and plants.

To reach the *northern section* of the Humber and James Gardens, proceed west from the intersection of Dundas and Jane Streets 4/10 mile to the next light, and turn north on Scarlett Road. Continue north one mile until the road crosses the river. The river flats at this point are a gathering place for ducks, gulls, and shorebirds. A section of the river valley is accessible on foot from here, and also from Lawrence Avenue and Raymore Drive, further north on Scarlett Road. Just beyond the bridge, turn left on Edenbridge Drive, proceed 8/10 mile to *James Gardens*, and turn into the parking area on the left of the road. These very attractive public gardens are bounded by a fine deciduous woodland.

For the *central, "Old Mill" section* of the river, proceed from the Dundas-Jane intersection 9/10 mile west, crossing the river on the high-level Lambton bridge. At the western end of the bridge turn sharply left and drive down the hill to enter the Humber Valley Park. The road follows the river southward. Watch for ducks, shorebirds, gulls, and migrant land birds. The gulls should be carefully scrutinized for a possible Little Gull, as odd birds of this species occur regularly. The road through the park ends at Old Mill Road. Turn left (east) and go down the hill, crossing the Humber bridge. A parking area is located on the north side of the road, and the east bank of the river can be covered on foot from this point.

To visit an easily accessible portion of the *lower Humber* proceed west on Bloor Street 1/10 mile from the Bloor-Jane intersection, and turn south at the light onto the South Kingsway. Drive one mile and park just beyond the point where the road merges with Riverside Drive. Note the colony of Bank Swallows and look out over Humber marshes No. 2 and No. 3 for marsh birds. Hooded Mergansers occur in spring and fall, and Dunlin and Rusty Blackbirds chiefly in fall. For the naturalist who is prepared to do some scrambling, much of the lower Humber is accessible on foot, although waterproof footwear should be worn. Access can be gained from the east side of the Bloor Street bridge. Sycamore and Sassafras occur and the area is rich in marsh flora.

GRENADIER POND (in High Park). Located in the west end of Toronto, between Bloor and Queen streets, Grenadier Pond is at the west end of High Park (Toronto's largest park). During the spring and fall migration it is an excellent place to observe many species of ducks, grebes, and swallows. A small stream enters the north end, where there is a good-sized cattail marsh; the north end usually stays open in winter and is often productive of wintering waterfowl, Redwinged and Rusty Blackbirds and Swamp Sparrows. The brushy tangles at the north end and along the west side are good places to look for most of our common winter birds. An interesting association of plants can be found growing on the sandy hillside above the northeast end of the pond.

SUNNYSIDE BEACH (Toronto lakefront). This mile-long stretch extends along Lake Ontario between the mouth of the Humber River on the west and Palais Royale parking lot on the east. It may be reached from either direction via Lakeshore Road. There is plenty of free parking in lots adjacent to the beach, where observation can be done from one's automobile (a good feature on cold winter days!). This area is best known for wintering waterfowl including visitors such as King Eider, Ruddy Duck, Canvasback, Redhead, and Glaucous and Iceland Gulls. This is a good place to look for Brant and Whimbrel in late May.

TORONTO ISLAND. Proceed by automobile or street car to the foot of Bay Street where the island ferries run across the bay to the island (actually several islands joined by bridges and separated by lagoons). Frequent ferry service is available from May to December; less frequent service by ice-breaking tug is provided during the balance of the year.

The island is being converted into a large park with extensive gardens and picnic areas, entailing the gradual removal of many summer homes. The best place for the naturalist is the 75-acre wildlife sanctuary just north of the filtration plant between Centre Island and Hanlan's Point. The willow scrub here is probably the best place in North America for Saw-whet Owls during the last half of October and early November. Up to 45 have been banded in a single day. A permanent banding station was established in 1962, under the supervision of the staff at the Island Natural Science School, where Grade 6 pupils of Toronto schools spend two weeks studying nature in ideal surroundings. There are thousands of wintering Old-squaw on the lake, a colony of Black-crowned Night Herons on Mugg's Island, and migrating shorebirds in late summer and fall at the airport and the adjacent beach.

PURPLEVILLE. Drive north on Highway 400 from Highway 401 to the Maple sideroad (4 miles north of Highway 7). Proceed west ½ mile to the first north-south road (Concession 6) and west a further 1½ miles to the next north-south road (Concession 7). Eastern Bluebirds are regular inhabitants in this area north of the Maple sideroad and along Concessions 6 and 7. The Toronto Field Biologists' Club have 40–50 wooden nesting boxes placed on trees and fence-posts along fencelines up to 2½ miles north of the Maple sideroad. Other interesting breeding birds to be found in the area include Ruffed Grouse, Grasshopper Sparrow, Western Meadowlark (occasional), Loggerhead Shrike, Pileated Woodpecker, Red-shouldered Hawk, and Red-tailed Hawk.

D. E. BURTON
G. M. FAIRFIELD
C. E. GOODWIN

 **WEST LORNE**

THE WEST ELGIN Nature Club's territory consists of the townships of Dunwich and Aldborough in Elgin County and the bank of the Thames River which borders these townships in Middlesex. The southern boundary of the territory is Lake Erie. Both banks of the Thames are included, thus bringing in a small portion of Ekfrid and Mosa townships of Middlesex. These areas can be reached by Highway 2 through Melbourne to Wardsville, and

Highway 3 from Iona to New Glasgow. Connecting links between Highways 2 and 3 are Highway 76 from Eagle to Woodgreen, and county roads from New Glasgow to Wardsville and
Wallacetown to Eaton's Corners.

The area consists of general farming and grazing land on the
northern sections and mainly tobacco and general farming in the
area close to Lake Erie. Woodlots are well dispersed throughout
the territory with some large stands in the West Lorne district.

The West Elgin Nature Club holds approximately three to four
meetings a year in West Lorne. Visitors may contact Dougald
Murray, R. R. 3, Melbourne; V. Earl Lemon, West Lorne; or Mrs.
Horace Mylrea, Secretary, Rodney.

MURRAY'S WOODS, SOUTH EKFRID. These woods are good for woodpeckers, especially Red-bellied and Pileated, and ducks in
spring and fall. This site can be reached from Highway 2, 3
miles west of Melbourne. Turn south on eighth sideroad of
Ekfrid Township for a distance of another 3 miles to corner at
River Road. Access by permission of Mr. Murray.

NEW GLASGOW MEMORIAL PARK AT LAKE ERIE. In early spring
ducks and flying Whistling Swans may be seen from this vantage spot. By county road it is 1½ miles south of New Glasgow
on Highway 3.

WATERWORKS PARK ON LAKE ERIE. Located one mile south of Eagle
(Highway 3), this park will bring to view ducks and Whistling Swans in season.

TYRCONNELL. This area on Lake Erie may be reached from Wallacetown on Highway 3. It gives access to good views of Lake
Erie.

BANKS OF THAMES RIVER. These may be reached from sideroads
running north from Highway 3. Fringed Gentians grow here,
and Bobwhite may be seen along the shrubby roadsides.

*West Elgin Nature Club*

# Sources and Indexes

# ❈ SOURCES OF IDENTIFICATION OF PLANTS AND ANIMALS

INCLUDED HERE are a few manuals for the identification of plants and animals in the range covered by the guide.

## PLANTS

BRITTON, NATHANIEL LORD, and ADDISON BROWN, An Illustrated Flora of the Northern United States, Canada and the British Possessions from Newfoundland to the Parallel of the Southern Boundary of Virginia, and from the Atlantic Ocean Westward to the 102d Meridian (New York Botanical Garden, New York, 1943), vol. I, pp. i–xxix, 1–680; vol. II, pp. i–iv, 1–735; vol. III, pp. 1–637.

CANADA, DEPT. OF NORTHERN AFFAIRS AND NATIONAL RESOURCES, FORESTRY BRANCH, Bulletin 61, Native Trees of Canada, 5th ed. (1956), pp. i–xvii, 1–293.

COBB, B., A Field Guide to the Ferns (Houghton Mifflin Co., Boston, 1956), pp. i–xviii, 1–281.

DURAND, HERBERT, Field Book of Common Ferns (G. P. Putnam's Sons, New York, 1949), pp. 1–223.

FERNALD, MERRITT LYNDON, Gray's Manual of Botany, 8th ed. (American Book Co., New York, Boston, 1950), pp. i–lxiv, 1–1632.

GROVES, J. WALTON, Edible and Poisonous Mushrooms of Canada (Canada, Dept. of Agriculture, Research Branch, 1962), pp. i–iv, 1–298.

MARIE-VICTORIN, FRÈRE, Flore laurentienne (Les Frères des Ecoles Chrétiennes, Montreal, 1947), pp. 1–916; supplement, pp. 1–63.

MONTGOMERY, F. H., Native Wild Plants (Ryerson Press, Toronto, 1962), pp. i–iv, 1–193.

PETRIDES, G. A., A Field Guide to Trees and Shrubs (Houghton Mifflin Co., Boston, 1960), pp. i–xxix, 1–431.

POMERLEAU, RENE, and H. A. C. JACKSON, Mushrooms of Eastern Canada and the United States (Les Editions Chantecler Ltée., Montreal, 1951), pp. 1–302.

RICKETT, HAROLD WILLIAM, The New Field Book of American Wild Flowers (G. P. Putnam's Sons, New York, 1963), pp. 1–414.

SOPER, JAMES H., and MARGARET L. HEIMBURGER, 100 Shrubs of Ontario (Ontario, Dept. of Commerce and Development, 1961), pp. i–xiii, 1–100.

THOMAS, WILLIAM STURGIS, Field Book of Common Mushrooms (G. P. Putnam's Sons, New York, 1948), pp. i–xx, 1–369.

WHERRY, E. T., Wild Flower Guide (Doubleday and Co. Inc., New York, 1948), pp. i–xv, 1–202.

WHITE, J. H., and R. C. HOSIE, The Forest Trees of Ontario and the More Commonly Planted Foreign Trees (Ontario, Dept. of Lands and Forests, Division of Reforestation, 1957), pp. i–v, 1–81.

FISH

SCOTT, W. B., Freshwater Fishes of Eastern Canada (University of Toronto Press, Toronto, 1955), pp. i–xiv, 1–128.

HUBBS, CARL L., and KARL F. LAGLER, Fishes of the Great Lakes Region (Cranbrook Institute of Science, Bloomfield Hills, Mich., 1958), pp. i–xi, 1–213.

AMPHIBIANS AND REPTILES

CONANT, ROGER, A Field Guide to Reptiles and Amphibians (Houghton Mifflin Co., Boston, 1958), pp. i–xv, 1–366.

LOGIER, E. B. S., The Amphibians of Ontario, Royal Ontario Museum of Zoology Handbook 3 (1937), pp. 1–16.

—— The Reptiles of Ontario, Royal Ontario Museum of Zoology Handbook 4 (1939), pp. 1–63.

—— The Frogs, Toads and Salamanders of Eastern Canada (Clarke, Irwin and Co. Ltd., Toronto, 1952), pp. i–xii, 1–127.

—— The Snakes of Ontario (University of Toronto Press, Toronto, 1958), pp. i–x, 1–94.

BIRDS

KORTRIGHT, FRANCIS H., The Ducks, Geese and Swans of North America (Wildlife Management Institute, Washington, 1942), pp. i–ix, 1–476.

PETERSON, ROGER TORY, A Field Guide to the Birds (Houghton Mifflin Co., Boston, 1947), pp. i–xxiv, 1–290.

SNYDER, L. L., and T. M. SHORTT, Ontario Birds (Clarke, Irwin and Co. Ltd., Toronto, 1951), pp. i–x, 1–248.

MAMMALS

BURT, WILLIAM HENRY, and RICHARD PHILIP GROSSENHEIDER, A Field Guide to the Mammals (Houghton Mifflin Co., Boston, 1952), pp. i–xxi, 1–200.

CROSS, E. C., and J. R. DYMOND, The Mammals of Ontario, Royal Ontario Museum of Zoology Handbook 1 (1929), pp. 1–55.

INSECTS

KLOTS, ALEXANDER B., A Field Guide to the Butterflies (Houghton Mifflin Co., Boston, 1951), pp. i–xvi, 1–349.

LUTZ, F. E., Field Book of Insects (G. P. Putnam's Sons, New York, 1948), pp. 1–510.

SWAIN, RALPH B., The Insect Guide (Doubleday and Co. Inc., New York, 1948), pp. i–xlvi, 1–261.

URQUHART, F. A., Introducing the Insect (Clarke, Irwin and Co. Ltd., Toronto, 1949), pp. i–x, 1–287.

ADDER'S-MOUTH, Bog-, 179
Alder, Green, 27, 29
　Speckled, 27
Alewife, 33
Anemone, 32
　Rue, 84
Apple, 57
　Baked-, 32
Arbutus, Trailing, 75, 110
Arnica, Wilson's, 80
Arrow-Arum, Green, 132
Arrow-grass, Seaside, 100
Ash, Black, 26, 156
　Blue, 71, 156, 158
　Prickly, 110
　Red, 73
　Showy Mountain-, 27, 29
　White, 24, 83, 166
Aspen, Large-toothed, 27
　Trembling, 26, 29, 83, 90, 179
Aster, Large-leaved, 27
　Swamp, 148
Asphodel, False, 179
Avens, 32

BAKED-APPLE, 32
Balsam-Fir, 25, 27, 29, 39, 43, 77, 83, 107, 179
Balsam-Poplar, 26, 29, 68, 77, 90
Basswood, 24, 26, 83, 166
Bear, Black, 31, 39, 104, 161
　Polar, 33, 69
Bearberry, 32
Beaver, 31, 39, 43, 88, 106, 107, 121, 123, 146, 150, 160, 161, 169, 176
Bedstraw, 27
Beech, 24, 26, 83, 119, 147, 163, 166, 171
　Blue, 24

Beech-drops, 96, 181
Bellflower, Tall, 158
Bilberry, 31, 32
Birch, Dwarf, 31, 89, 91, 100
　Gray, 109, 171
　Ground, 32
　White, 26, 29, 39, 43, 57, 77, 83, 90, 107, 161, 169, 179
　Yellow, 26, 39, 77, 83, 171
Bistort, 32, 179
Bittern, American, 96, 98
　Least, 96, 167
Bittersweet, 25
Blackbird, Brewer's, 34
　Redwinged, 28, 133, 158, 167, 174, 184
　Rusty, 81, 183, 184
Bladder-Campion, 32 (*Melandrium apetalum*), 35 (*Silene cucubalus*)
Bladdernut, 25, 71
Bladderwort, 148
Blazing-star, 71
Blue Beech, 24
Bluebell, Virginia, 71
Blueberry, 29
Bluebird, Eastern, 71, 146, 161, 185
Blueweed, 35
Bobolink, 28, 34, 43, 77, 96, 161
Bobwhite, 26, 71, 186
Bog-Adder's-mouth, 179
Bog-Laurel, 31
Brant, 184
Buckthorn, 56
Bunchberry, 27, 29, 84
Bunting, Indigo, 28, 46, 78, 176
　Snow, 33, 95, 96, 161
Burning-bush, 25
Bush-Clover, Hairy, 171

Buttercup, 32
  Common Field, 35
Butterfly, Giant Swallow-tailed, 158
Butternut, 24, 27, 166
Butterwort, 179
Buttonbush, 121, 167

CABBAGE, Skunk-, 78, 150
Calypso, 75, 78, 146
Campion, Bladder-, *see* Bladder-Campion
Canvasback, 71, 101, 184
Cardinal, 34, 75, 158
Cardinal-flower, 83, 98, 121, 155
Caribou, 31, 34
Carp, 35
Carrion-flower, 78
Carrot, Wild, 35
Catbird, 28, 76
Catbrier, Bristly, 25
Cedar, Red, 24, 156, 158
  White, 24, 27, 57, 61, 75, 83, 138, 179
Chat, Yellow-breasted, 26, 158, 167
Cherry, Black, 24, 171
  Choke-, 25, 27, 57
  Pin-, 27, 171
Chestnut, 24, 71 (sprouts)
Chestnut-Oak, 24, 158, 166
Chickadee, Black-capped, 39, 75
  Boreal, 31, 39, 41, 43, 78
Chicken, Prairie, 119
Chickweed, 32
Chicory, 35
Chipmunk, Eastern, 26, 31
  Least, 31
Chives, Wild, 179
Choke-Cherry, 25, 27, 57
Chubsucker, Lake, 25
Cicely, Sweet, 158
Cinquefoil, 35
Cliff-Brake, Purple, 134
  Slender, 100, 182
  Smooth, 81
Clover, Hairy Bush-, 171

Club-moss, Bristly, 29
  Shining, 182
Coot, American, 73, 110, 182
Coral-root, Early, 75
  Spotted, 75
Cormorant, Double-crested, 172, 177
Cottontail, Eastern, 28, 181
Cottonwood, 158
Cowbird, Brown-headed, 28
Coyote, 169
Crab, Wild, 24
Cranberry, Ground, 150
  Mountain-, 32
Crane, Sandhill, 167, 178
Creeper, Brown, 75, 180
Creeper, Virginia, 57
Crossbill, Red, 46
  White-winged, 46, 78, 107
Crow, Common, 28, 105
Crowberry, 32
Currant, Wild Black, 25
  Skunk-, 27, 31

DAISY, Ox-eye-, 35
Deer, White-tailed, 28, 34, 39, 85, 115, 160, 167, 179
Dickcissel, 167
Dogwood, Drummond's, 158
  Flowering, 24, 55, 71
  Red-osier, 75
  Round-leaved, 27
Dove, Mourning, 28, 34, 46
Duck, Black, 42, 43, 57, 58, 81, 96, 172
  Ruddy, 71, 184
  Wood, 28, 46, 58, 121, 146, 173, 181
Dunlin, 70, 183

EAGLE, Bald, 39, 58, 73, 101, 111, 113, 118, 132, 146, 150, 167, 173, 178, 179
  Golden, 66
Earth Star, Many-mouthed, 158
Ebony-Spleenwort, 171
Egret, Common, 72, 73, 110

Eider, King, 70, 184
Elder, Red-berried, 27
Elm, White, 24, 26, 77, 149, 166

FALCON, Peregrine, 121
Fern, Hart's-tongue, 67, 74, 182
    Interrupted, 181
    Maidenhair-, 74, 134
    Ostrich-, 90, 147, 181
    Rattlesnake-, 27
    Royal, 121
    Walking, 74, 100, 134, 154, 182,
        183
Fescue, Rough, 78
Finch, Purple, 46
Fir, Balsam-, 25, 27, 29, 39, 43, 77,
    83, 107, 179
Fisher, 29, 31, 39
Fleabane, Hyssop-leaved, 80
Flicker, Yellow-shafted, 28
Flycatcher, Acadian, 26, 167
    Great Crested, 26, 28
    Olive-sided, 42, 63, 135
    Traill's, 154, 182
    Yellow-bellied, 31
Fox, Arctic, 33, 69
    Gray, 34, 169
    Red, 28, 39, 85, 105, 169, 179,
        181
Frog, Cricket, 25, 158
    Leopard, 28
    Wood, 33

GALE, Sweet, 41
Gallinule, Common, 62, 96, 110,
    167, 182
Gentian, Closed, 78
    Fringed, 83, 148, 186
    Macoun's, 80
Ginger, Wild, 90, 134
Gnatcatcher, Blue-gray, 26, 54,
    110, 111, 158, 167
Goldeneye, Common, 81, 101, 179
Goldenrod, 33
Golden-seal, 71
Goldfinch, American, 28
Goldthread, 27, 75

Goose, Blue, 72, 146
    Canada, 31, 72, 89, 97, 101, 104,
        146
    Snow, 33, 70, 72
Gooseberry, Prickly, 25, 27
Goshawk, 39
Grackle, Common, 105
Grass, Lyme-, 32
Grasshopper, Seaside, 158
Grass-of-Parnassus, 148
Grass-pink, 75, 148
Grebe, Pied-billed, 62, 110
    Red-necked, 78, 107, 159, 182
Grosbeak, Evening, 46, 78, 135
    Pine, 31
    Rose-breasted, 28, 42, 46, 74, 78,
        173
Groundsel, 33
Grouse, Ruffed, 39, 46, 98, 113,
    185
    Sharp-tailed, 29, 107
    Spruce, 31, 34, 39, 41, 43
Gull, Bonaparte's, 95, 107, 161
    Glaucous, 94, 184
    Great Black-backed, 94
    Herring, 61, 62, 94, 172, 174
    Iceland, 94, 184
    Little, 183, 184
    Ring-billed, 61, 62, 94, 163, 172
Gum, Black, 71
    Sour, 24

HACKBERRY, 71, 156, 158
Hare, European, 35
    Snowshoe, 28, 31, 179
Hawk, Broad-winged, 46, 103
    Marsh, 142, 161
    Pigeon, 78
    Red-shouldered, 74, 98, 185
    Red-tailed, 74, 185
Hawkweed, Orange, 35
Hawthorn, 57, 76
Hazel, American, 25
    Beaked, 27
    Witch-, 25
Heal-all, 36
Helleborine, 36

Hemlock, 24, 27, 39, 42, 61, 74, 83, 109, 138, 147
Heron, Black-crowned Night, 73, 96, 172, 174, 185
  Great Blue, 50, 57, 58, 62, 73, 121, 150
  Green, 58, 75, 96, 98, 181
  Louisiana, 167
Hickory, Bitternut, 166
  Shagbark-, 24, 166, 171
Honeysuckle, Bracted, 29
  Bush-, 27
  Fly-, 27
Hop-tree, 71, 158

Iris, Dwarf, 67, 148
  Yellow, 71
Ironwood, 24, 26
Ivy, Poison, 25, 153

Jack-in-the-pulpit, 78
Jack-Pine, 27, 29, 39, 76
Jaeger, Parasitic, 33, 70
Jay, Blue, 28, 39, 158
  Gray, 31, 39, 78, 179
Junco, Slate-colored, 75
Juniper, 32
  Creeping, 179

Katydid, Northern, 158
Killdeer, 28, 142
Kingbird, Eastern, 28
Kingfisher, Belted, 46, 81
Kinglet, Ruby-crowned, 63

Labrador-tea, 29, 31, 32, 41, 75, 95, 107, 180
Lady's-slipper, Pink, 180
  Ram's-head, 75
  Showy, 75, 180
  Stemless, 75, 80
  Yellow, 148, 180
Lambkill, 95
Lamprey, Sea, 33
Lark, Horned, 142
Laurel, Sheep-, 63
  Bog-, 31

Leather-leaf, 31, 41
Leatherwood, 25
Licorice, Wild, 133
Lily-of-the-valley, Wild, 27
Lobelia, Great, 83
Longspur, Lapland, 70, 96, 142
Loon, Arctic, 33
  Common, 42, 61, 62, 114, 179
  Red-throated, 33
Loosestrife, Purple, 181
  Swamp-, 121
Lotus, American, 72
Lungwort, 32
Lyme-Grass, 32
Lynx, 31

Maidenhair-Fern, 74, 134
Mallard, 57, 58, 85
Mallow, Swamp-, 158
Maple, Manitoba, 73
  Mountain-, 27
  Red, 24, 26, 57, 60, 74, 156
  Striped, 27
  Sugar-, 24, 26, 39, 57, 77, 83, 166, 171
Marten, 29, 31, 39
Massasauga, Eastern, 63, 73, 133
Meadowlark, Eastern, 28, 34, 43
  Western, 34, 77, 185
Merganser, Common, 42, 81
  Hooded, 43, 183
Milfoil, 35
Milk-Vetch, 32
Milkweed, Poke, 134
  Swamp-, 121
Mink, 39, 169
Miterwort, 29
Mockingbird, 26, 167
Mole, Eastern, 26, 158
  Hairy-tailed, 28
Moonwort, 32
Moose, 31, 34, 39, 43, 104, 107, 161, 176, 179
Moosewood, 71
Moss, Beard, 179
  Bristly Club-, 29
  Shining Club-, 182

Sphagnum, 31, 58, 75, 89, 113, 120, 140
Mountain-Ash, Showy, 27, 29
Mountain-Cranberry, 32
Mountain-Maple, 27
Mouse, Deer, 28, 31
  House, 35
  White-footed, 26, 28
  Woodland Jumping, 28
Mulberry, Red, 24, 158, 166
Muskellunge, 171
Muskrat, 85, 107, 110, 161, 169, 181

NUTHATCH, Red-breasted, 63, 75, 135
  White-breasted, 75

OAK, Black, 166
  Bur, 27, 77, 178
  Chestnut-, 24, 158, 166
  Red, 24, 26, 42, 74, 83, 171
  Swamp-White, 24
  White, 24, 171
Oldsquaw, 33, 101, 185
Opossum, 34, 169
Orchid, Hooker's, 75
  Round-leaved, 75
Oriole, Orchard, 26, 158, 167
Osprey, 39, 46, 58, 98, 99, 100, 150
Ostrich-Fern, 90, 147, 181
Otter, 39
Ovenbird, 26
Owl, Barred, 39, 161
  Boreal, 31
  Great Gray, 31
  Great Horned, 75, 110
  Hawk, 161
  Saw-whet, 184–85
  Screech, 28
  Short-eared, 96
  Snowy, 33, 84, 161

PARNASSUS, Grass-of-, 148
Partridge, Gray, 35, 111, 142
Partridge-berry, 27

Pawpaw, 24, 71
Pear, Prickly, 158
Pelican, White, 167
Pewee, Eastern Wood, 26, 46, 80, 173
Phalarope, Northern, 70
  Wilson's, 80
Pheasant, Ring-necked, 35
Phenacomys, Eastern, 31
Pin-Cherry, 27, 171
Pine, Jack-, 27, 29, 39, 76
  Pitch-, 171
  Prince's 75
  Red, 27, 39, 77
  White, 24, 27, 39, 58, 61, 77, 83, 138, 150, 166, 171, 179
Pink Grass-, 75, 148
Pintail, 57
Pipewort, 98
Pipit, Water, 33, 95, 96, 142
Pitcher-plant, 45, 75, 95, 113, 120, 148, 150, 154, 180
Pitch-Pine, 171
Plantain, Rattlesnake-, 75, 96
Plover, Black-bellied, 72
  Golden, 72
  Piping, 167
  Upland, 52, 77, 96
Plum, Canada, 78
Pogonia, 45, 148
Polygala, Fringed, 75
Polypody, Common, 74
Poplar, Balsam-, 26, 29, 68, 77, 90
Porcupine, 28, 31
Potato-vine, Wild, 158
Praying Mantis, European, 171
Primrose, Bird's-eye, 67, 80
Primula, 148
Ptarmigan, Willow, 33
Puccoon, Hoary, 78

RACCOON, 26, 85, 158, 181
Racer, Blue, 25
Rail, King, 167
  Virginia, 96, 167
  Yellow, 51
Rat, Norway, 34

Rattlesnake, Swamp, *see* Massa-
    sauga, Eastern
Rattlesnake-Fern, 27
Rattlesnake-plantain, 75, 96
Raven, Common, 31, 39, 78, 80,
    105, 135, 176
Redhead, 71, 101, 184
Redpoll, Common, 31
Redstart, American, 26
Rice, Wild, 78, 85, 167
Robin, 28
Rose, Prickly, 29
Rosebay, 32
Rue Anemone, 84
Rush, Flowering, 133, 171, 181


St. John's-wort, 35
Salamander, Jefferson's, 80
Sandpiper, Pectoral, 70
    Semipalmated, 70
    Stilt, 70
Sandwort, 32
Sapsucker, Yellow-bellied, 98
Sarsaparilla, 27, 29
Sassafras, 24, 54, 86, 110, 158, 166,
    169, 184
Scaup, 101
Seal, Bearded, 69
Selfheal, 36
Shagbark-Hickory, 24, 166, 171
Sheep-Laurel, 63
Shoveler, 57, 107
Shrew, Little Short-tailed, 26
Shrike, Loggerhead, 28, 185
    Northern, 161
Siskin, Pine, 41
Skink, Blue-tailed, 158, 169
Skunk, Striped, 28, 181
Skunk-cabbage, 78, 150
Skunk-Currant, 27, 31
Snake, Brown, 28
    Fox, 158, 169
    Garter, 28, 31
    Water, 110
Snipe, Common, 51, 96, 105, 110,
    142

Snowberry, 25, 27
Soapberry, 32
Solomon's-seal, Three-leaved
    False, 31
Sora, 96, 167
Sorrel, Wood-, 27
Sparrow, Clay-colored, 34, 76, 77
    Chipping, 28
    Field, 28, 76, 141
    Fox, 31
    Grasshopper, 43, 51, 96, 185
    Henslow's, 182
    House, 35
    LeConte's, 51, 77
    Lincoln's, 80, 133
    Savannah, 28, 43, 76, 96
    Song, 28, 76
    Swamp, 184
    Tree, 31, 75
    Vesper, 43, 76, 96
    White-crowned, 31
    White-throated, 28, 31, 39, 45,
        46, 180
Sphagnum, *see* Moss, Sphagnum
Spicebush, 25, 158, 167
Spleenwort, Ebony-, 171
    Maidenhair, 74, 134
Sponge, Fresh-water, 80
Spruce, Black, 25, 27, 29, 31, 58,
    68, 76, 89, 91, 113, 140, 161,
    179
    White, 25, 27, 29, 31, 68, 75, 77,
        83, 90, 91, 138
Spurge, Flowering, 158
Squashberry, 29
Squirrel, Eastern Gray, 26, 28, 29,
    112
    Franklin's Ground, 29
    Northern Flying, 28
    Red, 28, 31
Star, Blazing-, 71
    Many-mouthed Earth, 158
Star-flower, 27, 29
Starling, 35, 105
Stickleback, Three-spined, 33
Stoneroot, 25
Strawberry-bush, Running, 25

Sugar-Maple, 24, 26, 39, 57, 77, 83, 166, 171
Sumac, Fragrant, 167
Sundew, Linear-leaved, 80
Sunfish, Green, 25
Swallow, Bank, 173, 183
  Barn, 28
  Cliff, 74, 98
  Rough-winged, 28, 78
Swamp-Loosestrife, 121
Swamp-Mallow, 158
Swamp-Milkweed, 121
Swamp-White Oak, 24
Swan, Whistling, 62, 72, 74, 114, 115, 148, 167, 178, 186
Swift, Chimney, 161
Sycamore, 158, 166, 184

TAMARACK, 25, 27, 29, 31, 32, 42, 45, 68, 75, 89, 91, 95, 100, 113, 180
Tanager, Scarlet, 26, 28, 29, 74, 173, 176
  Summer, 167
Tea, Labrador-, 29, 31, 32, 41, 75, 95, 107, 180
  New Jersey, 171
Teal, Blue-winged, 57, 58, 96
Tern, Arctic, 33
  Black, 57, 62, 63, 96, 110, 133, 167, 181
  Caspian, 100, 148, 172
  Common, 62, 100, 161, 163, 172
Thrasher, Brown, 28, 46, 76
Thrift, 32
Thrush, Gray-cheeked, 31, 46
  Hermit, 31, 43, 45, 135
  Swainson's, 31, 43, 135
  Wood, 26, 28, 43, 74
Titmouse, Tufted, 26, 167
Toad, American, 28
  Fowler's, 158, 169
Towhee, Rufous-sided, 28, 141
Trillium, Large-flowered, 109, 121
  Nodding, 78, 90, 148
Trout, Speckled, 81
Tulip-tree, 24, 55, 71, 166

Turkey (Wild), 26, 101
Turnstone, Ruddy, 106
Turtle, Bell's Painted, 78
  Blanding's 42, 158
  Map, 158
  Spiny Soft-shelled, 158, 169
Twinflower, 27, 29, 75, 84
Twisted-stalk, 27

VEERY, 28, 43, 150, 180
Vetch, Milk-, 32
Viburnum, Maple-leaved, 25
Violet, Smooth Yellow, 90
  White Dog's-tooth-, 71
Vireo, Red-eyed, 26, 42, 98
  Solitary, 42, 80
  Warbling, 28, 98
  Yellow-throated, 28, 110
Virgin's-bower, 25
Vole, Meadow, 28
  Pine, 26
  Red-backed, 31
Vulture, Turkey, 34, 66, 74, 98, 111, 146, 182

WALLEYE, 121
Walnut, Black, 24, 158, 166
Warbler, Bay-breasted, 31
  Black-and-white, 42, 98, 180
  Blackpoll, 31
  Black-throated Blue, 28, 46
  Black-throated Green, 42, 75, 78, 98
  Blue-winged, 26, 111
  Canada, 180
  Cape May, 31, 63, 78
  Cerulean, 26, 54, 99, 103, 110, 167
  Connecticut, 107
  Golden-winged, 99, 111, 154
  Hooded, 26, 167, 173
  Magnolia, 63
  Myrtle, 28, 63
  Nashville, 75, 180
  Palm, 107
  Parula, 63, 80, 179

Pine, 28
Prairie, 55
Prothonotary, 26, 158, 167
Tennessee, 31
Yellow, 28
Waterleaf, Appendaged, 158
Waterthrush, Louisiana, 26, 167
Northern, 55, 110, 180
Waxwing, Bohemian, 150
Cedar, 46, 150, 182
Weasel, Long-tailed, 28
Whale, White, 33
Whimbrel, 159, 184
Whip-poor-will, 46
Widgeon, American, 107
Wintergreen, Large-flowered, 32
One-flowered, 95
Witch-Hazel, 25
Wolf, Brush, 34, 160
Timber, 31, 39
Woodchuck, 28
Woodcock, American, 84, 118, 120

Woodpecker, Black-backed Three-
toed, 31, 39, 46, 179
Downy, 75, 78, 98
Hairy, 75, 78, 98
Northern Three-toed, 31, 39
Pileated, 39, 46, 55, 78, 98, 103,
110, 173, 182, 185, 186
Red-bellied, 26, 167, 186
Red-headed, 28, 179
Woodsia, Rusty, 45
Wood-Sorrel, 27
Wren, Bewick's, 158
Carolina, 26, 158, 167
House, 28
Long-billed Marsh, 96, 110, 167,
181
Short-billed Marsh, 142
Winter, 42, 43, 66, 74, 78, 180

YAM VINE, Wild, 25
Yellowthroat, 80, 180
Yew, American, 27

References in italic indicate articles on the area.

ABBEY DAWN, 97
Abitibi River, 91, 92
Abitibi Slough, 80
Achray, 40
Adelaide Island, 170
Agawa River, 81
Albany, 88, 90, 92
Albion Falls, 85
Aldborough Township, 185
Aldershot, 86, 87
Algonquin (Michigan), 178
Algonquin Park, 28, *39–45*, 46
Allanburg, 134
Allandale Station, 49
Alps Road, 110
Altrieve Lake, 110
Ameliasburg Inlier, 53
Amherst Island, 93, 95
Amherstburg, 72
Ancaster, 84, 87
Angus, 50
Apsley, 46, 47, 48, 151
Arran Lake, 60
Atikokan, 81, 164
Attawapiskat, 68, 88, 92
Aubrey Island, 170, 171
Aunt Sarah's Lookout, 123
Aurora, 180

BACKUS WOODS, 25, 55
Baie du Doree, 60
Bald Lake, 155
Balls Falls, 66, 134
Bancroft, *45–49*
Bannister's Marsh, 110–11
Barrie, *49–52*
Barriefield, 95
Barrie Lake, 110

Barrow Bay, 62
Barry's Bay, 46, 48
Bat Cave, 81
Bath, 93
Bayer's Creek, 133
Bayfield Sound, 120
Bay View Bog, 94–95
Beamers Falls, 134
Bear Creek, 174–75
Beatty Township, 107
Beau Rivage Island, 170, 171
Beausoleil Island, 81–83
Beaver Dams, 66
Beaver Valley, 8, 67, 143, 145
Bedford Mills, 99
Belle River, 72
Belleview Park, 175
Belleview Quarry, 176
Belleville, *52–53*, 162
Bell's Swamp, 96
Beverly Swamp, 86, 111
Beverly Township, 86, 111
Bicroft Mine, 47, 48
Big Creek, 72, 73
Bighead Valley, 143, 145–46
Black Ant Island, 171
Black Bay, 179
Blackburn, 140
Black Fox Lake, 43, 45
Black Rapids, 103
Blanche River, 104, 105
Blantyre, 147
Blenheim, 71
Blind River, 11, 12
Bloomingdale, 109
Blueberry Marsh, 150
Bluejay Creek, 118
Blue Mountains, 8, 74, 143

Boat Lake, 62
Bobs Lake, 149
Bognor, 146
Bognor Wildlife Sanctuary, 146
Bolton, 180
Bond Township, 107
Bonnechère Graben, Ottawa-, 6, 9, 13
Boshkung Lake, 123
Boulevard Lake, 80
Bowden's Woods, 70–71
Bradford, 51
Bradley's Marsh, 72
Brampton, 180, 181
Brant County, 53
Brantford, 53–55, 111
Breithaupt Park, 108–9
Brewery Creek, 136
Bridgeport Dam, 109
Brighton, 162
Brock Monument, 66, 128
Brockville, 55–59, 170, 171
Bruce County, 60–63, 142
Bruce Mines, 177
Bruce Peninsula, 60–63, 83, 84, 117, 142, 143
Bruce Trail, 63–67, 147
Brule Bay, 78
Buckhorn, 151, 155
Buck Lake, 99
Bullock's Corners, 86
Burgess, 150
Burgoyne, 60
Burleigh Falls, 46, 48, 151, 153, 154
Burlington, 66, 87
Burnham Park, 155
Burnt Root, 40
Buttermilk Falls, 85, 123
Buttermilk Hill, 176
Byrnes Avenue Woods, 74–75
Byron Bog, 113

Cache Lake, 42
Caledon Hills, 67, 181
Caledon Hills Farm, 181–82
Camden East, 93

Camelot Island, 170
Canadian Locks (Sault Ste. Marie), 175
Canatara Park, 174
Canoe Lake (Rideau Lakes), 99
Cape Henrietta Maria, 32, 33, 67–70, 89
Cape Nemaskamagow, 70
Cardiff, 48
Carleton University, 139
Carlisle, 86
Carlsbad Springs, 140
Carnarvon, 123
Casey Township, 104
Cataraqui, 93
Cataraqui River, 93, 95, 96
Catchacoma, 46
Catfish Creek, 172
Causeway, 110
Cavan Swamp, 154
Cavern Lake, 81
Cedar Island, 170
Central Experimental Farm, 139
Centre Island, 184
Chaffeys Locks, 100
Champlain Bridges, 139
Chantry Island, 61
Charing Cross, 71
Chatham, 70–73, 174
Chaudière Falls, 140
Cheddar Road, 47, 48
Cheminis Mountain, 106
Cheltenham, 181
Chepstowe, 60
Chesley, 60
Chippewa Park, 78
Christie Lake, 149, 150
Clay Belt, 29, 92, 104
Cobalt, 11
Cobourg, 159–60, 162
Cochrane, 90, 91, 104, 107
Coldspring Valley, 86
Collingwood, 73–76, 143
Collins Bay, 94
Colpoy's Bay, 143
Combermere, 49
Conestogo River, 108

Coniaurum Lake, 161
Connecticut Warbler Swamp, 107
Constance Bay, 141
Constance Creek, 141
Constance Island, 170
Constance Lake, 141
Coote's Paradise Marsh, 85–86
Coot Lake, 42
Copetown Bog, 54
Coral Rapids, 91
Cornwall, 57
Costello Creek, 45
Cottam, 72
Courtland, 115
Craigleith, 67, 75–76
Cranberry Creek, 176
Cranberry Marsh, 150
Cressman's Woods, 109
Crosby, 99
Crowe Lake, 155
Cruickston Park Farm, 110
Crystal Beach, 133
Culver Park, 106–7
Current River, 80
Cyrville, 140

DAWSON TRAIL CAMPGROUNDS, 163, 164, 165
Dean Bay, 119
Decew Falls, 66, 134
Dee River, 121
Deer Lake Nature Trail, 42
Delaware, 113
Delhi, 115
Desert Lake, 98, 99
Desjardins Canal, 86
Detroit River, 72–73
Devil Lake, 99
Devil's Glen, 67
Devils Punchbowl, 66
Dobbinton, 60
Don Valley, 15
Doon, 109, 110
Dorcas Bay, 63
Dorchester Swamp, 113
Dorion Hatchery, 80–81
Dorset, 46, 49, 121

Dover, 72
Dow's Lake, 138, 139
Drummond Centre, 150
Drummond Township, 150
Duck Creek, 68
Dunbar Experimental Station, 178
Dundas, 8, 66, 84, 86
Dunnville, 131, 133
Dunwich Township, 185
Durham County, 159
Dyno Mine, 47, 48
Dwight, 46

EAGLE, 186
Eaton's Corners, 186
Echo Bay Flats, 177
Eel's Creek, 47, 48, 154
Eel's Lake, 48
Ekfrid Township, 185, 186
Ekwan Point, 69
Elderslie Island, 60
Elgin County, 172, 173, 185
Elizabethville, 159
Elk Lake, 104
Elliott Lake, 11
Elmsley, 150
Elora, 60
Emo, 81
Empire Elevator, 77
Endymion Island, 170
Erieau, 167
Essex County, 155

FELKERS FALLS, 66
Fanshawe Park, 114
Faraday Mine, 47, 48
Fermoy, 99
Fifteen Mile Creek, 66, 134
Fishing Islands, 61–62
Flesherton, 145
Flowerpot Island, 63, 81, 83–84
Foleyet, 162
Forest Glen Woods, 175
Forks-of-the-Credit, 66
Fort Erie, 133
Fort Frances, 81
Fort William, *76–81*, 163, 164

Forty Mile Creek, 66, 133, 134
Freelton, 111
French Falls, 164
French Lake, 163, 164, 165
French Lake Nature Trail, 164
Frenchman's Bay, 182

GAGE PARK, 87
Galt, 54, 110, 111
Gami Lake, 105
Gamitagama Lake, 81
Gananoque, *93–103*, 170, 171
Ganaraska Conservation Area, 159–60
Garden River, 177
Gatineau Hills, 8, 9, 135, 136, 140
Gatineau River, 136
Georgian Bay, 8, 12, 15, 39, 62, 63, 82, 117, 145, 146
Georgian Bay Islands National Park, 63, *81–84*
Georgina Island, 170, 171
Gibbons Park, 112
Glamorgan, 159
Glenhurst Gardens, 53, 54
Glen Morris, 111
Glenora, 52
Glen Williams, 181
Goat Island, 129
Godfrey, 99
Gooderham, 46, 47
Gordon Island, 170
Gore Bay, 119
Goulais River, 176
Grafton, 160
Grand River, 53, 108, 109, 131, 133
Grant's Creek, 150
Gravenhurst, 121
Great Lakes, v, 15, 33, 126, 143, 174, 190
Greenock Swamp, 60
Green's Creek, 140
Grenadier Island, 170, 171
Grenadier Pond, 184
Grey County, 5, 9, 60, 142
Griersville, 145
Grimsby, 66, 132, 133, 134

Grimsby Beach, 133
Grimston Flats, 60
Gros Cap, 175–76
Grosse Ile, 73
Guelph, 108, 143

HAINS MEMORIAL LOOKOUT, 4
Haliburton County, 12, *45–49*
Hall's Lake, 123
Hamilton, 66, *84–87*, 131, 132, 134
Hanlan's Point, 184
Harrison Park, 147
Hartington, 98
Hastings County, *45–49*
Hawkcliff, 173
Hell Holes, 100
Hendrie Forest, 50, 52
Hendrie Park, 85
Hepworth, 61, 148, 149
Heron Creek, 41
Hiawatha Park, 176
High Park, 184
Hill Island, 101
Hockley Valley, 67
Hog's Back, 139, 141
Holland Marsh, 51
Holleford Lake, 98
Homer Watson Memorial Park, 109
Honey Harbour, 82
Hope Bay, 62
Hornings Mills, 67
Howdenvale, 62
Howe Island, 93
Hudson Bay, v, 14, 21, 32, 68, 69, 88
Hudson Bay Lowlands, 6, 8, 31, 87–92
Huff's Island, 52
Humber River, 182–84
Huntsville, 40, 46, 120
Huron Highlands, 8

INDIAN POINT BRIDGE, 120
Inglis Falls, 147
Iona, 186
Iroquois, 57

Isaac Lake, 62
Ivy Lea, 101, 170, 171

JACK LAKE TRAIL, 42
Jack's Lake, 75
Jackson Park, 152
James Bay, 14, 68, 69, 70, 87, 88, 91, 92
James Gardens, 183
Jardun Mine, 177
Jerseyville Road, 87
Johnston Property (Brockville), 56
Johnstown, 137
Jones Creek, 59
Jones Falls, 100
Jordan Harbour, 133, 134

KAGAWONG RIVER, 119
Kaministikwia River, 76, 78
Kars, 141
Kawagama, 40
Kawartha Lakes, 150
Kearns, 106
Kempenfelt Bay, 49
Kemptville, 137, 141
Kendal, 159
Kenogami, 90
Kent Bridge, 70
Kettle Creek, 172
Killaloe, 46
Killean, 109
Kincardine, 60
King Mountain, 135
King's Forest Park, 85
Kingston, *93–103*, 137, 149, 170, 171
Kingston Mills, 100
Kin Park, 80
Kirkland Lake, 9, 11, 12, *103–7*
Kirkland Lake Dump, 105
Kitchener, *108–11*
Kolapore Creek, 145
Komoka, 113
Kwinabiskak Lake, 70

LAC DES CHENES, 140
Lake Chipican, 174

Lake Erie, v, 24, 33, 53, 55, 115, 131, 132, 155, 169, 173, 185, 186
Lakefield, 152, 153
Lake Gibson, 134
Lakehead Airport, 77
Lake Huron, 11, 12, 15, 24, 60, 61, 62, 63, 82, 83, 117, 118, 142, 143, 148, 174
Lake Ira, 62–63
Lake Lavieille, 40
Lake Marie Louise, 179
Lake Muskoka, 121
Lake Nipissing, 8, 13
Lake Ontario, 15, 24, 33, 52, 84, 131, 132, 134, 159, 160, 162, 180, 184
Lake on the Mountain, 52
Lake Opeongo, 43, 45
Lake of Two Rivers, 43
Lake River, 70
Lake St. Clair, 111
Lakeshore Slimes, 105
Lake Simcoe, 8, 49
Lake Superior, 26, 29, 76, 80, 175, 179
Lake Superior Park, 81
Lake Timiskaming, 6
Lake Wolsey, 120
Lanark, 149, 150
Lansdowne, 103
Larder Lake, 103, 106
La Salle, 73
La Salle Park, 87
Latta, 53
Laurentian Hills, 135
Lavender, 67
Leamington, 155, 156
Leeds, 93
Lee's Pond, 58, 59
Lett's Grove, 150
Lillabelle Lake, 107
Lily Bay, 58–59
Lily Lake, 152
Limberlost, 121
Lindsay, 46, 47, 162
Little Cape, 68, 69

Little Cataraqui River, 94
Little Current, 117, 119, 120
Little Driftwood Creek, 107
Little Lake, 50–51
Little Lake Cemetery, 151–52
Little Madawaska River, 42
Logan Sills, 11
London, 70, *111–14*, 165
Long Beach, 59
Long Lake, 41
Long Point, 25, 53, 55, *115–16*
Long Swamp, 57–58 (Brockville),
    150 (Perth)
Long Swamp Heronry, 147–48
Lookout Nature Trail, 164
Lookout Trail, 43
Lyn, 58, 59
Lyndhurst, 103


MADAWASKA, 8, 9, 46, 49
Madawaska River, 43
Madoc, 46
Madoma Marsh, 97
Major's Hill Park, 138
Mallorytown Landing, 59, 170, 171
Mammamattawa, 90
Manitoulin Island, *117–20*, 177
Manitou River, 118
Manotick, 141
Maple, 185
Maple Grove Swamp, 54
Mar, 62
Markham, 180
Marl Lake, 52
Marmora, 155
Massie, 147
Matachewan, 103, 104–5
Matheson, 107
Mattagami River, 92
Mattawa River, 39
Maynooth, 46, 48, 49
McArthurs Mills, 46
McIntyre Park, 161
McIntyre River, 77, 80
McKenzie River, 80
McNab Lake, 148

Meaford, 145, 146
Melbourne, 185, 186
Meldrum Bay, 120
Memorial Park (Huntsville), 120
Mer Bleue, 140
Mermaid Island, 170, 171
Mersea Township, 155
Mew Lake, 43
Michael Bay, 118
Middlebrun Bay, 179
Middlesex County, 185
Midland, 82
Millhaven, 95
Milton, 180
Mindemoya, 118, 119
Minden, 46, 47, 49, 121, 123
Miners Bay, 47
Miner's Sanctuary, 71–72
Minesing, 50, 52
Mink Lake Nature Trail, 165
Missinaibi River, 92
Mission Bay, 78
Mississauga Lakes, 46
Mississippi River, 150
Mohawk Park, 54
Moira River, 53
Mono Mills, 67
Montreal River, 103, 105
Moose Factory, 88, 91–92
Moose Lake, 107
Moose River, 14, 91, 92
Moose River Crossing, 91
Moosonee, 88, 90, 91, 92
Morpeth, 165
Morrisburg, 137
Mosa Township, 185
Mountain Lake, 104, 146
Mountjoy, 160, 161
Mount McKay, 12, 78–80
Mount Nebo, 155
Mount Nemo, 66
Mud Lake, 150
Muggs Island, 185
Mukataship River, 69
Murray's Woods, 186
Muskoka, 12, 49, *120–23*
Muskoka River, 39

NAPANEE, 93, 100
Narrows Lane, 59
Nassau, 152
Nattabisha Point, 92
Neebing River, 77
Nepean Point, 138
New Glasgow, 186
New Liskeard, 103, 104
Newtonville, 159
Niagara Escarpment, 6, 8, 13, 14, 64, 66, 84, 117, 124, 131, 134, 143, 180, 181
Niagara Falls, 6, 8, 84, *123–31*, 132
Niagara Glen, 124, 128
Niagara Gorge and River, 15, 123, 126–30, 131, 134
Niagara-on-the-Lake, 132, 133
Niagara Peninsula, 25, 66, *131–35*
Nipigon, 11
Nipissing Lowlands, 9
Nith River, 108
Norfolk County, 53
Norland, 46
North Bay, 40, 90, 104
Northern Lakes (Gananoque), 101–3
Northumberland County, 159, 160
Northumberland Forest, 160
Norval, 181
Norwood, 151
Nottawasaga Bay, 74, 142
Nottawasaga River, 50, 52, 74
Nym Lake, 81

ODESSA, 93
Ogoki, 88
Old Fort Erie, 133
Old Fort Henry, 94, 95, 96, 97, 99
Old Goulais Road, 176
Old Monk Road, 48
Oliphant, 61, 62, 148
Omemee, 155
One-sided Lake, 81
Opeongo, 40
Orangeville, 143

Orr Lake, 51
Orr's Lake, 110
Orwell, 173
Osborne Corners, 54
Osler Bluff, 8, 74
Otonabee River, 151, 152, 155
Ottawa, 40, 46, 92, 100, 135–42, 149
Ottawa-Bonnechère Graben, 6, 9, 13
Ottawa River and Valley, 8, 9, 13, 15, 39, 55, 135, 136, 138, 140, 141
Otter Lake, 98, 100
Otto Lake, 106
Otty Lake, 150
Ouimet Canyon, 80
Outlet, 103
Owen Sound, 67, *142–49*
Ox Narrows, 123
Oxtongue River, 41

PAGWA, 90, 92
Paisley, 60
Paris, 54
Partridge Lake, 123
Paudash Lake, 47, 48
Pearl Lake, 161
Pembroke, 40
Penetangore River, 60
Peninsula Lake, 120
Perth, *149–50*
Peterborough, 15, 46, *150–55*, 159
Peterborough Game Preserve, 48
Petrolia, 175
Pickering, 180, 182
Pickford, 178
Pike Bay, 61, 62
Pike Lake, 150
Pinafore Park, 172
Pinehurst Park, 54, 111
Pioneer Logging Museum, 45
Point de Meuron, 78
Point Edward, 174
Point Pelee National Park, *155–58*
Pond Mills, 112

Poplar, 119
Porcupine District, 9, *160–62*
Porcupine Lake, 161
Portage Bay, 119
Port Arthur, *76–81*, 164, 178, 179
Port Bruce, 173
Port Burwell, 173
Port Colborne, 133
Port Credit, 181
Port Dalhousie, 133
Port Elgin, 60–61
Port Hope, *159–60*
Port Huron (Michigan), 174
Port Lambton, 6
Portland, 99, 100
Port Maitland, 133
Port Rowan, 115
Port Severn, 82
Port Stanley, 173
Port Weller, 133
Pottageville Swamp, 180
Potter, 107
Pottohawk Point, 115
Presqu'ile Provincial Park, *162–63*
Pretty Valley, 67
Prince Edward County, 52
Providence Bay, 118
P.U.C. Reservoir (St. Thomas),
    172
Purpleville, 185
Puslinch Lake, 109–10

QUEENSTON, 64, 131, 132
Quetico Provincial Park, 81, *163–
    65*
Quinte, 53

RAINY RIVER, 28, 81
Rattlesnake Point, 66, 86–87
Rattray's Marsh, 180–81
Red Bay, 148
Red Hill Creek, 66
Redwing Caves, 145
Remie Rapids, 140
Renison, 91
Rice Lake, 151, 155, 159
Richmond, 141–42

Rideau Canal, 95, 96, 100, 136,
    137, 138, 139, 141, 149
Rideau Lake, 149
Rideau Lakes, 97–99, 100
Rideau River, 136, 137, 139, 141
Ripple Rocks, 177
Roblin, 100
Rock Chapel, 86
Rockcliffe Park, 138
Rockford, 146
Rock Lake, 43 (Algonquin), 177
    (Sault Ste. Marie)
Rockway (Falls), 66, 134
Roger's Creek, 118
Rondeau Bay, 165, 166
Rondeau Provincial Park, 25, *165–
    69*
Roseville Swamp, 110
Round Lake, 105
Royal Botanical Gardens, 85
Rudyard, 178
Rupert's House, 87, 91
Rydal Bank, 177

ST. CLAIR RIVER, 173, 174
St. Davids, 129, 131
St. Edmunds Marsh, 63
St. Joseph's Island, 177
St. Lawrence Islands National
    Park, 59, 94, *170–72*
St. Lawrence River and Valley, v,
    15, 33, 56, 57, 58, 93, 101, 170,
    171
St. Nora's Lake, 123
St. Peter's Cemetery, 58
St. Thomas, *172–73*
St. Williams Forestry Station, 55
Sandbanks Area (Belleville), 52
Sarnia, *173–75*
Saskatchewan Lake, 123
Sauble Beach, 61, 148, 149
Sauble Elm, 149
Sauble River, 60, 61, 149
Sault Ste. Marie, *175–78*
Savigny Creek, 80
Scarborough Bluffs, 15
Schomberg River, 51

Scott's Mills, 155
Schumacher, 160, 161
Scuttle Hole, 53
Searchmount Road, 176
Serpent Mounds Park, 155
Severn, 88, 92
Shallow Lake, 148
Shannonville Inlier, 53
Sharp-tailed Grouse Muskeg, 107
Sherwood Forest, 56
Shillington, 107
Shipsands Island, 92
Shoal Cove, 62
Sibley Provincial Park, 12, 80, 178–79
Silver Islet, 179
Silver Lake Provincial Park, 149
Simcoe, 53, 55
Simcoe County, 49, 51,
Simcoe Island, 93
Sinclair's Woods, 71
Skye Lake, 62
Sleeping Giant, 12, 179
Smith Lake Road, 45
Smoke Lake, 42
Southampton, 60, 61
South Baymouth, 117, 118, 119
South Ekfrid, 186
South Lake Area (Gananoque), 103
South March, 141
South Nation River, 142
South Porcupine, 160
South River, 39
Speed River, 108
Spencer Creek, 66
Spottiswood, 111
Springbank Park, 112
Springwater Pond, 173
Squaw Point, 94
Stalwart Ridge, 178
Stanley, 77–78
Stayner Speedway, 52
Steckle's Woods, 109
Stella, 95
Stewart Park, 149
Stinson's Lake, 99–100

Stinson's Swamp, 99–100
Stokes Bay, 62
Stoney Creek, 66, 133
Stoney Creek Falls, 134
Stovin Island, 170, 171
Sucker Lake, 98
Sudbury Basin, 12
Sulphur Springs Road, 87
Sunnidale, 50
Sunnyside Beach, 184
Sunset Point Park, 73
Sutton River, 68, 69
Swastika, 106
Sydenham, 93
Sydenham River, 143, 147

TALBOTVILLE, 165
Table Rock House, 128
Tay River, 149
Tee Harbour, 179
Tehkummah, 118
Tews Falls, 66
Thames River, 70, 71, 72, 111, 112, 114, 185, 186
Thamesville, 165
Thornbury, 145
Thousand Islands, 93, 101, 103, 170
Thorold, 66
Three Mile Creek, 121
Three Mile Lake, 121
Thunder Bay, 12, 76, 179
Thunder Cape, 179
Tilbury, 72
Tillsonburg, 115
Timmins, 12, 107, 160, 161, 162
Tobermory, 63, 64, 83, 117
Toronto, 15, 66, *180–85*
Toronto Island, 184
Trent River and Canal, 8, 152
Trowbridge Falls, 80
Turkey Point, 25, 55, 115
Twelve Mile Creek, 134
Twenty Mile Creek, 66, 133, 134
Twin Locks, 66
Two Rivers Basin, 43
Tyrconnell, 186

UFFORD, 121
Upper Rideau Lake, 100
Ussher's Creek, 132
Utterson, 121

VESPRA TOWNSHIP, 50, 51
Vicker's Heights, 78
Vicker's Park, 77, 78
Victoria, 181
Victoria Mine, 177
Victoria Park, 108 (Kitchener),
    109 (Galt), 112 (London)
Virginiatown, 103, 106

WAINFLEET SWAMP, 133
Walker Ponds, 112–13
Walkerton, 60
Wallacetown, 186
Walpole Island, 71, 72
Walrus Island, 68
Walters Falls, 67, 146–47
Wardsville, 185, 186
Warsaw Caves, 153–54
Wasaga Beach, 52, 75
Waterdown, 86
Waterloo, *108–11*
Waterloo Park, 108
Waterworks Park, 186
Waubaushene, 15
Websters Falls, 66, 86
Welland Canal, 66, 134
Wellesley Island, 101
Wellington, 52
West Bay, 119
Westdale Ravine, 85
West Lorne, *185–86*

Westport, 99
Whirlpool (Niagara), 128, 129,
    130
Whiskey Jack Creek, 104
Whitefish Falls, 117
Whitefish Lake, 78
White's Woods, 25, 173
Whitney, 40, 45, 46, 160
Wiarton, 61, 62, 67, 148
Wicklow, 160
Wilberforce, 46
Wilke's Bush, 110
Willowbark Lake, 68
Willow Beach, 159
Willow Creek, 50, 51
Windermere, 121
Windigoostigwan Lakes, 164
Windsor, 70, 72, 143, 156, 165,
    174
Winisk, 68, 88, 92
Wintergreen Flats, 128
Wolfe Island, 93, 96–97
Wolfe Lake, 99
Wonnacott's Farm, 113
Woodgreen, 186
Woodslee, 72
Wren Lake, 121
Wright-Hargreaves Slimes, 106
Wrigley Corners, 111

YARKER, 93
York County, 51
York Road, 87
Young Lake Waterfowl Sanctuary,
    120
Young's Point, 153